What Your Colleagues Are Saying . . .

I am thrilled that Maria has released her new book, *More Ramped-Up Read Alouds: Building Knowledge and Boosting Comprehension*! We used her book *The Ramped-Up Read Aloud* as a foundation for my school district's interactive reading lessons. Maria selects the absolute *best* books and has carefully thought out lessons that beautifully align with our state standards. This book has transformed the way our teachers read aloud to their students. Read alouds are no longer a time for kids to passively listen. They are 100% ramped up! Kids are actively thinking, talking, and questioning throughout these lessons while being exposed to higher levels of text and rich vocabulary. Thank you, Maria!

Dr. Stefanie Steffan, Coordinator of Elementary Literacy and Title Programs
Rockwood School District

Maria's book *The Ramped-Up Read Aloud* was a gift to educators everywhere. Her follow-up *More Ramped-Up Read Alouds* is equally incredible. At a time when book bans are at an all-time high, Maria sets students up to thoroughly experience an engaging, interactive, and joyful read aloud.

Vera Ahiyya, Author of *Rebellious Read Alouds* (Corwin Literacy) and Educator

As a fellow lover of picture books, I absolutely love this book! Packed full of great titles, structured lessons, extension ideas, and suggestions for paired texts, Maria Walther takes the guesswork out of read alouds and puts the research back in. This is a must-have resource for every literacy classroom.

Kayla Briseño, Coauthor of *Text Structures from Picture Books* and the forthcoming
Text Structures from Nonfiction Picture Books (Corwin Literacy)

In *More Ramped-Up Read Alouds* Maria Walther provides another exceptional series of reading experiences that perfectly marry the art and science of learning to read! The carefully curated lessons are anchored with text, weaving the components of the Reading Rope together so seamlessly that students can't help but fall in love with reading!

Andrea Burkiett, Director of Elementary Curriculum & Instruction
Savannah–Chatham County Public School System

More Ramped-Up Read Alouds respectfully and ambitiously flaunts the power of a read aloud, taking an even deeper dive into increasing the ability to expand critical thinking, language, prior knowledge, dialogic interactions, and foundational skills all through the culturally diverse and responsive titles that allow our students to see themselves represented, fostering confidence, self-advocacy, and compassion for others. . . . The thoughtfully laid out resources make this a professional development title that will be a favorite for all.

Hilda Martinez, RTI Coordinator
San Diego Unified School District

More Ramped-Up Read Alouds represents our current understanding of all the reasons we *love* reading aloud. Maria masterfully guides us through all the benefits and gives us so many practical and pedagogical reasons to make reading aloud a part of our daily classroom routine. The books used are current, which will mean I need to expand my ever-growing collection of the best read alouds available. The books reflect all of the things we strive to model for children. You need to get *More Ramped-Up Read Alouds* for yourself, your teacher friend, or the newest teacher on staff. You will be glad that you did. Happy reading!

Katrina Murphy, Grade 2 Teacher
Chignecto Central Regional Center of Education
Nova Scotia, Canada

Imagine this resource as a direct line to Maria Walther's heart and mind! Through her thoughts on the most recent research and invitation to lean on literature to nurture children's curiosity, every empowered educator will find a text and run with it to share with their learners.

Dr. Noor Shammas, Instructional Coach
Naperville Community Unit School District 203

MORE RAMPED-UP READ ALOUDS

To Whitney Wheeler and her amazing third-grade class at North Grove
Elementary School in Sycamore, Illinois:

Henry, Mackenzie, Evan, Nixon, Ella, Alexis, Kellan, Lillian, Hazel, Eliza, Morgan, Jaxon, Jordyn, Weston, Andy, Jameson, Connor, Mark Anne, Quinn, Carter, Novi, Adela, Everleigh, Mariah, and Fiona

Thanks for inviting me to read, think, and learn with all of you!

MORE RAMPED-UP READ ALOUDS

BUILDING KNOWLEDGE AND BOOSTING COMPREHENSION

50 NEW READ-ALOUD EXPERIENCES

MARIA WALTHER

CORWIN Literacy

FOR INFORMATION:

Corwin
A SAGE Company
2455 Teller Road
Thousand Oaks, California 91320
(800) 233-9936
www.corwin.com

SAGE Publications Ltd.
1 Oliver's Yard
55 City Road
London EC1Y 1SP
United Kingdom

SAGE Publications India Pvt. Ltd.
Unit No 323-333, Third Floor, F-Block
International Trade Tower Nehru Place
New Delhi 110 019
India

SAGE Publications Asia-Pacific Pte. Ltd.
18 Cross Street #10-10/11/12
China Square Central
Singapore 048423

Vice President and
  Editorial Director: Monica Eckman
Executive Editor: Tori Mello Bachman
Content Development Editor: Sharon Wu
Product Associate: Zachary Vann
Production Editor: Tori Mirsadjadi
Copy Editor: Talia Greenberg
Typesetter: C&M Digitals (P) Ltd.
Proofreader: Dennis Webb
Indexer: Integra
Cover Designer: Gail Buschman
Marketing Manager: Margaret O'Connor

Printed in the United States of America

Library of Congress Cataloging-in-Publication Data

Names: Walther, Maria P., author.

Title: More ramped-up read alouds : building knowledge and boosting comprehension / Maria P. Walther.

Description: Thousand Oaks, California : Corwin, a SAGE Company, [2025] | Series: Corwin literacy; volume 1 | Includes bibliographical references and index.

Identifiers: LCCN 2024019738 | ISBN 9781071931240 (paperback ; acid-free paper) | ISBN 9781071962633 (epub) | ISBN 9781071962596 (epub) | ISBN 9781071962602 (pdf)

Subjects: LCSH: Oral reading. | Reading (Elementary) | Literature—Study and teaching (Elementary) | Language arts (Elementary)—Activity programs. | Group reading.

Classification: LCC LB1573.5 .W347 2025 | DDC 372.45/2—dc23/eng/20240624

LC record available at https://lccn.loc.gov/2024019738

This book is printed on acid-free paper.

24 25 26 27 28 10 9 8 7 6 5 4 3 2 1

Contents

① Chapter 1: Maintain a Happy and Caring Learning Community All Year Long   39

② Chapter 2: Focus on Foundational Skills: Phonological Awareness, Skillful Decoding, Vocabulary, Fluency, and Comprehension Monitoring   75

Chapter 3: Strengthen Listening Comprehension   107

Visit the companion website at
https://resources.corwin.com/more-rampedup-readalouds
for downloadable resources.

Note From the Publisher: The author has provided web content throughout the book that is available to you through QR (quick response) codes. To read a QR code, you must have a smartphone or tablet with a camera. We recommend that you download a QR code reader app that is made specifically for your phone or tablet brand.

Acknowledgments

I've had a writing deadline for a quarter-century! After completing my dissertation in 1998, I collaborated with colleagues on a college reading textbook (a daunting task!). The textbook led to an opportunity to coauthor a professional book, which inspired another and another . . . the book you're holding in your hands is number 12! I will forever be grateful for the cumulative wisdom I've gained along my writing journey from brilliant editors, insightful coauthors, and all the folks who work tirelessly behind the scenes to produce, publish, and promote my work. A huge shout-out also goes to the dedicated educators who put their own spin on my ideas and make them come to life in their classrooms. I am a better writer, educator, and human because of the guidance and expertise of these individuals and of the following people who cheered me on during the writing of *More Ramped-Up Read Alouds*:

- Katherine Phillips-Toms: We've taught together, written books together, laughed, cried, and pondered together since 1995 (or, as the kids say, since back in the 1900s!) Your kindergarten classroom is my happy place. You work tirelessly to create caring and joyful space for children to flourish. Spending time each week learning alongside you and your students keeps me grounded and is a constant reminder of the fast-paced life of teachers. Our mutual love of organization and planning has seeped into these pages.

- Whitney Wheeler: From the first time I visited, I felt at home in your classroom. It was like stepping back into my own. I appreciate your willingness to let me "go with the flow" and see where each read-aloud experience led your learners. Your third-graders' insights and feedback were invaluable.

- Karen Biggs-Tucker: You have been a constant in my teaching and writing journey. Whether we're presenting, listening to a conference speaker, or running around an exhibit hall in search of books, I always learn something from you. You are a treasured friend and Lenny and I enjoy the time we spend together with both you and Brian.

- The friends, colleagues, and students I've had the pleasure of learning alongside during my tenure and continued partnership with IPSD 204, in Aurora, Illinois: Thank you for continuing to welcome me into your classrooms, libraries, and schools. A special shout-out goes to Kathy Williams for inviting me into her first-grade classroom to dabble with ideas for this book!

- Tori Bachman: Well, here we are again, ready to send another book out into the world. You seem to know exactly when I need a gentle nudge or encouraging word. Your keen editorial insights and unwavering commitment to supporting teachers have guided me in creating an impactful resource for educators.

- Lisa Luedeke, Sharon Wu, Zack Vann, and the rest of the Corwin team: From proposal to finished book, I know I can count on you to make my ideas shine.

- The following publishers who provided me with many of the titles that I included in this book: Candlewick, Disney/Hyperion, Holiday House, Macmillan Publishing Group, Penguin Random House, Simon & Schuster, and Scholastic.

- The librarians at the West Branch of the Aurora Public Library: Without knowing it, you made this book possible. Week after week, I ordered the picture books you had just processed so that I could stay on top of the latest and greatest. Kudos to you and to librarians everywhere!

When this book hits the shelves, I will have been happily married for 35 years. I can always count on my husband, Lenny, for his unwavering support of my writing and of the work I do as a traveling teacher. More importantly, he pulls me away from my office and into the real world. I treasure your adventurous spirit and love traveling with you. Our daughter Katie and newly minted son-in-law Brian are often part of our experiences. Whether we're hiking up a mountain, reading in a park, or enjoying a meal out, every small moment we spend together as a family brings me joy. Now that I've written a dozen books, it's time to take a much-needed break and make more memories!

Publisher's Acknowledgments

Corwin gratefully acknowledges the contributions of the following reviewers:

Melissa J. Black
Teacher and Education Consultant, Whittier Elementary School (DCPS)
Washington, DC

Tiffany Coleman
Chair of Literacy, retired, Educational Consultant, Georgia Gwinnett College
Way Loganville, GA

Katie Keier
Kindergarten Teacher, Fairfax County Public Schools
Alexandria, VA

Hilda Martinez
RTI Coordinator, San Diego Unified School District
Chula Vista, CA

Connie Obrochta
Literacy Coach, National Louis University
Chicago, IL

Viviana Tamas
Literacy Coach
White Plains, NY

About the Author

Photo by Latrice Murphy Design & Photography

Maria Walther is a seasoned educator, author, and literacy consultant with over three decades of experience teaching first grade. Her practical yet engaging approach to classroom instruction has made her a trusted partner for educators seeking effective teaching strategies. With a doctoral degree from Northern Illinois University, Maria is an avid researcher who continues to further her knowledge of literacy instruction. Maria is a strong advocate for reading aloud and has been honored for her dedication to fostering a love of reading in children with the Illinois Reading Educator of the Year and the ICARE for Reading Award. One of Maria's most cherished awards is The Most Influential Educator, given to her by a former student turned colleague. This speaks to the lasting impact she has on those she teaches. As a prolific writer, Maria aims to provide busy teachers with practical resources. Her best-selling books *The Ramped-Up Read Aloud* and *Shake Up Shared Reading* offer actionable insights into creating engaging reading experiences for kids. Collaborating with Karen Biggs-Tucker, Maria coauthored *The Literacy Workshop*, which helps educators seamlessly integrate reading and writing instruction. In *A Year for the Books*, cowritten with her daughter Katie, Maria shares routines and mindsets for building student-centered reading communities from kindergarten to eighth grade. Educators can learn more about Maria's consulting work and find helpful resources on her website, mariawalther.com, or connect with her on Instagram and X (previously Twitter) @mariapwalther and @ayear4thebooks.

Photo by Whitney Wheeler

Welcome! I appreciate you joining me and my colleagues—the creators who've poured their passion into the texts that are highlighted in the pages that follow. Their words and illustrations inspire kids to dream big, be kind, ask questions, reflect on the past, and forge new paths into the future.

The How and Why of Effective Interactive Read Alouds
From Research to Practice

Tucked on a shelf in classrooms and libraries there's a gateway that connects young minds to essential knowledge, while, at the same time, fueling imagination, and nourishing empathy. This portal is—you guessed it—none other than a picture book. When we joyfully share picture books with children, the power of the author's words brought to life by our spoken voice has the ability to shape their hearts and foster a lasting love of learning, literature, and connection. I'm inferring you selected this text to add to your professional book stack because you're already a read-aloud enthusiast. Or, perhaps you recognize that read aloud is powerful, but you want to fine-tune your techniques to make read-aloud experiences even more dynamic for your students. Welcome! I appreciate you joining me and my colleagues—the creators who've poured their passion into the texts that are highlighted in the pages that follow. Their words and illustrations inspire kids to dream big, be kind, ask questions, reflect on the past, and forge new paths into the future. When those same words and illustrations are studied and discussed during an interactive read aloud, they provide students with the wealth of knowledge needed to become insightful readers, writers, and citizens of the world.

I have dedicated nearly 40 years to studying picture books and considering their instructional possibilities. Based on what I've learned and observed, I have an unwavering belief in the power of read aloud. I believe a read-aloud experience can and should be both entertaining and educational at the same time. You might be wondering what I mean by a read-aloud experience. To clarify, here's my definition:

A Read-Aloud Experience Is . . .

A carefully planned learning event where you joyfully celebrate a text and demonstrate skilled, expressive reading by reading *to* children while they listen, notice, and wonder. During a read-aloud experience, you typically have the text in your hands and your listeners nearby. As you are reading, you strategically pause and pose open-ended questions that engage learners in collaborative conversations to help them uncover the meaning and/or message of the text.

I have dedicated nearly 40 years to studying picture books and considering their instructional possibilities.

I crafted each read-aloud experience in this book as a multifaceted learning event so that you can creatively use the components to enhance your instruction. Be confident that when you share these read-aloud experiences in the way that works best for your learners you will not only be nurturing lifelong readers, but also helping kids progress toward standards-based learning goals.

In the years since *The Ramped-Up Read Aloud* was published, the landscape of reading instruction has shifted and realigned to match the most current evidence-based findings. Throughout this shift, one instructional constant has been proven essential—a well-planned interactive read-aloud experience (Conradi Smith et al., 2022; D. Fisher et al., 2023; Wright, 2019). In fact, the Association for Supervision and

Curriculum Development (ASCD) Scientific Advisory Committee recommends that educators give read alouds a central role because they help students build knowledge as they grapple with complex ideas and vocabulary (ASCD, 2023b). When we view read alouds as one way to build knowledge, we see benefits across grade levels and subject areas. In the social studies realm, a picture book like *Stars of the Night: The Courageous Children of the Czech Kindertransport* (Stelson, 2023), told from the collective perspective of the children, gives upper elementary grade readers a unique insight into one aspect of the Holocaust that may not be covered in a social studies program. To enhance a first-grade science unit on the phases of the moon, read aloud *Thank You, Moon: Celebrating Nature's Nightlight* (Stewart, 2023a) to help children understand how the moon influences wildlife. I could go on listing knowledge-building books forever because finding picture books to illuminate a topic or concept is one of my favorite nerdy pastimes. In fact, I frequently get emails that begin with, "Can you recommend a good book for . . . ?"

The point here is that, due to their undisputed benefits, read-aloud experiences are a high-priority literacy routine. They should hold a permanent timeslot (or, in my opinion, timeslots) in your daily schedule. The 50 exemplar read-aloud experiences in this book will help you seamlessly enhance the components of an evidence-based read aloud and, when coupled with responsiveness to your students' needs, improve its instructional quality (D. L. Baker & Santoro, 2023). Through adaptable approaches and real-world examples, you'll learn how to make read-aloud experiences a staple of your teaching toolkit. We'll begin by thinking through the comprehension conversations that add value to a read aloud.

Every word you read aloud has the potential to inspire an enthusiastic reader.

Comprehension Conversations: The Key to Interactive Read-Aloud Experiences

After reading Linda Liu's *Hidden Gem* (2023) aloud to third graders, I prompt, "Talk to your neighbor about the title *Hidden Gem*. Have you ever heard that phrase before? What do you suppose it means?" I overhear snippets of conversation:

> Cai turns to his neighbor, "I think a hidden gem is something special because the rock decided it was special."

> Brylee chimes in, "Me too! Remember the part in the book when the rock saw its reflection in the big gem? I think that's when it started to feel special."

The dialogue continues as learners build on each other's thinking and, in the process, uncover the theme of the story. One of the key features of a quality read aloud is text-based discourse where we, as teachers, strategically prompt listeners to discuss the pertinent parts that will lead them to understanding (D. L. Baker & Santoro, 2023). Encouraging learners to engage in comprehension conversations during read alouds is a proven instructional routine for enhancing language development (Burkins & Yates, 2021) and so much more!

Encourage learners to engage in comprehension conversations.

I want to be clear that there are many times during my day or week when I read aloud because it's just plain fun, letting students' reactions drive the conversation. Oftentimes, we read the books in what Lester Laminack (2016) refers to as the "movie read" (p. 39) or in a theatrical fashion without any pauses or interruptions. If you have time in your teaching day, you may choose to read the books featured here in "movie read" style first, and then reread to engage in the comprehension conversation. The key takeaway is that learners' interactive conversations elevate read aloud to a comprehension-building instructional approach. Research shows that when we lead discussions that promote student talk and comprehension these conversations do the following:

- Invite learners to co-create knowledge
- Develop stronger textual understanding
- Build and reinforce knowledge and comprehension
- Are effective for a wide range of learners, including multilingual learners
- Gain power when paired with students writing about their reading

(Scientific Advisory Committee, ASCD, 2023a)

Let's quickly review the two main aspects of these interactions—teacher talk and listener's conversations.

Teacher Talk During Interactive Read-Aloud Experiences

Effective interactive read-aloud experiences are a carefully orchestrated dance among the enjoyment of the text, adult discourse, and children's interactive conversations. During dialogic read alouds, teachers encourage and extend students' comments, ideas, interpretations, and questions that are shaped by their lived experiences (Varelas & Pappas, 2006). To remember the four ways to spark students' conversations during read aloud, I created the acronym T.A.L.K.

- **T**hink aloud: Explain the mental processes you use to decode text, understand words, and construct meaning.
- **A**sk open-ended questions: Pose questions and/or prompts that have more than one possible response.
- **L**isten and give descriptive feedback: Listen carefully to students' responses and offer feedback that is focused on their effort or strategy use. The goal of descriptive feedback is to point out behaviors that the child can approximate when they are reading independently.
- **K**eep the conversation going: Ask follow-up questions that prompt listeners to think critically, revise their initial ideas, provide text evidence for their claims, consider the author's purpose, make connections, and so on.

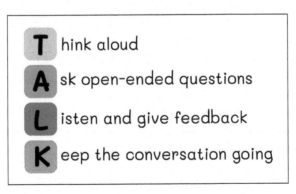

T hink aloud

A sk open-ended questions

L isten and give feedback

K eep the conversation going

T. A. L. K. to spark interactive conversations.

As you will see when you peruse the exemplar read-aloud experiences, I use these discussion-provoking questions and prompts sparingly so as to not interrupt the flow of the book. To narrow your focus and select key stopping points when creating your own read-aloud experiences, keep your learning targets in mind. Once you've started the conversation with your questions and prompts, the next step is to teach listeners how to effectively converse with one another.

Four Ways to Spark Interactive Conversations

Think Aloud	Ask Open-Ended Questions	Listen and Give Descriptive Feedback	Keep the Conversation Going
When I look at the cover of a book, I ask myself, "What can I learn from this cover that will help me better understand what might happen in the book?"	What do you notice on the cover?	You worked hard to notice details I missed. Noticing details makes reading more interesting.	Why do you think the illustrator chose to design it this way?
I'm thinking about what the words say and noticing the character's facial expressions; when I put these together, I can infer . . .	What are you thinking?	That's a new way to think about this. How did you come up with that idea?	I wonder if your thinking will change as we continue reading.
When I'm reading a nonfiction book, I check in with myself to make sure I'm understanding the main idea and details.	Why do you think learning about this topic is important?	I noticed you used the title of the book to help you figure out the main idea. Are there other ways to figure out the main idea?	How does what you've learned connect to something else in the world or in your life?

Listener's Conversations During Interactive Read-Aloud Experiences

What happens when you invite your listeners to turn and talk? In my experience, without guidance, children typically talk *at* each other and the volume gets louder and louder until I attempt to call them back together. To facilitate students' active listening and their ability to build on each other's thinking, it's helpful to teach kids some questions and phrases to use as they converse with one another. Here's a demonstration lesson that I've found helpful:

- Invite a colleague or another vocal student (you know the one!) to sit next to you as you read aloud.
- Bring some plastic math links or paperclips to use as a visual.

- Pose a question about the book. Then, use the questions or phrases to demonstrate a two-way conversation.

- Add a link to the chain each time a person talks to show that as you build on each other's thinking, your learning grows (Walther & Phillips, 2012).

- Demonstrate your two-way conversations a few times at the beginning of the read aloud, and then turn the responsibility over to partnerships as you finish the book.

I wish I could tell you that this one mini-lesson will work magic and kids will instantly use these questions and phrases. The reality is that you will have to consistently demonstrate, practice, scaffold, and give feedback throughout the year to make two-way conversations a habit.

Another way to emphasize the importance of partner dialogue is to refrain from routinely asking a few students to share out to the whole group after learners complete their peer discussion. This teaching move places more value on the ideas they're building together, emphasizing dialogic learning. In addition, it nudges children to actively engage in the conversation with their peers rather than focusing solely on what they plan to say to the whole group.

Finally, drawing attention to the importance of peer conversations is beneficial for your quieter students who typically prefer smaller interactions than talking in front of the whole class. To keep tabs on students' discussions, circulate among them gathering snippets in your teacher notebook to refer to later or to highlight during the read aloud if it will move their understanding of the text forward. Spotlighting the smart thinking of your quiet students helps boost their confidence to share during future whole-class discourse. Keep the idea of interactive conversations in focus as we move on to the "why" or "research-y" section of this introduction; remember that every word you read aloud has the potential to inspire an enthusiastic reader, an inquisitive learner, and a compassionate citizen.

Coach students as they link their thinking.

Eight More Evidence-Based Reasons
to Engage in Interactive Read-Aloud Experiences

The purpose of this section is twofold. First, to provide a clear rationale for dedicating instructional time to interactive read alouds. Second, to offer actionable ideas that will ramp up your read-aloud experiences. Part of our role as educators is to stay in tune with the latest research and teaching practices by reading about and listening to experts in our field. The knowledge we gain from ongoing study helps us to hone our instruction to better address the needs of our learners. *The Ramped-Up Read Aloud* (2019) included a detailed, research-based rationale for reading aloud. Readers of that book will recognize these 10 compelling reasons. We read aloud to:

- Promote reading

- Foster a strong sense of community

- Celebrate the written (and illustrated) word

- Build a foundation for future learning

- Expand vocabulary

- Showcase a proficient reader's strategy use

- Support budding writers

- Spark collaborative conversations

- Encourage perspective-taking and empathy

- Open windows to other worlds

In the time since that book published, I've continued studying the benefits of interactive read aloud. Here, I'll expand on the original rationale and add updated evidence. To provide a framework for organizing the eight additional reasons to read aloud, I'll use constructs that appear in the model developed by Nell Duke and Kelly Cartwright (2021) called the *Active View of Reading*. The Active View of Reading is a theory that expands on the *Simple View of Reading* (Gough & Tunmer, 1986), is based on a synthesis of research, and includes these four features:

- Lists contributors to reading and potential causes of reading difficulty

- Depicts word recognition and language comprehension as overlapping and explicitly identifies the processes that bridge the two

- Includes active self-regulation

- Explains how instruction in each construct can improve reading comprehension

When we examine the read-aloud experience through the lens of some of the constructs that appear in the Active View of Reading, we clearly see how this time-honored practice plays a critical role in reading instruction today and into

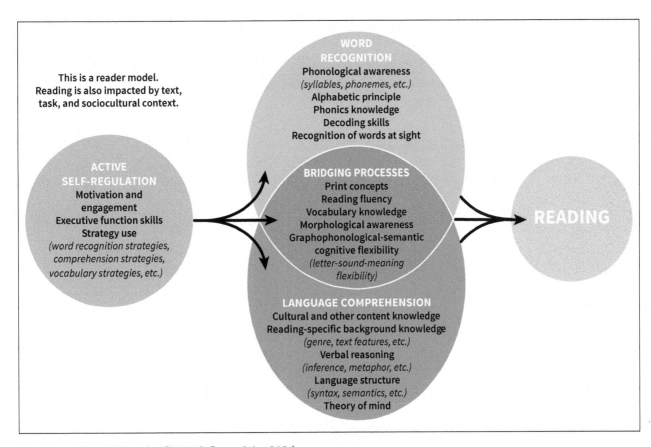

The Active View of Reading (Duke & Cartwright, 2021)

Source: Duke, N. K., & Cartwright, K. B. (2021). The science of reading progresses: Communicating advances beyond the Simple View of Reading. *Reading Research Quarterly, 56*(S1), S25–S44. https://ila.onlinelibrary.wiley.com/doi/full/10.1002/rrq.411. Used with permission of John Wiley & Sons; permission conveyed through Copyright Clearance Center, Inc.

the future. View this section of the chapter as a quick-reference guide to the research that confirms the importance of intentional, interactive read-aloud experiences. Use the evidence found here to validate your professional decision making and to convince stakeholders that children should engage in *daily* read-aloud experiences (Rasinski, 2017; Venegas & Guanzon, 2023) not only during language arts, but also across the school day (Wright, 2019).

So that you can quickly zoom-in on the section that meets your needs, you'll find a brief synopsis of the four broad categories found in the Active View of Reading: word recognition, bridging processes, language comprehension, and active self-regulation. Then, under each of the broad categories, I'll outline the corresponding evidence-based reasons to engage in interactive read-aloud experiences. To make the research actionable, each of these sections follows a predictable structure to define, summarize the importance, and share ways you can leverage read alouds to elevate each of the eight constructs.

Eight More Evidence-Based Reasons to Engage in Read-Aloud Experiences	
Active View Components	**Evidence-Based Reasons**
Word Recognition	• Enhance phonological awareness • Support skillful decoding
Bridging Processes	• Foster fluency • Build vocabulary knowledge
Language Comprehension	• Broaden content knowledge • Impart reading-specific background knowledge
Active Self-Regulation	• Enrich efficient strategy use • Spark motivation and engagement

Word Recognition

Is it possible to enhance some aspects of word recognition using a picture book? I would argue a resounding, YES! Under the umbrella of word recognition in the Active View of Reading, you find phonological awareness, alphabetic principle, phonics knowledge, decoding skill, and recognition of words at sight. While all of these competencies are essential, phonological awareness and skillful decoding are the two components of word recognition highlighted in this section and in read-aloud experiences in Chapter 2. I want to be crystal clear before we move on that the read-aloud experiences in this book are designed to enhance, *not replace*, the structured, systematic instruction of these competencies.

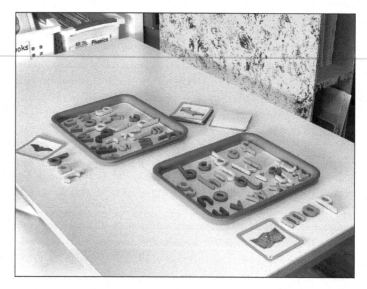

Read alouds enhance, not replace, structured, systematic word recognition instruction.

Obviously, most picture books include well-chosen words. To enhance students' phonics knowledge during read aloud, isolate and decode a few key words. This intentional teaching move will give your read alouds the extra *oomph!* they need to reinforce phonics skills for literacy learners. Making connections between systematic word study instruction and the texts you're reading aloud emphasizes that the purpose of learning about letters and sounds is to be able to read and understand engaging books.

Effective word recognition techniques to incorporate after a read-aloud experience include playful practice with words. To do this, simply select and study words from the text that have common word families; sort a sampling of words with similar phonetic features; or collect, define, and display relevant vocabulary (Rasinski, 2017). I've included many ideas like these in the *Extend the Experience* portion of exemplar interactive read alouds found in Chapters 1–5. With a clear understanding of the construct guiding your way, you will find opportunities to highlight the sounds, letters, and words as you share a book. You'll look at your texts with new eyes, and so will your students.

Enhance Phonological Awareness

- **Phonological awareness is** the ability to recognize and manipulate sounds in spoken language. Typically, phonological awareness develops from larger units of language (words) to the smallest unit (phonemes). Phonemic awareness is the most essential aspect of phonological awareness and because of this, phonemic awareness should be systematically taught. Children who are phonemically aware can hear, generate, isolate, blend, segment, and manipulate sounds.

- **Phonological awareness is essential** because it is the building block for both decoding and spelling (International Literacy Association, 2020).

- **To enhance phonological awareness while reading aloud**: Read aloud picture books that contain playful words and/or onomatopoeia. Invite students to chorally read with you, and then identify familiar letter sounds in the noisy words. Other books to add to your phonological awareness collection include those that rhyme, are written with alliteration, and alphabet books where children can match the sounds to the letters.

Read These! Noisy Books to Enhance Phonological Awareness

Title/Author	About the Book
The Animal Song (Howley, 2023)	Animal band members Croc, Bear, and Weasel fill the forest with music all summer long. When winter blows in, all of the animals ask them to stop so they can go to bed. With a "snap-poom-jingle-jangle," the band moves on to entertain in town (where it never sleeps!). The band members perform for the townspeople until they're exhausted and return to the forest just in time for spring. But now instead of playing, the band wants to sleep!
Ear Worm (Knowles, 2022)	Little Worm has this song stuck in his head: "Shimmy shimmy, no-sashay, shimmy shimmy, no-sashay!" Owl explains that a tune stuck in your head is called an "ear worm" and then performs his ear worm. When Little Worm goes on a quest to find the origin of the melody, he gathers a merry band of singing animals, each with their own unique ditty. After Papa Worm tucks him in for his nap and returns to his chores, Little Worm discovers where he heard the song before.
Song in the City (Bernstrom, 2022) [See Read-Aloud Experience on page 78]	Emmalene navigates the world with a National Federation for the Blind (NFB) white cane. On her way to church with Grandma Jean, she hears a busy city symphony, but her grandmother calls it a commotion. Once in church Grandma enjoys the music while Emmalene pouts because Grandma Jean won't listen to her city music. Finally, she covers Grandma Jean's eyes and, together, they listen to the city song.

Support Skillful Decoding

- **Decoding is** the ability to use the knowledge of the connections between letters (graphemes) and sounds (phonemes).

- **Decoding is essential** for readers because it is "the bridge between phonics knowledge and proficient word reading" (Lindsey, 2022, p. 34). In other words, decoding is the way children get the spellings of words in their memory so they can read those words by sight. When readers can automatically connect letters to sounds in words that are seen and heard, that helps them retain those words in their memory (Ehri, 2020).

- **To enhance skillful decoding during and after a read aloud**: Now and then, pause to demonstrate sound-by-sound decoding in single-syllable words. For instance, after studying the short /o/ sound, introduce the title of the Caldecott-winning book *Hot Dog* (Salati, 2022). Demonstrate how to decode the words *hot* and *dog* and remind students that sound-by-sound decoding is an effective way to figure out unknown words. Alternatively, reinforce students' knowledge of the long /i/-silent e, as you enjoy the repetition of the title: *MINE!* (Fleming, 2023). See page 84 for a read-aloud experience featuring this book.

Language Comprehension

Language comprehension is also known as listening or linguistic comprehension and is comprised of cultural and other knowledge, reading-specific background knowledge, verbal reasoning, language structure, and theory of mind.

Theory of mind is the ability for readers to understand that people's beliefs, desires, and emotions drive their actions and that other people's mental states might be different than theirs. While reading aloud narrative texts, you can boost comprehension by highlighting the social knowledge children need to have in order to make inferences (D. Fisher et al., 2023). Here are a few questions and prompts that foster theory of mind:

- Can you infer how that character is feeling at this point in the story? Use the clues in the text and in the illustrations. Which words would you use to describe that emotion?

- Imagine how you would feel in this situation. Describe that emotion.

- How did the character react to that event? Explain how you would react.

- Notice how the character's feelings have changed. What caused the change?

- Ponder the themes or big ideas in this story. Did you learn any lessons you can use in your own life?

Listening comprehension is a crucial element of reading because it enables learners to derive meaning from text and it improves parallel with decoding skills. Children develop linguistic knowledge through exposure to language in their environment and their development is enhanced with explicit instruction. As students progress through elementary school, the significance of language comprehension continues to grow (Silverman et al., 2020). Interactive read-aloud experiences shine the light on language comprehension because they offer rich, immersive opportunities to introduce children to ideas and information they might not typically come across in their daily experiences. Plus, sharing appealing fiction and nonfiction picture books gives listeners the chance to experience material that might be too challenging for them to read on their own, yet well within their capacity to understand when it's read to them (McClure & Fullerton, 2017; Silverman & Keane, 2022). As learners engage with a story, follow along with the plot, and work to understand the meaning that is conveyed through pictures and words; they are steeped in rich vocabulary and storytelling patterns. Although read aloud helps to strengthen all of the aspects of language comprehension, we will further explore content knowledge and reading-specific knowledge here.

Broaden Content Knowledge

- **Content knowledge are** understandings related to the natural and social world.

- **Content knowledge is essential** for readers because students who have content knowledge about a topic can better understand a text about that topic (Cabell & Hwang, 2020). Readers can use their knowledge to make connections within and beyond the text, visualize what is happening, and remember what they've read (Cervetti & Hiebert, 2018).

- **Read aloud builds content knowledge by** introducing students to a broad range of texts and genres. When you intentionally integrate read alouds into your content area instruction by creating text sets of conceptually or thematically related materials, and choose books with characters from a broad range of cultures and backgrounds, you are building content knowledge (Wright, 2019). I've always been a collector of text sets because they offer children wider exposure to the same topic or experience. If you follow me on social media, you'll see that I post pairs, trios, and sets of books that you can share and compare. To guide you in gathering text sets, I've included a sampling of text sets in Appendix A. You can find additional multigenre text sets in *Shake Up Shared Reading* (Walther, 2022).

Build content knowledge by extending the read-aloud experience.

A Sampling of Content-Rich Read Alouds

Topic	Title and Summary
Engineering: Bridges	*Bridges* (Majewski, 2023) Marc Majewski begins this ode to bridges with a collection of structures that have opposing physical characteristics: a high bridge—a low bridge, a long bridge—a short bridge. Then, he transitions to the ways that bridges connect us, mark history, and tell stories. Each page identifies the bridge's country and gives a one-sentence fact sparking questions and investigations on Google Earth to pinpoint its exact location. A brief paragraph about each bridge appears in the backmatter. Pairs perfectly with *A Book of Bridges: Here to There and Me to You* (Keely, 2017), featured in *The Ramped-Up Read Aloud* (Walther, 2019).
Science: Food Chain	*Creep, Leap, Crunch! A Food Chain Story* (Shaffer, 2023) Like the book, I wrote this summary to the tune of "There Was an Old Lady Who Swallowed a Fly." Get ready to sing. . . . There was a cumulative tale about temperate deciduous forest that reads like a song with a repeated chorus. The repeated chorus highlights the food chain while animals gobble and munch again and again. There's also a part where resiliency is featured as animals scramble to evade the larger creature. And then it's done!
Math: Exponential Growth	*One Chicken Nugget* (Bentley, 2023) Frank, the purple monster, loves the chicken nuggets from Celeste's food truck so much he scares away her customers and eats all of her inventory. To solve her problem, Celeste poses the "Double or Nothing Nugget Eating Challenge." To win free chicken nuggets for life, the contestant has to eat double the number of nuggets as the previous day for 30 straight days. Read to find out who wins! The back endpapers explain the origin of the folktale and exponential numbers.

Impart Reading-Specific Background Knowledge

- **Reading-specific background knowledge is** an understanding of how both narrative and informational texts work. Children who have reading-specific background knowledge can differentiate among genres, identify story elements, recognize various nonfiction text structures, access text features to help them grasp information, and contemplate the author's craft and purpose.

- **Reading-specific background knowledge is essential** because it supports readers in comprehending texts and reading strategically and critically.

- **Read aloud imparts reading-specific background knowledge** when you share informational texts and draw students' attention to the way in which the author teaches the reader about the topic and how their choice of print and visual features reflects their purpose. As you emphasize and analyze the inner workings of informational texts, students begin to recognize the presence of argument and persuasion (McClure & Fullerton, 2017). Dedicating read-aloud time to unpacking the distinctive formats of nonfiction texts empowers students to explore and gain a deeper appreciation for them. As an added bonus, instruction on text structure enhances overall comprehension (Young et al., 2023). To help students distinguish between the genres of fiction and nonfiction, share and compare paired texts on the same topic. Read-aloud experiences that focus on reading-specific background knowledge are powerful tools for enriching students' reading abilities and fostering a deeper understanding of the written word.

Paired Texts on the Same Topic

Topic	Fiction Title	Nonfiction Title
Foxes	*How to Find a Fox* (Magruder, 2016)	*How to Find a Fox* (K. Gardner, 2021)
Storms	*I Am the Storm* (Yolen & Stemple, 2020)	*Disasters by the Numbers: A Book of Infographics* (S. Jenkins, 2021)
Puffins	*When the Fog Rolls In* (Fong, 2023)	*Puffin* (M. Jenkins, 2022)

Bridging Processes

As the term implies, the bridging processes impact both of the categories we've already discussed—word recognition and language comprehension. The bridging processes include print concepts, reading fluency, vocabulary knowledge, morphological awareness, and graphophonological-semantic-cognitive flexibility, or "the ability to simultaneously consider and actively switch between letter-sound (graphophonological) and meaning (semantic) features in printed words" (Duke & Cartwright, 2021, p. 535).

When designing reading instruction, it's important to consider these bridging processes, as they effect both decoding and linguistic comprehension. The two bridging processes highlighted in this book because they are strengthened during read aloud are reading fluency and vocabulary knowledge. Before delving into these two constructs, I'd like to emphasize the role read aloud also has in developing the bridging process of print concepts. Print concepts include initial proficiencies such as noticing print and recognizing it has meaning; to more developed concepts like directionality and the ability to contrast letters, words, and sentences; to the most advanced—finger pointing to track print. Our goal in teaching print concepts is for children to use the knowledge they gain to navigate and create texts (Lindsey, 2022). With this aim in mind, take a moment here and there during a read-aloud experience to show and demonstrate how print works by naming basic book parts, highlighting the role of the author and illustrator, or pointing out the purpose of elements like punctuation, speech bubbles, captions, and so on. When we intentionally refer to the text and demonstrate how it functions, learners make substantial gains in print knowledge (Wright, 2019).

Foster Fluency

- **Fluency is** the ability to automatically decode the words within a written passage and read those words with appropriate intonation and phrasing (prosody) that mirrors the text's intended meaning.

- **Fluency is essential** for readers because "there is a strong correlation between prosodic oral reading and silent reading comprehension" (Rasinski, 2017, p. 520). That is, when children are able to read with expression, they grasp the meaning and message of the text more efficiently.

- **To foster fluency during and after read-aloud experiences** add a few fluency-enhancing practices like choral reading and performance. Choral reading is a scientifically validated method for improving fluency. Rereading portions of or an entire text in unison gives students a feel for the author's language. Predictable, cumulative, and repetitive texts naturally encourage choral reading. Listeners will sing along with the cumulative pattern borrowed from "There Was an Old Lady Who Swallowed a Fly" as a ravenous pea eats his way across the royal dinner table in *The Princess and the (Greedy) Pea* (Hodgkinson, 2023).

An authentic after-reading approach to developing fluency through repeated reading is performance. Whether children are performing a poem or preparing for Readers Theater, trust they are improving not only their fluency, but also their word decoding and even comprehension (Rasinski et al., 2020). A few of my favorite books for Readers Theater are listed in the chart below.

Read These! Books That Are Perfect for Readers Theater

Title/Author	About the Book
Hurry, Little Tortoise, Time for School! (Finison, 2022)	It's Little Tortoise's first day of school, so she paints on her racing stripes, grabs her Super Tortoise lunch box, and is on her speedy way. First, Cheetah races by. Cheetah is followed by a llama, a group of monkeys, a pangolin (I think!), and a snail. Just as Little Tortoise is nearing the school, Cheetah races by and knocks her over, shell side down. Fortunately, her teacher, Mr. Sloth, is also a slow mover. Together, they arrive just in the nick of time. But a surprise awaits . . . you'll have to read the book to find out!
The Red Jacket (Holt, 2023)	Bob, the seagull, is feeling left out and lonely. When a cheery, chirping bird notices Bob's glumness, he gives him his red jacket (with french fries in the pocket). Bob is so thrilled with his "swanky stylish" coat that he enthusiastically greets his fellow sea creatures. When a wave whooshes the jacket away, his new friends help him find it. Bob pays the kindness forward by gifting the red jacket to a gloomy turtle.
Somewhere in the Bayou (Pumphrey, 2022b)	An opossum, a squirrel, a rabbit, and a mouse are looking for a place to cross the bayou. They spot a floating log. But what's lurking in the water next to the log? A long, green tail. Rabbit makes assumptions about the tail. First, it thinks the tail is sneaky. So, opossum tries to quietly sneak by. Next, rabbit presumes it's scary. So, squirrel loudly squeaks across. Then, rabbit determines the tail is mean and pokes it on his way across. Alone, mouse discovers that the tail is actually stuck and frees the alligator.

Build Vocabulary Knowledge

- **Vocabulary knowledge is** both knowing the correct pronunciation and monitoring whether the text that includes that particular word makes sense (Duke & Cartwright, 2021).

- **Vocabulary knowledge is essential** for readers because knowledge is vital to comprehension. As we've already learned, readers need to acquire orthographic or word-reading knowledge. In addition, they need linguistic knowledge and general knowledge. In the area of linguistic knowledge, vocabulary is essential because understanding the individual words in a text helps readers better understand the text (Castles et al., 2018).

- **Read aloud builds vocabulary knowledge by** providing the opportunity to highlight and define useful words. A sensible vocabulary-building strategy I learned from Patricia Cunningham (2017) is *Three Read-Aloud Words*. The three words are selected from one read-aloud selection each week as "Goldilocks" words—words that are not *too easy* and generally known by most of your students or words that are not uncommon, obscure, or *too hard*. This idea echoes *Bringing Words to Life: Robust Vocabulary Instruction,* where the authors state, "An excellent source of words that will expand young students' vocabularies are trade books that are designed to be read aloud to children" (Beck et al., 2013). They call the words *Tier Two* words and define Tier Two words as those important and useful words that are unfamiliar to children yet they can define them using words they already know. Tier Two words provide new, more precise labels for established concepts (Beck et al., 2002). For instance, most kids understand the concept of being mad, but they may not be as familiar with words like *aggravated, furious,* or *disgruntled*. For each read-aloud experience in this resource, I selected *up to* three key vocabulary words using the Tier Two criteria. Depending on the needs of your students, you can choose to teach the words before, during, or after the read-aloud experience by adapting the during-reading procedure on page 18.

Highlight and define key vocabulary.

Teaching Key Words During Read-Aloud Experiences

1. Before reading, show the key vocabulary words to your students, one at a time. Teach your students to pronounce each word, but *do not* ask them to share the meanings for two reasons: First, several students guessing the meaning of the word wastes precious instructional time that could otherwise be used for them to hear a precise, kid-friendly definition. Second, students are likely to retain the incorrect word associations they've heard, making it more challenging for them to grasp the true meaning (Beck et al., 2013).

2. Place the words where your students can see them.

3. Read aloud the text and invite listeners to show a silent "stop" signal when they hear one of the key vocabulary words in the book. At this point, pause and help students learn the meaning of the word using the steps below. While this sequence includes seven steps, once you give it a try, you'll be able to incorporate your own language, seamlessly integrating vocabulary teaching into your read-aloud experiences.

The example that follows uses the word *vanished* from the *Song in the City* read-aloud experience found on page 78.

1. Read the word in the text.	"Emmalene left Grandma Jean and she *vanished* out the back."
2. Review the story context for the word.	See how the people are walking away out the back door. Once they're outside, you can't see them—they've *vanished*.
3. Provide a kid-friendly definition of the word.	*Vanished* means something you can't see anymore.
4. Ask children to say the word.	Say the word *vanished* with me.
5. Offer examples of the word used in familiar contexts different from the story context.	Our sidewalk chalk drawings *vanished* when it rained.
6. Engage children in activities to get them to interact with the word.	Tell your partner something that *vanished*. Say, "_____ *vanished* when . . ."
7. Invite students to say the word again to reinforce its phonological representation and meaning.	What's the word that means disappeared from being seen?

4. Showcase the key vocabulary words alongside the book cover and encourage students to be on the lookout for these words. Place a tally mark next to each word that a student reads, hears, or notices in print. Additionally, challenge yourself to incorporate these words into your conversations over the course of the week.

Active Self-Regulation

The act of reading is complex and multidimensional. Each unique reader uses a coordinated, interconnected, and orchestrated set of processes and actions (Compton-Lilly et al., 2023). When you reflect on the components that we've explored thus far—word recognition, language comprehension, and the bridging processes—it's hard to believe that there's another set of processes and actions that proficient readers employ, but active self-regulation is crucial to reading success, too.

Active self-regulation has three constructs: strategy use, motivation and engagement, and executive functioning. I'll address the role read aloud plays in enriching effective strategy use and sparking motivation in the sections that follow. First, though, we'll unpack executive functioning and how it supports comprehension.

Executive functioning skills include cognitive flexibility, inhibition (self-control), and working memory. You might be curious how these skills play out as children listen to a narrative:

- **Cognitive flexibility** is the ability to switch attention back and forth between concepts; listeners use this as they ponder story events and compare them to their own experiences.
- **Inhibition or self-control** is a reader's ability to control their impulses and ignore distractions.
- **Working memory** helps children remember the events that have happened so far while continuing to listen to the story (DeBruin-Parecki & Cartwright, 2023).

There are simple and effective ways to nurture students' executive functioning skills during read alouds. To build listeners' cognitive flexibility, pause and prompt them to think about a time when they've had a similar experience. Ask them how they would react to the event in the book. You can develop students' working memory by stopping mid-book to ask, "Catch me up, what happened so far?" As you're engaging in book experiences, informally assess learners' executive functioning skills and then continue to provide additional scaffolding and support during read aloud and beyond.

Enrich Efficient Strategy Use

- **Strategies that help readers are** the thinking processes that they use to recognize words, define unknown vocabulary, read fluently, comprehend texts, and regulate themselves and their interaction with texts.
- **Enriching efficient strategy use is essential** for readers because proficient comprehenders use strategies. Some children learn these thinking processes naturally while others benefit from explicit instruction (Duke et al., 2021).
- **Read aloud enriches efficient strategy use** when you demonstrate how you use reading strategies such as making predictions, asking questions, and summarizing, students begin to understand and interpret texts more effectively, leading to improved reading comprehension. During read-aloud experiences, pause to figure

out the main idea, identify story elements, think critically, and analyze the text. This cultivates higher-order thinking skills and encourages students to make connections and draw conclusions. Whether reading fiction or nonfiction, the comprehension strategy of inferring has been proven essential for successful comprehension (DeBruin-Parecki & Cartwright, 2023), should be modeled and explicitly taught starting in the early grades (Cervetti & Hiebert, 2018; Hwang et al., 2023), and can be fostered during discussion about children's literature (Kelly & Moses, 2018).

I've included a few tips I learned from combing through the research on how read alouds can help children enrich comprehension, specifically by teaching them the strategy of inferring. Then, in the comprehension conversations in each read-aloud experience, you'll find book-specific ideas for enriching efficient strategy use.

Inferring During Read Alouds

Kid-friendly explanation of inferring:

To infer, pay attention and connect events or ideas across a text. Think about what you already know, your schema, and use the clues in the text and illustrations to fill in the ideas or information the author left out. Some people call this "reading between the lines."

The subskills involved in inferring include:

- Attending to key details.
- Remembering events or information across a text using working memory.
- Paying attention to when things aren't making sense.
- Supporting inferences with textual and visual details.

To support students in forming inferences:

- Ask high-level questions that invite children to access prior knowledge, go beyond the text, and connect to ideas, situations, and experiences using their cognitive flexibility.
- Encourage dialogue where students offer evidence, examples, clarification, and elaboration.
- Explicitly demonstrate how to make inferences. Here are a few examples:
  - I read *this*. I saw *this* in the illustrations. When I put these two ideas together, I can infer *this*.
  - I remember *this fact* from earlier in the book. Now I learned *this fact*. I can infer that the two facts are connected because . . .
  - When I had a similar experience, I felt *like this*. The character said *this* and looks like *this*. I can infer the character is feeling *like this* because . . .

Select picture books that invite inferring:

- Stories with open-ended conclusions for inferring the ending.
  - *Down the Hole* (Slater, 2023) Can you infer what happened to the fox?
- Stories that illuminate social-emotional competencies like identity, feelings, friendship, giving, kindness, and so on to infer the author's message, themes, or big ideas.
  - *How This Book Got Red* (Greanias, 2023)

(Kelly & Moses, 2018)

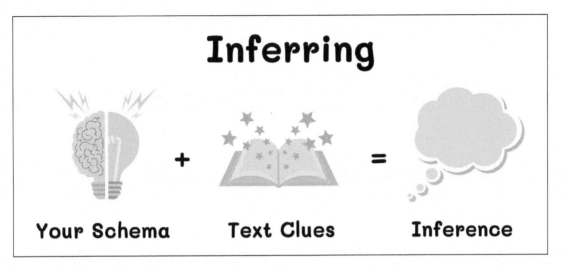

Explicitly teach inferring.

Spark Motivation and Engagement

- **Motivation is** the internal and external factors that drive a child to initiate, sustain, and direct their efforts toward completing a task—in this case, reading.

- **Engagement occurs** when children actively participate in and invest their attention in the act of reading.

- **Motivation and engagement are essential** for readers because motivated students are more likely to participate in reading activities willingly and with enthusiasm. Therefore, motivation is a crucial factor influencing reading comprehension (Duke et al., 2021). When researchers examined various approaches to enhancing reading motivation including guidance on self-regulation (refer to page 19), initiatives to cultivate students' reading interests, instilling in them an appreciation for the value of reading, and encouraging a shift in their mindsets around reading successes and challenges as readers, there were positive effects on word reading, reading fluency, and reading comprehension (Duke & Cartwright, 2021). Engaged readers are also more likely to comprehend and retain information. When students are actively engaged in the reading process,

Engaged readers interact with and respond to the material.

they are better able to connect with the text, make sense of the content, and remember key information. Engagement goes beyond reading and includes a willingness to interact with and respond to the material.

- **Read aloud sparks motivation and engagement by** fostering positive attitudes about both reading and learning, as well as forging lasting connections with books. Selecting read-aloud texts that match students' interests, lived experiences, and learning needs heightens their motivation. Consider polling your learners about their favorite picture books and including them in your selections during the year. Frequent read-aloud experiences cultivate a positive and supportive environment, another factor that enhances motivation and engagement. Finally, the thought-provoking questions and prompts you pose during a read aloud challenge students to think deeply, thereby enhancing their interest and engagement.

Read These! Books That Portray the Joys of Reading

Title/Author	About the Book
Everything in Its Place: A Story of Books and Belonging (David-Sax, 2022)	Nicky feels safe spending her recess shelving books in the school library. When she learns that the librarian, Ms. Gillam, is going to a conference, she begins to worry about spending a whole week outside at recess. After school at her mother's café, Nicky notices the people who are there alone. Her favorite solo customer is motorcycle-riding Maggie, with whom she shares a love of reading. When Nicky asks Maggie if it is scary riding a motorcycle, Maggie replies, "Everything in life is a risk." Later, when Maggie shows up at the café with her motorcycle "sisters," Nicky begins to realize that you don't have to be exactly the same as your friends to belong. In the end, while reading a poem by Mary Oliver, Nicky finds a fellow poetry lover to hang out with at recess.
This Is a Story (Schu, 2023)	The story told in Lauren Castillo's illustrations goes this way: A father and his two children are off to enjoy a day together. First, they stop by the park to fly a seahorse kite. Then, they head to the library. There, they are met by the librarian, who resembles the author and former school librarian, John Schu. Seeing the child's seahorse kite and fish shirt, the librarian picks out *Sea Horse: The Shyest Fish in the Sea* by Chris Butterworth and that child, in turn, picks out *City Cat* by Kate Banks for their sibling, who is carrying a cat stuffie. John Schu's sparse, lyrical text celebrates the connection between a book and a reader and the limitless possibilities of the world of reading.
¡Vamos! Let's Go Read (Raúl the Third, 2023)	In the fourth installment of the *¡Vamos!* series, Little Lobo and friends embark on a library adventure during a book festival. The story celebrates the wonders found inside a library, showcasing classes, digital resources, and the librarians who open doors to a world of free entertainment and information. The distinctive artwork includes labels in both Spanish and English. Readers will pore over the engaging illustrations, spotting new details each time they reread.

With all of these benefits, it's easy to see why the International Literacy Association (2018) declared that, "Reading aloud is undoubtedly one of the most important instructional activities to help children develop the fundamental skills and knowledge needed to become readers" (p. 2). While research is helpful in guiding our instructional decision making, the reality of classroom life is that we need reliable and sensible strategies for putting that research into action. The book you hold in your hands does just that. I'll round this introduction out with some techniques to ramp up your read alouds along with a quick book tour.

Read aloud helps children develop the skills and knowledge needed to become readers.

Six More Secrets to a Successful Interactive Read-Aloud Experience

In *The Ramped-Up Read Aloud* I outlined six secrets to successful read-aloud experiences. Here's a quick recap of the key ideas:

- **Strategic book selection:** As you can see from the list of criteria on page 24, many factors go into selecting texts to read aloud. While these criteria offer valuable guidance, your overarching consideration should always be the interests, lived experiences, and needs of the group of children sitting in front of you.

Criteria for Strategic Book Selection

- Characters and creators with varied voices
- Rich language
- Fascinating illustrations
- Thought-provoking themes
- Kid-appealing content
- Original premise
- Unique perspectives
- Horizon-broadening topics

Source: Walther (2019)

- **A comfy place to read and listen:** Create a space where all learners can feel comfortable, see, and hear. If your kids will be sitting on the floor, you might consider adding some inexpensive plastic footstools to give a boost to those seated in the back.

- **Expressive oral reading:** Read aloud is a performance art. Find a style that works for you. Match the tone of your voice to the mood of the text; vary your pitch; use pacing pauses, and volume, for dramatic effect; and read rhyming texts and poetry with a toe-tapping beat.

- **Frequent brain breaks:** Always leave students wanting more. In other words, don't be afraid to stop in the middle of a read-aloud experience if interest and enthusiasm are waning. Simply say, "I'm going to leave you in suspense until next time." Then, take a brain break!

- **Joyful and purposeful classroom climate:** I'm a fan of strategic seating during read aloud. Using what I've learned about my students, I give them designated "places for learning." These places are flexible, change often, and facilitate pairing students with supportive turn-and-talk partners.

- **Meaningful technology connections:** While there are many meaningful technology connections you can use to extend your read-aloud experience, I want to offer a word of caution about playing video recordings of read alouds. Remember all the insights we gained regarding the interactive nature of a comprehension-building read aloud? When your students watch someone else reading aloud, your opportunity to question, prompt, and give feedback is lost. Also missing is the emotional bond that is developed between reader and listener. In addition, unless the video is produced by the author or publisher, the content may infringe on the rights of the creators. Instead of turning on the screen, visit your school or public library to borrow the books you want to share.

Next, I want to add six additional secrets I've learned from my ongoing study of read aloud and from reading to students across the grade levels and around the country.

Secret #1: Read-Aloud Picture Books Across the Grades

During her session at the Colorado Council International Reading Association (CCIRA) conference, Dr. Sonja Cherry-Paul (2023) said, "Picture books are short stories that belong in all classrooms." So true! I never thought about picture books as short stories, but her analogy makes perfect sense, especially for children in the upper elementary grades. Here are just a few of the many reasons why picture books are essential across the grades:

- **Present a variety of narrative structures:** When you read aloud narrative picture books, students experience the entire arc of a story numerous times over the course of a week or month. The varied plot structures presented in these shorter stories are helpful in building the story grammar needed to understand the arc of a novel. For instance, you could use a picture book like *When You Can Swim* (Wong, 2023) as a touch point for future discussions about figurative language.

- **Enhance comprehension:** Rich ideas and sophisticated themes in many picture books offer opportunities for readers to locate evidence in the text and images to support their inferences, synthesize information in a nonfiction text, critique the text by expressing their opinions, and back those opinions with textual evidence.

- **Build content knowledge:** Informational picture books with rich visual images help learners build background knowledge for content-area topics. In science, you can zoom-in on a concept like ocean-floor ecosystems with the picture book *Whale Fall* (Stewart, 2023b), which details this little-known subject with visual examples and extensive backmatter. Picture books make history come alive. When learning about the Civil Rights Movement, a biography like *Love Is Loud: How Diane Nash Led the Civil Rights Movement* (Wallace, 2023) helps listeners make personal connections and better empathize with the situations Black people faced during that time period.

- **Inspire inquiry:** I can't tell you how many times I've fallen down a research rabbit hole after reading a picture book. The same can be true for your students. Whether they want to learn more about the topic, the time period, the creator, or to research unanswered questions, picture books naturally lead to micro-inquiry investigations.

- **Improve visual literacy:** An increasing amount of information is conveyed through infographics and images, making it even more important that children acquire the ability to comprehend visuals alongside written text. While reading informational texts, prompt readers to notice whether the message is mainly carried in the text, in the illustrations, or in a careful combination of both. Compare books on similar topics illustrated in different ways. As you enjoy stories, invite readers to consider the illustrator's artistic and storytelling style.

- **Serve as mentor texts for writers:** Picture books showcase how authors of informational books synthesize extensive research into an accessible and information-filled text. For writers of fiction, picture books are complete ideas expressed with originality and attention to each individual word, providing a scaffold for writers as they experiment with literary language.

- **Increase motivation and engagement:** Listeners of all ages enjoy hearing a picture book read aloud. The social collaboration that occurs as you share a picture book with your upper elementary grade learners is a motivator.

- **Are an economical use of instructional time:** Keeping all of the previously listed benefits in mind, it is clear that reading aloud picture books is an efficient and effective way to do more in less time.

Using picture books across the grades proves to be a rich and versatile way to enhance your literacy instruction.

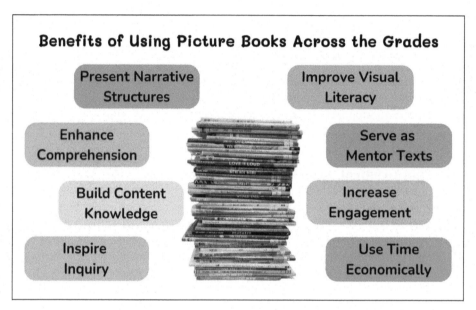

Picture books are a rich and versatile way to enhance literacy instruction across the grades.

Secret #2: Make Multimodal Connections

After listening to the book *One Tiny Treefrog: A Countdown to Survival* (Piedra & Joy, 2023) Tanisha exclaims, "That reminds me of our butterflies. We started with 20 caterpillars and now we only have 15 butterflies!" Tanisha saw the similarities between what happened in *One Tiny Treefrog* and the scientific phenomenon that had occurred in her classroom. Building bridges across the curriculum and among the texts you read aloud expands students' content knowledge. When we model and guide children as they make intertextual links, we are helping them see themselves as both teachers and learners who make connections to better make sense of their world (Varelas & Pappas, 2006). It is also essential to connect with students' "funds of knowledge" (Moll & Gonzalez, 1994, p. 443), or culturally developed everyday experiences. A culturally responsive and brain-friendly way of doing this is by tapping into multimodal resources related to the topic or theme of the featured book (Z. Hammond, 2015). You might choose to show a real object, locate the setting on Google Earth, listen to a song, display an image, or view a quick videoclip related to your upcoming read-aloud text. Making multimodal connections is essential for multilingual learners.

For all readers—but particularly those in the upper elementary grades—making connections between and among texts, including multimodal texts, is important as they learn to synthesize understandings across a variety of sources. This is where the *Similar Titles* feature in every read-aloud experience comes in handy. This feature includes two additional picture books that you can share to highlight the same learning targets as the featured selection. Then, invite students to find and investigate similarities and differences. In this volume, you'll notice texts marked with a ☆ that are a bit more complex than the main text to extend the learning or use with students in Grades 3–5. If you are looking for another idea-packed resource for incorporating multimodal texts, check out Pam Koutrakos's book *Mentor Texts That Multitask* (2022).

I'd like to emphasize that while this resource is primarily aimed at teachers of Grades preK–5, your colleagues who work with middle and high school readers can also benefit from integrating picture book read alouds into their literacy instruction. Don't hesitate to champion the idea of using read alouds when you talk with teachers across grade levels and during collaborative planning with multilevel teams!

Secret #3: Read the Whole Book—Notice and Share Unique Book Design Elements

Taking the time to notice and share unique book design elements enhances the read-aloud experience by inviting learners to study the intentional decisions the author, illustrator, and book designers make when creating a complete text. This knowledge transfers over to students' writing. Below, you'll find an overview of the parts of a picture book. To guide your whole-book conversations, take note of the information found in the *Notice the Cover Illustration* section of each read-aloud experience. There, I point out design features to share with your readers.

Read the Whole Book

Source: Walther (2021)

Notice and Share Unique Design Elements

Book Part With Definition	What to Notice in These Exemplar Texts
Jacket/Dust Jacket: The paper wrapping around a hard case cover of a hardcover book.	*This Is a Story* (Schu, 2023) *All Are Neighbors* (Penfold, 2022) **Notice:** The insides of both of these book jackets are also posters.
Wraparound Cover: A continuous cover illustration that spans across the front and back cover.	*Beneath* (Doerrfeld, 2023) **Notice:** The wraparound book jacket is different than the wraparound case cover and shows the loss this family has experienced.
Case Cover: The outer wrapping of a hardcover book. Some people call this the undies!	*I Made These Ants Some Underpants!* (Wilder, 2023) **Notice:** The hilarious case cover!
Title Page: Usually includes the title, creators' names, and publisher's logo.	*Gibberish* (Vo, 2022) **Notice:** The illustration darkens as Dat and his mom travel to their new home. The same is true for the copyright page.
Copyright Page: Found in the front or back of book and includes the book's identifying information.	*The Together Tree* (Saeed, 2023) **Notice:** Important details in the illustration. The story begins on the copyright page.
Endpapers: The glued pages at the beginning and end of a hardcover book.	*Something, Someday* (Gorman, 2023) *The Welcome Home* (Bates, 2023) **Notice:** The endpapers in both books show the setting before and after the events that transpired in the book.
Back Cover Blurb: A short, persuasive statement about the book.	*Mysterious, Marvelous Octopus* (Towler, 2024) **Notice:** The rhyming, poetic blurb.
Gutter: The center fold line in the middle of an open book that runs from the top to the bottom where the two pages meet.	*This Book Just Ate My Dog* (Byrne, 2014) **Notice:** The characters disappear into the gutter.
Backmatter: Supplementary material in the end of the book.	*I Was: The Stories of Animal Skulls* (Hocker, 2024) **Notice:** The human skull diagram and accompanying text that compares the parts of human and animal skulls.

Secret #4: Model, Explain, and Think Aloud

Recall the T. A. L. K. acronym on page 5. The *T* stands for think aloud. When you pause during a read aloud to model, explain, or verbalize your thought processes, you are demonstrating the metacognitive strategies that your readers can use as they coach themselves (Afflerbach et al., 2008). By showcasing these intentional mental actions, you provide learners with a blueprint of how to strategically approach their own reading. Thinking aloud encourages them to become more aware of the strategic actions they can use when faced with challenging texts or unfamiliar content. As an added bonus, thinking aloud builds a sense of agency and self-regulation. Without a doubt, the act of pausing to model and explain becomes a valuable instructional strategy that extends beyond immediate comprehension, contributing to the development of life-long learning skills. To help you keep this important practice at the top of your mind, there are frequent instances of inner monologue in the comprehension conversations throughout this resource.

Secret #5: Highlight Creators With Varied Voices

I intentionally selected the picture books in this volume to highlight creators with varied voices. We know from the work of Dr. Rudine Sims Bishop the importance of offering self-affirming books to our readers, books where they see their lived experiences reflected as an integral part of the broader human experience. In her words,

> Books are sometimes windows, offering views of worlds that may be real or imagined, familiar or strange. These windows are also sliding glass doors, and readers have only to walk through in imagination to become part of whatever world has been created and recreated by the author. When lighting conditions are just right, however, a window can also be a mirror. Literature transforms human experience and reflects it back to us, and in that reflection we can see our own lives and experiences as part of the larger human experience. Reading, then, becomes a means of self-affirmation, and readers often seek their mirrors in books. (Bishop, 1990, p. ix)

To take this a step further, look for ways to help readers see and connect with these creators. Throughout the year, display creators' photos and quotes from their books (G. Muhammad, 2020). Update your author and illustrator studies with creators like Anituke, Daniel Bernstrom, Minh Lê, Oge Mora, Kenard Pak, LeUyen Pham, and Christian Robinson. For additional books and ideas for highlighting creators with varied voices, I recommend *Rebellious Read Alouds: Inviting Conversations About Diversity With Children's Books* (Ahiyya, 2022) and *Antiracist Reading Revolution: A Framework for Teaching Beyond Representation to Liberation* (Cherry-Paul, 2024).

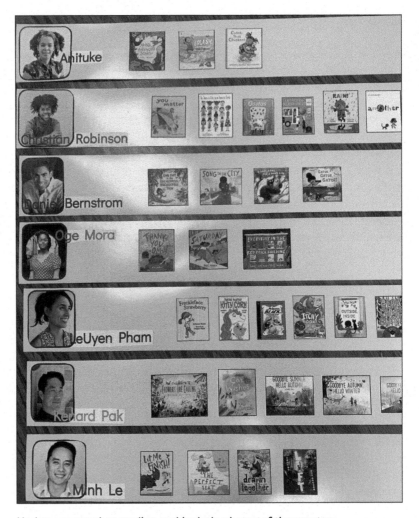

Update your author studies and include photos of the creators.

Secret #6: Embrace a Blank Sheet of Paper

Students can do a lot with a blank sheet of paper. When you offer learners a "blank slate" on which to respond to their reading or learning, you are strengthening decision making, inviting innovation, and fostering creativity. Here are ways to extend the read-aloud experience using a blank 6 x 18-inch strip of white construction or drawing paper:

- After enjoying a story, fold the strip in thirds and have children record the beginning, middle, and end.

- After reading a biography, readers can use an unfolded strip to create a timeline of a person's life.

- After learning from an informational book, fold the strip into fourths and ask students to record the main idea and three key details.

In the *Extend the Experience* section, you will find ideas that use a blank sheet of paper and a few printable templates that feature response ideas. I worked to make the printable templates as open-ended as possible so that your students could easily replicate them using a blank sheet of paper. View each template as one example of what your learners might do rather than the only option.

If you work with upper elementary grade readers, you might occasionally choose to have readers track their thinking *during* a read-aloud experience on a blank sheet of paper in a spiral notebook we call a *Literacy Notebook* (Walther & Biggs-Tucker, 2020). To do this, decide on the standard or big idea you want to target and then pause a few times for students to record their thinking. Like any during–read aloud processing, be mindful to limit the number of times you ask students to stop so you do not interrupt the flow of the book. You'll find a few ideas to get you started below.

Embrace a blank sheet of paper.

Possible During-Read Aloud Literacy Notebook Responses

Standards-Based Big Idea	Literacy Notebook Response Idea
Describe a character using thoughts, words, and actions (works well while reading character-driven, realistic fiction books).	• Before Reading: Invite students to create a T-chart labeled with the headings: *I noticed* and *I learned this about the character.* • During Reading: Pause on a few key pages where the character's thoughts, words, or actions offer insight into the character. • After Reading: Students use read-aloud notes to discuss or create a product that represents the character.
Describe the relationship between a series of historical events (works well while reading biographies).	• Before Reading: Show learners how to orient their *Literacy Notebook* landscape and draw a line. • During Reading: Pause so that listeners can record key historical events on their timeline. • After Reading: Use the timeline to converse about the connection among the events and the impact of those events on the subject of the biography.

Now that you've added a few more strategies to your read-aloud toolkit, I'll highlight the features found in Chapters 1–5.

Features You Can Count on
From *The Ramped-Up Read Aloud*

I taught with a lively and quick-witted first-grade teacher named Larry who watched the way I worked and would frequently ask, "Why are you always reinventing the wheel?" Reflecting on that question, I realize that planning with colleagues and reimagining instructional possibilities is another one of my favorite nerdy pastimes. With that said, although I reinvented many parts of this new volume, there are a few features of the read-aloud experiences that have worked well for teachers and librarians, so why change them? In this book, I have followed basically the same format as *The Ramped-Up Read Aloud.* (Larry would be so proud of me!)

Standards-Focused Read-Aloud Experiences

Like my other books, the learning targets in this volume are rooted in standards. If you've spent as much time studying standards as I have, a quick glance at the learning targets provided in the *Read-Aloud Experiences At-A-Glance Charts* that appear at the beginning of each chapter will confirm that ELA Standards were on a screen in front of me as I crafted each read-aloud experience.

Providing one alignment document that reflects standards in all 50 states and Canada is challenging due to the slight variations. Therefore, instead, you'll find a complete *Learning Target Chart* located on the companion website that includes all of the featured book titles, standards-aligned learning targets, key vocabulary words, similar book titles, and any pertinent resource links. Use this chart to guide your planning and selection of read-aloud experiences to match your specific standards and curriculum. (Visit the companion website at resources.corwin.com/more-rampedup-readalouds.)

Predictable Lesson Format

As you can see from the infographic on pages 34–35, each read-aloud experience follows the same, predictable format that appears in both *The Ramped-Up Read Aloud* and *Shake Up Shared Reading.* This easy-to-follow format has proven helpful for classroom teachers, literacy coaches, librarians, and even substitute teachers.

Robust Comprehension Conversations

In the review of the research earlier in this chapter, we learned the significance of a thoughtfully planned and interactive comprehension conversation. This effective teaching strategy creates a dynamic learning environment for both you and your students. As children actively participate in growing comprehension together, you're nurturing a community and fostering collaboration. To that end, you can expect that comprehension conversations, the heart of the interactive read aloud-experience, are filled with open-ended questions, cues for listeners to co-create knowledge, and follow-up questions aimed at promoting critical thinking. Drawing on the insights I've learned from researching for this volume, I must confess I may have slightly reinvented the collaborative conversations to make sure they are even better than last time!

What's New in *More Ramped-Up Read Alouds?*

One of the most frustrating aspects of writing a professional book is that as soon as it's published, you can think of a handful of ways you would like to revise it. In writing this volume, I've done my best to improve upon the content in *The Ramped-Up Read Aloud* in a few, specific ways. I hope you find these upgrades valuable as you read aloud in the company of children!

Recently Published Picture Books

I've always challenged myself to include an updated selection of picture books in every professional resource I've written. To that end, the 50 featured texts and most of the similar titles are different than those found in either *The Ramped-Up Read Aloud* or *Shake Up Shared Reading*. This gives you the flexibility, if you have my other books, to mix and match for a grand total of 201 read-aloud experiences to best meet the needs of your learners and your literacy curriculum. If you don't have the other resources, you are holding a book with teaching ideas for 50 of the best picture books I could find at this moment in time.

Timely Topics

Instead of focusing on the community-building concepts that we typically highlight during the first months of school like those found in *The Ramped-Up Read Aloud*, Chapter 1 is aimed at promoting ongoing conversations to maintain a happy and caring learning environment all year long.

And now that you know the importance of building content knowledge, you'll be excited to learn that this volume includes a chapter on integrating read-aloud experiences into science, technology, engineering, art, and math or STEAM learning with an eye toward standards-based science, engineering, and math practices. The books in Chapter 4 introduce readers to the thinking practices of scientists, engineers, artists, and mathematicians.

Ideas for Upper Elementary Grade Readers

I've met many teachers who learn alongside students in Grades 3–5 and have successfully enhanced the ideas in *The Ramped-Up Read Aloud* to meet the needs of their learners. As we discussed these modifications, we came to the conclusion that the comprehension conversation that occurs before, during, and after the read aloud typically works as it is written. It is the ideas in the *Extend the Experience* section that are easily adjusted to match the expectations for upper elementary grade learners. I also know the reality of your busy teaching day, so I've helped you out in this volume by including an additional, innovative *Upper Elementary Extend the Experience* ideas for each of the 50 featured titles.

Read-Aloud Experiences at a Glance

Read-Aloud Experience Title:

To assist you in intentionally selecting picture books for your read-aloud experiences, I've categorized each read-aloud title by strategy and learning target. A complete list of titles and learning targets appears in the Learning Target Chart found on the companion website (resources. corwin.com/more-rampedup-readalouds). It's nearly impossible to put a well-crafted picture book neatly into one category. My hope is to give you a starting point knowing that you'll let your students and their responses to the books be your guide.

Book Title: The 50 titles featured in this resource were selected to represent a range of recently published books and spotlight those written and illustrated by people who are from underrepresented and/or marginalized backgrounds.

About the Book: Here I include a teacher-focused summary of any insights I've learned about the author, illustrator, or behind-the-scenes tidbits about the creation or design of the book.

Learning Targets: This section will help you zero in on what you are aiming for students to be able to know and do as a result of the experience.

Let Your Talents Shine

Book Title: *Kick Push: Be Your Epic Self* (Morrison, 2022)

About the Book: Ivan, nicknamed Epic because of his epic skateboard tricks, moves into a new home. When Epic's tricks aren't grabbing the attention of the kids in the neighborhood, he tries fitting in by playing other sports. After this strategy doesn't go as planned, he takes his parents' advice and skates over to the bodega for a treat. There he finds a new crew and, together, they head out for a skateboarding session.

To find a book like this one, look for the following:

- Characters who embrace individuality
- Characters who are passionate about their hobbies

 Comprehension Conversation

Before Reading

Notice the Cover Illustration:

Learning Targets:

- I notice and track the actions and feelings of characters.
- I pay attention to my own actions and feelings.
- I talk, write, or draw about how a person's actions and feelings make them unique.

What is the boy on the cover doing? [skateboarding] Do you see anything in the illustration that makes it seem like he's moving? In the creator's note, Frank Morrison tells us that he painted the illustrations using his "signature style of mannerism" to capture the vibe of skateboarding tricks. When artists use mannerism, they stretch out parts of a person's body or twist them in an exaggerated way to show movement. Mannerism gives the painting energy. See if you notice his style as we enjoy this story.

Set a Purpose: Just like Frank Morrison, we all have a "signature style" because we do just about everything in our own, unique way. As you probably predicted by looking at the cover, in *Kick Push: Be Your Epic Self*, you're going to meet a boy who loves to skateboard. Pay careful attention to how his actions and feelings change over the course of the story. Let's go for a ride!

During Reading

- *Front endpapers:* Take a look at the front endpapers. Can you figure out what is going on? [It looks like someone is moving to a new home.] Let's start reading to see if we can figure out which character is moving.
- *A new day in a new neighborhood* page: Use the clues from the text and illustrations to infer how Epic is feeling at this point in the story. [excited, confident, happy] Share the clues you used with a partner.
- *KICK PUSH PLOP* page: Uh-oh! What's changed? Trade ideas with your *compadres*. The word *compadres* on this page means buddies or friends. How would you feel in this situation?

Comprehension Conversation

Before Reading

Notice the Cover Illustration:

Take a moment to glance at the book cover that appears with each read-aloud experience. In this part, I guide you in previewing the book. This preview might include noticing the artistic and design techniques used on the book jacket and, if applicable, on the case cover (the hard cover underneath the paper book jacket), pondering the connection between front and back cover, discussing the title, and exploring other ideas to build excitement and invite wonder.

Set a Purpose: View the purpose statement like an invitation to your listeners to inquire and investigate something in the book. The purpose statement will align with the learning target(s).

Bracketed Text

The text that appears in brackets includes teaching tips and other insights that are directed at you, the teacher, rather than the students.

During Reading

Because most picture books don't have page numbers, I use the first few words on the top of the left-hand page to point you in the right direction. The questions and prompts are designed to be asked *after* you've completed reading the entire two-page spread. As to not disrupt the flow of your read aloud, I've included only a handful of questions at critical key points. In my opinion, asking too many questions distracts your listeners. It is better to let the author and illustrator magic do the job!

Embrace Individuality

- *Bright and cheerful, Epic decided to try fitting in with the neighborhood kids* page: Epic is following his dad's advice and keeping an open mind. Does it look like it's working? Why or why not? What would you tell him to do next?
- *Epic hopped inside the bodega and grabbed his favorite snack* page: How do you think Epic feels when the kids in the bodega say, "Sick moves, bro"?

After Reading

- Share something you learned about Epic by paying attention to his actions and feelings.
- Epic loves skateboarding. Do you have any activities that you enjoy? How do you feel when you're doing them?

 Extend the Experience

- As we skated along with Epic, we noticed that his feelings changed at different points in the story. Let's revisit three key events in the story to identify and record Epic's emotions. [Revisit the pages that begin with these sentences to record Epic's emotions:
  - *A new day in a new neighborhood?*
  - *"What's going on, Epic?" Dad wants to know.*
  - *Back home they started a gnarly game of Skate.*]

  How does tracking a character's actions and feelings help you as a reader?

- Think back to a story you've just read, a movie you've watched, or a recent experience. Design a diagram to track the events and emotions that happened during that story, movie, or personal experience.

Similar Titles

🔵 *Skater Cielo* (Katstaller, 2022) [Spanish Edition: Cielo la patinadora]

About the Book: When Cielo skates, nothing can stop her except a deep pool called *The Whale*. After falling hard while trying to skate *The Whale*, Cielo loses her confidence and stuffs her skateboard into the back of her closet. Then, Cielo meets Mia and Miro, who cheer her on until she overcomes her fear of *The Whale*—one fall at a time.

🔵 *When Langston Dances* (Langley, 2021)

About the Book: Langston likes basketball, but he loves to dance. Inspired by a performance of the Alvin Ailey American Dance Theater he begins practicing until he's ready for his first day of dance school. Encouraged by his mother, he joins the class clad in his basketball gear. The teacher, Ms. Marie, gives him a pair of black ballet slippers, advises him to work hard, and he does!

Chapter 1: Maintain a Happy and Caring Learning Community All Year Long ● 43

Key Vocabulary and Kid-Friendly Definitions:

- cheerful: filled with happy feelings
- defeated: feeling like you've lost or haven't been able to do something
- drenched: soaking wet

Upper Elementary Extension:

Skateboarding was added as an Olympic sport in 2020. Curious learners can research past and future Olympic skateboarding events and/or athletes and share their findings with the class.

Key Vocabulary and Kid-Friendly Definitions:
When highlighting vocabulary during a read aloud, it is helpful to provide kid-friendly definitions. In this feature, you will find key words along with a definition to share with your learners.

Extend the Experience:
The extension will differ based on where the text and conversation naturally lead. For consistency and to assist you with your planning, they will follow this pattern: the first extension will align with the learning target and purpose statement, and the second extension will vary.

Similar Titles:
I scoured my independent bookstore and public library shelves to find related titles with comparable themes that lead students to similar read-aloud conversations. You might choose to read these titles to reinforce learning targets, compare and contrast with the featured title, or continue the conversation with a small group of students. Titles marked with this icon ☆ are more suitable for upper elementary grade listeners.

Upper Elementary Grade Extension:
This extension is written to you, as the teacher, and offers a suggestion to enrich your upper elementary grade students' book experience. These suggestions are designed to expand learners' content knowledge by inviting them to inquire, write, create, and explore ideas beyond the text.

After Reading
The concluding questions and conversation starters bring the experience full circle by drawing students' attention back to the purpose of the read aloud (other than simply for fun!). Their intention is to prompt students to apply what they've learned from this book to their lives, their learning, or their own writing.

Kid-Friendly Definitions for Key Vocabulary Words

The teaching sequence outlined on page 18 emphasizes the importance of sharing kid-friendly definitions of the key vocabulary words. Studies indicate the importance of presenting children with accessible definitions when teaching individual words (Cobb & Blachowicz, 2014).

However, that is easier said than done. I often find myself stumped to formulate an on-the-spot definition. To assist you in defining the key vocabulary words in this book, I've provided child-friendly definitions comprised of words typically familiar to young children. To enhance the explanation, consider incorporating a relevant example or displaying a corresponding image.

How to Find More Time to Read Aloud

Teachers often ask, "How do I fit read-aloud experiences into my already packed schedule?" Here are a few ideas on how you can *flexibly* use the read-aloud experiences in this resource:

- Split a picture book read-aloud experience into sections like you would a chapter book. Then, read the beginning in the morning, the middle after lunch, and the conclusion at the end of the day. This strategy provides more time for students to converse and also offers an opportunity for listeners to recap what they've learned so far from a nonfiction book or retell the story bit by bit—strengthening working memory.

- Integrate read-aloud experiences into your content-area instruction. Supplement your science or social studies materials with a picture book to build or extend students' knowledge about the topic. See the sample first-grade schedule during a science unit on animals. Notice that all of the books focus on animal characters or include animal facts.

- Weave read-aloud experiences into a published reading series. Add picture book read alouds to build background knowledge about the theme, topic, or focus strategy. Extend the learning by sharing similar books to compare and contrast with the publisher's selection.

Reading Aloud Across a First-Grade Day

Schedule	Read-Aloud Experience
Morning Meeting Learning Target: I think of ways to spread kindness.	*The Red Jacket* (Holt, 2023)
Reading & Social Studies Learning Target: I infer characters' feelings.	*How This Book Got Red* (Greanias, 2023) [See Bonus Read-Aloud Experience on the companion website (resources.corwin.com/more-rampedup-readalouds)]

Reading Aloud Across a First-Grade Day (Continued)

Schedule	Read-Aloud Experience
Snack Time or After Lunch Learning Target: I like reading funny books about animals!	*Lucky Duck* (Pizzoli, 2024)
Writing & Science Learning Target: I notice patterns in nonfiction texts while I learn about animal characteristics.	Read aloud *one or two pages of Butt or Face?* (Lavelle, 2023) [See Read-Aloud Experience on page 184]
End of Day Learning Target: I use clues to guess an animal.	Read aloud *one poem from Champion Chompers, Super Stinkers and Other Poems by Extraordinary Animals* (Ashman, 2023) [See Read-Aloud Experience on page 202]

Weaving Ramped-Up Read Alouds Into a Publisher's Reading Program

Day 1	Day 2	Day 3	Day 4	Day 5
Introduce theme and/or strategies using a picture book from *More Ramped-Up Read Alouds*.	"Shared reading" of story of the week per publisher's directions.	"Close reading" of story of the week per publisher's directions.	"Response to reading" with story of the week per publisher's directions.	Share and compare story of the week with a picture book from *More Ramped-Up Read Alouds*.

Let the Reading Begin!

With the confidence that comes from knowing exactly why we must redouble our efforts to share high-quality interactive read-aloud experiences with children, it's time to pull a picture book off the shelf. Savor the illustrations. Study the text. Then, with enthusiasm and intention, let the reading begin!

"Sari-sari means 'a good variety'—just look around and you'll see. What help can you give your community?"

—Lolo's Sari-Sari Store
by Sophia N. Lee and Christine Almeda

Maintain a Happy and Caring Learning Community All Year Long

Read Beyond the Pages

Picture books expand learners' horizons and extend the boundaries of your teaching space. During the interactive read-aloud experiences in this chapter, listeners will meet children, caregivers, and a few creatures. Guided by your questions and prompts, students step into the lives of these characters, fostering social awareness and comprehension. The narrative-focused conversations help children appreciate the viewpoints, thoughts, and emotions of others—developing their theory of mind. As learners explore characters' mindsets, they have opportunities to reflect on their own perspectives, fostering a deeper awareness of themselves and their peers. The learning events in Chapter 1 will not only enhance your students' literacy development, but they will also help to support a community where empathy, resilience, and kindness flourish as you introduce readers to characters who do the following:

- Embrace individuality
- Reach for goals
- Face challenges
- Nurture relationships
- Spread joy and kindness

Together, let's cultivate a vibrant learning environment where thought-provoking stories nurture a deep sense of connection and understanding. As educators, you play a pivotal role in steering students beyond the books as they create spaces where every individual is seen, heard, and valued.

Scan here to find a complete learning target chart with book-related online links, a bonus read-aloud experience, and printable resources.

https://qrs.ly/h5fv5pt

To read a QR code, you must have a smartphone or tablet with a camera. We recommend that you download a QR code reader app that is made specifically for your phone or tablet brand.

Big Idea: Featured Title	Learning Targets
Let Your Talents Shine: *Kick Push: Be Your Epic Self* (Morrison, 2022)	• I notice and track the actions and feelings of book characters. • I pay attention to my own actions and feelings. • I talk, write, or draw about how a person's actions and feelings make them unique.
Make Space for Yourself: *BIG* (Harrison, 2023)	• I notice and track the words, actions, and feelings of characters. • I pay attention to my own words, actions, and feelings. • I talk, write, or draw about how words and actions impact my feelings and the feelings of others.
Celebrate Strengths: *Spanish Is the Language of My Family* (Genhart, 2023)	• I think about the actions characters take to reach their goals. • I set my own goals.
Persist: *The Perfect Plan* (Gilbert, 2021)	• I predict the actions characters take to reach their goals. • I ponder whether a story is real or make-believe. • I set my own goals.
Be Confident: *Daddy Dressed Me* (M. Gardner & Gardner, 2023)	• I use details to describe characters and events. • I notice how characters react to events and challenges.
Be Optimistic: *The Bright Side* (Otis, 2023)	• I use details to describe characters' traits. • I explain how characters react to events and challenges. • I connect characters' actions to their traits.
Reach Out: *The Together Tree* (Saeed, 2023)	• I notice how characters' words and actions affect people around them. • I think about how my words and actions affect people around me. • I look for ways to reach out to people.
Compromise: *The Only Astronaut* (Jain, 2023)	• I notice how characters' words and actions impact people around them. • I think about how my words and actions impact people around me. • I look for ways to compromise.
Show Appreciation: *Stickler Loves the World* (L. Smith, 2023)	• I notice how characters' mindsets and actions impact people around them. • I think about how my mindset and actions impact people around me. • I look for ways to spread joy.
Share and Care: *All Kinds of Special* (Sauer, 2023)	• I notice how characters' mindsets and actions affect people around them. • I think about how my mindset and actions affect people around me. • I look for ways to spread kindness.
Bonus Lesson (online) Share and Care: *The Last Stand* (Eady, 2024)	• I notice how characters' mindsets and actions affect people around them. • I think about how my mindset and actions affect people around me. • I look for ways to spread kindness.

My Favorite Read Alouds for Creating Community

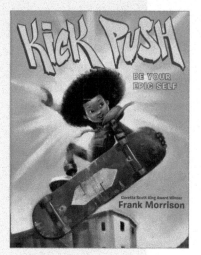

Let Your Talents Shine

Book Title: *Kick Push: Be Your Epic Self* (Morrison, 2022)

About the Book: Ivan, nicknamed Epic because of his epic skateboard tricks, moves into a new home. When Epic's tricks aren't grabbing the attention of the kids in the neighborhood, he tries fitting in by playing other sports. After this strategy doesn't go as planned, he takes his parents' advice and skates over to the bodega for a treat. There he finds a new crew and, together, they head out for a skateboarding session.

To find a book like this one, look for the following:

- Characters who embrace individuality
- Characters who are passionate about their hobbies

Comprehension Conversation

Before Reading

Notice the Cover Illustration:

What is the boy on the cover doing? [skateboarding] Do you see anything in the illustration that makes it seem like he's moving? In the creator's note, Frank Morrison tells us that he painted the illustrations using his "signature style of mannerism" to capture the vibe of skateboarding tricks. When artists use mannerism, they stretch out parts of a person's body or twist them in an exaggerated way to show movement. Mannerism gives the painting energy. See if you notice his style as we enjoy this story.

Set a Purpose: Just like Frank Morrison, we all have a "signature style" because we do just about everything in our own, unique way. As you probably predicted by looking at the cover, in *Kick Push: Be Your Epic Self,* you're going to meet a boy who loves to skateboard. Pay careful attention to how his actions and feelings change over the course of the story. Let's go for a ride!

During Reading

- *Front endpapers:* Take a look at the front endpapers. Can you figure out what is going on? [It looks like someone is moving to a new home.] Let's start reading to see if we can figure out which character is moving.
- *A new day in a new neighborhood* page: Use the clues from the text and illustrations to infer how Epic is feeling at this point in the story. [excited, confident, happy] Share the clues you used with a partner.
- *KICK PUSH PLOP* page: Uh-oh! What's changed? Trade ideas with your *compadres.* The word *compadres* on this page means buddies or friends. How would you feel in this situation?

Learning Targets:

- I notice and track the actions and feelings of characters.
- I pay attention to my own actions and feelings.
- I talk, write, or draw about how a person's actions and feelings make them unique.

- *Bright and cheerful, Epic decided to try fitting in with the neighborhood kids* page: Epic is following his dad's advice and keeping an open mind. Does it look like it's working? Why or why not? What would you tell him to do next?

- *Epic hopped inside the bodega and grabbed his favorite snack* page: How do you think Epic feels when the kids in the bodega say, "Sick moves, bro"?

After Reading

- Share something you learned about Epic by paying attention to his actions and feelings.

- Epic loves skateboarding. Do you have any activities that you enjoy? How do you feel when you're doing them?

Extend the Experience

- As we skated along with Epic, we noticed that his feelings changed at different points in the story. Let's revisit three key events in the story to identify and record Epic's emotions. [Revisit the pages that begin with these sentences to record Epic's emotions:

  o *A new day in a new neighborhood?*

  o *"What's going on, Epic?" Dad wants to know.*

  o *Back home they started a gnarly game of Skate.*]

    How does tracking a character's actions and feelings help you as a reader?

- Think back to a story you've just read, a movie you've watched, or a recent experience. Design a diagram to track the events and emotions that happened during that story, movie, or personal experience.

Similar Titles

 Skater Cielo (Katstaller, 2022) [Spanish Edition: *Cielo la patinadora*]

About the Book: When Cielo skates, nothing can stop her except a deep pool called *The Whale*. After falling hard while trying to skate *The Whale*, Cielo loses her confidence and stuffs her skateboard into the back of her closet. Then, Cielo meets Mia and Miro, who cheer her on until she overcomes her fear of *The Whale*—one fall at a time.

 When Langston Dances (Langley, 2021)

About the Book: Langston likes basketball, but he *loves* to dance. Inspired by a performance of the Alvin Ailey American Dance Theater he begins practicing until he's ready for his first day of dance school. Encouraged by his mother, he joins the class clad in his basketball gear. The teacher, Ms. Marie, gives him a pair of black ballet slippers, advises him to work hard, and he does!

Key Vocabulary and Kid-Friendly Definitions:

- cheerful: filled with happy feelings

- defeated: feeling like you've lost or haven't been able to do something

- drenched: soaking wet

Upper Elementary Extension:

Skateboarding was added as an Olympic sport in 2020. Curious learners can research past and future Olympic skateboarding events and/or athletes and share their findings with the class.

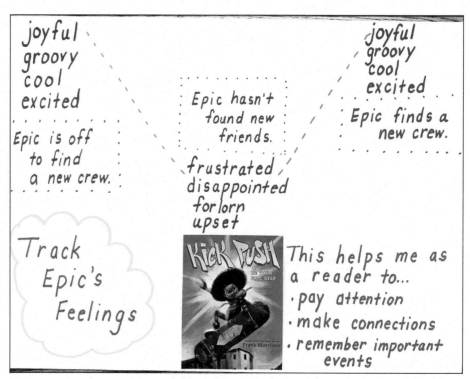

Track Character's Feelings Chart

Tracking Actions and Feelings About a Personal Experience Work Sample

My Favorite Read Alouds for Embracing Individuality

New York Times bestselling creator
VASHTI HARRISON

Learning Targets:

- I notice and track the words, actions, and feelings of characters.

- I pay attention to my own words, actions, and feelings.

- I talk, write, or draw about how words and actions impact my feelings and the feelings of others.

Make Space for Yourself

Book Title: *BIG* (Harrison, 2023)

About the Book: What does it mean when we say to a toddler, "What a big girl you are!"? How does the meaning of the word *big* change as girls grow older? Vashti Harrison explores these questions through the eyes of a child who finds enough strength and self-love to stand up for herself. *BIG* was the 2024 winner of the Caldecott Medal and a Coretta Scott King Award Author and Illustrator Honor book.

To find a book like this one, look for the following:

- Characters who embrace individuality
- Themes of self-acceptance

Comprehension Conversation

Before Reading

Notice the Cover Illustration

- What stands out when you first look at this book cover? [Discuss why they think Vashti Harrison made the title *BIG* stand out.] Vashti Harrison created the illustrations using digital tools and chalk pastel. Notice the colors she chose to use in her pictures.

- Let's peek at the back cover. Tell a friend something you learned about the girl. [She likes ballet.] [If you are able to reveal the case cover under the book jacket, discuss the words that appear there. Also, notice the phrase "I Love You" hidden among the scribbles on the endpapers.]

Set a Purpose: The title of this book, *BIG*, is a word that we use a lot like when we say things like, "It's no big deal!" or "Today's your big day!" Words can have different shades of meaning or make us feel differently depending on the situation. Keep that in mind as we read this story together.

During Reading

- *She learned her ABCs and 123s* page: Look at the girl's face. Can you infer how she's feeling? When the adults say, "What a big girl you are!" what do you think they mean?

- *until it wasn't* page: Tell a friend about what you see happening on these two pages. How is the meaning of the word *big* changing?

- *The words stung and were hard to shake off* page: How does this page make you feel? Explain what you've learned so far about the power of words.

- *and started to see things more clearly* page: Notice the words in her sea of tears. Which word is she picking up? Can you figure out what the author means by "she started to see things more clearly"?
- *These are yours* page: Why do you think she's giving some words back and keeping others? What has she discovered about herself?

After Reading

- What did you learn about the shades of meaning of the words we say to one another? How might you use what you learned when talking to your friends or to family members/caregivers?

- Did you notice that the girl didn't have a name? Why do you suppose Vashti Harrison chose not to name her?

Extend the Experience

- In the end, the girl makes space for herself and chooses adjectives like "smart, funny, and kind" to describe herself. Make a list of adjectives that you would use to describe yourself. Draw a self-portrait and write those adjectives around your picture. [If needed, co-create an Alphabet of Adjectives Chart to support your writers.]

- If you hear someone using words in a hurtful way, what can you do?

Similar Titles

 ***Baller Ina* (Casal, 2023)**

About the Book: Liz Casal's debut picture book features Ina, who loves basketball as much as she enjoys ballet. The rhyming text follows Ina from the ballet studio to the basketball court, where she encounters a player who questions her skills. Ina confidently replies, "Wait until you see me fly."

 ***Wallflowers* (Joy, 2023)**

About the Book: Written for all children who prefer to quietly watch and listen but still want to be seen, heard, and celebrated.

Key Vocabulary and Kid-Friendly Definitions:

- advice: ideas someone shares to help you solve problems

- exposed: feeling like everyone can see you without any protection

- judged: when people have opinions about you and/or your actions

Upper-Elementary Extension:

The word *big* took on nuanced meanings. Extend the idea of nuanced meanings by exploring words with multiple meanings. Have pairs of students illustrate the multiple meanings of words using the *Multiple Meaning Word Cards Printable*. [Located on the companion website (resources. corwin.com/ more-rampedup-readalouds).]

An Alphabet of Adjectives			
A athletic awesome artful amazing	B Bumpy bright brave beautiful	C colorful creative clever charming	D Dazzling delicious dependable delightful
E energetic easygoing enthusiastic enchanting	F fast Funny fluffy friendly fantastic	G gigantic grateful greasy grateful generous	H hard, happy high humorous helpful
I interesting Inventive intense incredible	J Jumpy Jolly juicy joyful	K Kind hearted knowledgable kooky kind	L loud lucky lovely loving
M messy magical merry	N nice Neat noisy	O outstanding outgoing original	P patient Playful polite
Q quirky quiet quick quaint	R rough respectful reliable responsible	S smart slimy soft sweet	T talented tall talented thoughtful
U unusual useful ultimate unbelievable	V valient valuable vast versatile	W witty warmhearted Wondering wonderful	XYZ young Yummy youthful zippy

Alphabet of Adjectives Chart

Multiple Meaning Words

Teacher Directions: Print word cards. Give one card to each pair of students. Invite them to work together to draw the different meanings of the word.

bark

bat

bowl

rock

Multiple Meaning Word Cards Printable

My Favorite Read Alouds for Embracing Individuality

_____
_____
_____
_____
_____
_____
_____
_____
_____
_____
_____
_____
_____
_____
_____
_____
_____
_____
_____
_____
_____
_____
_____
_____
_____
_____
_____
_____
_____
_____
_____
_____
_____

Celebrate Strengths

Book Title: *Spanish Is the Language of My Family* (Genhart, 2023) [Spanish Edition: El español es la lengua de mi familia]

About the Book: Manolo is the first to sign up for the Spanish Spelling Bee because Spanish is the language of his family. As his abuela helps him prepare, she shares stories from her childhood, when speaking Spanish was not allowed. After hearing the punishments that Abuela, her family members, and friends endured, Manolo is even more determined to win the spelling bee. In addition to the Spanish alphabet, backmatter includes an author's note and information about the National Spanish Spelling Bee, the prohibition of speaking Spanish in public schools, and Children's Day/Book Day on April 30.

To find a book like this one, look for the following:

- Characters who set goals
- Books that promote a love of words

Comprehension Conversation

Before Reading

Notice the Cover Illustration

Learning Targets:

- I think about the actions characters take to reach their goals.
- I set my own goals.

Who is under the spotlight? [a boy] Why do you suppose John Parra is highlighting this boy? [Perhaps he's the main character.] Use the details in John Parra's illustrations to infer what this boy might be doing.

Set a Purpose: The details in the cover illustration helped you predict that the boy is going to be in a *spelling bee*. A spelling bee is a competition in which the person who is able to spell the most words correctly wins. Let's R-E-A-D to hear about what the boy does and learns to get ready for the spelling bee.

During Reading

- *I don't know how to spell some words yet* page: What is Manolo's goal? Has he done anything to try and achieve his goal?

- *I work even harder* page: Why do you suppose he is working even harder now? [Because of the sad stories his abuela told him.] Tell us an adjective you would use to describe Manolo. [determined, hardworking, motivated, confident]

- *But studying all these words is hard* page: Have you ever felt frustrated or tired when you were trying to do or learn something? What could you do to cheer someone up who's experiencing these emotions? Swap ideas with a neighbor.

- *My first word is poderoso* page: The boy tells you exactly how he's feeling on this page. Let's reread to find the words he uses. [powerful, proud, strong] Why do you think his mood has changed at this point in the story?

After Reading

- How would you describe Manalo's mood when he achieved his goal?

- Predict what Manolo's next goal might be.

Extend the Experience

- Manolo had a goal and took action steps to reach his goal. Take a moment to think of a goal you have for yourself at school or at home. Write down that goal and the three things you will do to reach that goal on the *Goal Setting Printable*. [Located on the companion website (resources.corwin.com/more-rampedup-readalouds).]

- Go back through the text and find three words you want to learn how to spell in both English and Spanish. Practice the words with a friend.

Similar Titles

 ***Planting Stories: The Life of the Librarian and Storyteller Pura Belpré* (Denise, 2019) [Spanish Edition: Sembrando historias: Pura Belpré: bibliotecaria y narradora de cuentos]**

About the Book: In the 1920s, Pura Belpré shared her abuela's stories from Puerto Rico with the children who gathered at her feet in the New York Public Library. Pura sets her sights on publishing these stories and as she works toward this goal, she continues to plant story seeds across the country—seeds that change many young readers' lives.

 ***Words of Wonder from Z to A* (Avant-Garde, 2023)**

About the Book: In 2021, 14-year-old Zaila (ZI-eela) Avant-Garde became the first Black American to win the Scripps National Spelling Bee. In this reverse alphabet book, Zaila's passion for words and her positive, can-do attitude radiate off the colorful pages. The book begins with her first name and ends with her last name. In between, she highlights inspiring words like *resilience*, *optimism*, and *joy*. Each page features a quote about the word from a noteworthy individual. The backmatter includes the origins of all 26 words.

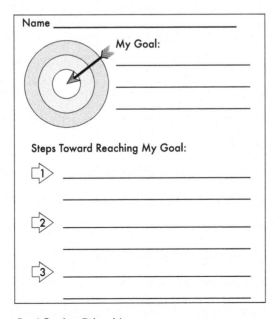

Goal Setting Printable

Key Vocabulary and Kid-Friendly Definitions:

- frustrated: feeling upset or angry when something is challenging

- shame: feeling like you did something wrong or bad

- triumphant: feeling happy and proud that you did or won something

Upper Elementary Extension:

In the backmatter, there is a note about Children's Day/Book Day on April 30. Invite interested students to plan and prepare a celebration of book joy. Find more information here:

Children's Day/Book Day Information
https://qrs.ly/1vfn8p2

Learning Targets:

- I predict the actions characters take to reach their goals.
- I ponder whether a story is real or make-believe.
- I set my own goals.

Persist

Book Title: *The Perfect Plan* (Gilbert, 2021)

About the Book: In order to make her dream of building the perfect tree fort come true, Maya researches, designs, plans, and gathers her supplies. Unfortunately, it proves a bit more challenging than she thought. Not willing to give up on her dream, Maya enlists the help of the forest animals and, together, they construct a treehouse that exceeds her imagination.

To find a book like this one, look for the following:

- Characters who set goals
- Characters who get help and persist

Comprehension Conversation

Before Reading

Notice the Cover Illustration

- Use the details in the cover illustration to help you predict what she is planning. Show a friend the details that helped you make that prediction.

- Front Endpapers: What do you think she's doing? [Looking at animal's homes.] How might that help her carry out her perfect plan?

Set a Purpose: Do you predict this story will be real or make-believe? Will her perfect plan work? There is only one way to find out the answers to these questions—let's read!

During Reading

- *Maya dreamed of having a fort* page: What is Maya's dream? [Having an incredible and wonderful tree fort.] Another word for a dream is a goal. Predict what Maya will have to do to build a tree fort.

- *But Maya wasn't ready to give up yet* page: Hmmm! What did Maya do to help her reach her goal? [Asked the beavers to help.] Could this happen in real life? Talk with a buddy.

- *Maya and her team hurried over to the moose* page: Look in the picture: The moose *lugged* the heavy branches. I lug my heavy backpack to school every day. Lugged is when you've pulled, lifted, or carried something heavy. Tell your neighbor something you've lugged around. Start with, "I've lugged around my ___." Say the word that means to have pulled, lifted, or carried something heavy. [lugged]

- *Maya and the animals studied the fort they had built together* page: Explain what keeps happening to Maya's plan. [Something goes wrong.] Does Maya give up? Predict what she's going to do now that it's raining.

After Reading

- Retell the steps Maya took to reach her goal of making a dream tree fort.

- Do you think this story is real or make-believe? Explain your reasons.

Extend the Experience

- Maya doesn't give up when trying to reach her goal. She's resourceful and figures out smart strategies. Let's look back over the story and jot down her strategies.

- Throughout the story, Maya enthusiastically describes her tree fort. Help me find the adjectives she chooses and record them on a chart. You can refer to this chart when you're looking for words to paint a clearer picture in the stories you're writing.

Similar Titles

 Jabari Tries (Cornwall, 2020) [Spanish Edition: *Jabari trata*]

About the Book: After overcoming his fears in *Jabari Jumps* (Cornwall, 2017), Jabari sets out to design a flying machine. His sister Nika wants to help. When Jabari resists, his dad steps in and encourages him to view his sister as his inventing partner. After a few attempts, a bit of frustration, and some wise advice from their dad, Jabari and Nika find success. [Find book experiences for *Jabari Tries* in *Shake Up Shared Reading* (Walther, 2022) and for *Jabari Jumps* in *The Ramped-Up Read Aloud* (Walther, 2019).]

Sal Boat: A Boat by Sal (Heder, 2022)

About the Book: Sal loves the water and decides to build himself a boat. He scours the seaside town for found materials and soon everyone has words of advice—sometimes too much! Determined to prove himself a worthy boat builder, he refuses to accept help until a girl asks, "So how are you going to launch it?" Then, Sal learns the value of teamwork and community.

Key Vocabulary and Kid-Friendly Definitions:

- eagerly: feeling happy or excited about something you want to do or get

- gasped: breathed in quickly because you were surprised

- heaved: lifted up

Upper Elementary Extension:

Have students draw a design for their dream fort either by hand or using a 3D design program.

Goal-Reaching Strategies Chart

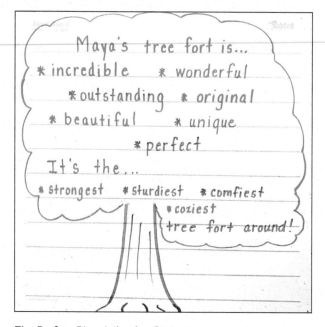

The Perfect Plan *Adjective Chart*

My Favorite Read Alouds for Goal Setting

Be Confident

Book Title: *Daddy Dressed Me* (M. Gardner & Gardner, 2023)

About the Book: Ava's dad is creative. He cooks, he builds, he decorates, but the thing he enjoys the most is sewing special outfits for Ava. At school, Ava finds out they will be celebrating "Move Up Day" by reciting a poem. Although she is excited about advancing to first grade, she's also apprehensive about missing her favorite kindergarten activities and "extra worried" about reciting a poem on stage. Daddy eases her fears by making her a special dress and helping her practice her poem. As he stitches and she rehearses, Ava gains confidence and performs her poem with pride.

To find a book like this one, look for the following:

- Characters or situations that are relatable to children
- Characters who face and overcome challenges

Learning Targets:

- I use details to describe characters and events.
- I notice how characters react to events and challenges.

Comprehension Conversation

Before Reading

Notice the Cover Illustration

Think about the title *Daddy Dressed Me* and look at the picture. How do you think these characters are related? [dad and daughter] Now, let's search the back cover for more clues. Here's a photograph of Michael and Ava Gardner—they are *coauthors* of this story. That means they wrote it together. Do you notice anything about their outfits? [they match]

Set a Purpose: Even before we started reading, we used clues from the cover illustration and photograph to learn a little more about the characters. Readers pay attention to details to get to know the characters in a book. Let's continue to be detail detectives as we enjoy *Daddy Dressed Me.*

During Reading

- *But, most of all, Daddy was best at sewing* page: What have you learned about Ava's daddy so far? Do you know any grown-ups who like to sew?

- *Ava's heart went thump, thump, thump* page: Ava is having mixed feelings about Move Up Day. Tell a neighbor one of Ava's emotions. Ask them to tell you another. Can you think of a time when you weren't sure how you were feeling and felt mixed up, like Ava?

- *Daddy held Ava close* page: Ava's daddy *assured* her that he would help her practice. That means he wanted her to know that she could feel safe and confident that he would truly help her. What else did he offer to do? [make her a special dress] How did Ava react to that?

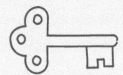
- *Back home Ava drew a picture of her dream dress* page: Turn and tell a neighbor how Daddy is thinking and explain the clues you used to figure it out. Why is it important to pay attention to characters' thoughts and moods?

After Reading

- What did Ava do when faced with the challenge of reciting a poem at Move Up Day? [practiced, worked hard, learned from her mistakes]

- What did Daddy do when faced with the task of making a complicated dress? [worked hard, learned from his mistakes]

Extend the Experience

- We all face difficult situations. Let's add to the strategies we learned from Ava and her dad. What else could you do when faced with a challenge?

- In this story, Ava's dad made her a dress to help her feel more confident and face the challenge of reciting a poem on stage. Design a piece of clothing that solves a problem. [If possible, display a few examples—I showed my zip-off hiking pants and a hat with an opening for a pony tail.] Begin by sketching your design on a whiteboard or piece of paper. Then, use construction paper or other materials to create your design.

Similar Titles

 Sydney's Big Speech (Newsome, 2024)

About the Book: *Sydney's Big Speech* is a celebration of self-discovery, empowerment, and the transformative power of words. It's the first day of school, and a shy girl named Sydney is unable to work up the courage to share anything about herself. When she hears that she has to give a speech, she's overwhelmed by fear that "the words won't come out." Sydney confides in her wise and supportive dad, who introduces her to the inspiring speeches of groundbreaking Black women: Kamala Harris, Condoleezza Rice, Carol Moseley Braun, and Shirley Chisholm. Through these videos, Sydney learns the impact of using wise, energetic, and powerful words.

 Walter Finds His Voice: The Story of a Shy Crocodile (Ha, 2023)

About the Book: Shy Walter floats just below the surface of the swamp. When he's nervous to sing with his friends or startled by their birthday surprise, Walter submerges himself. This changes when the heron twins decide to play catch with Walter's pal Turtle. Seeing Turtle in trouble prompts Walter to intervene and gives him newfound confidence.

Key Vocabulary and Kid-Friendly Definitions:

- complicated: needs more time or effort to do or understand; not simple

- confident: feeling sure and happy about yourself

- invincible: so strong that nothing can hurt you or make you feel bad

Upper Elementary Extension:

Provide students with the opportunity to practice and recite their favorite poems individually, in pairs, or in small groups.

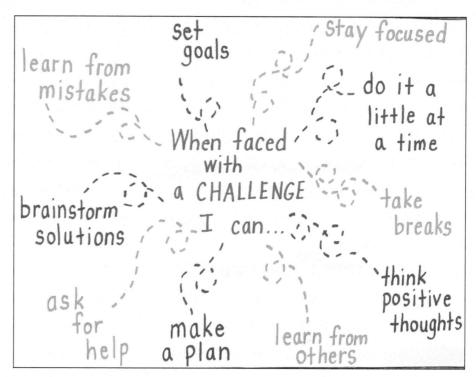

Strategies for Facing Challenges Chart

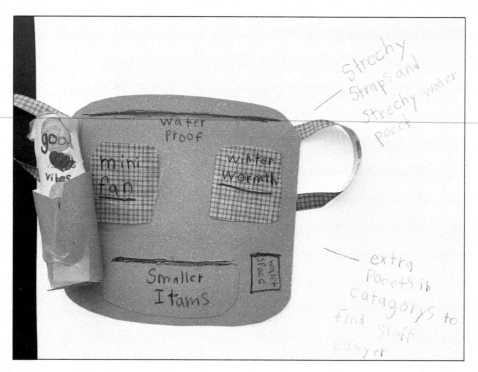

Clothing Design Work Sample

My Favorite Read Alouds for Facing Challenges

Be Optimistic

Book Title: *The Bright Side* (Otis, 2023)

About the Book: Based on the author's personal experience, a boy tells the story of leaving his house and living on a school bus. While on the bus, he is home-schooled. His family helps him think flexibly, use his imagination, and persist to overcome challenges. When he finally goes to school, he has a difficult time adjusting until his class is faced with an unexpected problem. Using his positive mindset and the skills he's learned from his prior experiences, he shows his teachers and classmates how to look at the bright side.

To find a book like this one, look for the following:

- Characters who face and overcome challenges
- Themes of positivity and persistence

Comprehension Conversation

Before Reading

Notice the Cover Illustration

Compare the school bus on the wraparound cover to a school bus you've seen or ridden on before. What is the same? Are there any differences? [Notice the household items that appear in the bus.] Along with the title, *The Bright Side,* the cover reads, "When your home is an old bus, optimism is your superpower!" When someone has *optimism* or is *optimistic,* they believe or hope that good things will happen. Why do you suppose the title of this book is *The Bright Side?*

Set a Purpose: In stories, the things that happen are called events. Like people, characters react differently to events. When you pay attention to a character's reactions, it helps you to get to know that character. Let's open the book and meet the main character of *The Bright Side.*

During Reading

- *It was hard saying goodbye to my friends* page: Notice the boy's reaction to leaving his friends. If you were in the boy's shoes, would you be able to look on the bright side?

- *You do something you didn't know you could do* page: What has the boy learned so far? If you had to describe him to a friend, what would you say? Take turns using the sentence stem, "The boy is _____." Do you notice anything different about the illustrations? [Colorful designs appear when he's looking on the bright side.]

- *I'm excited to finally make some new friends* page: Describe his reaction to going to "a real school."

- *I start to worry that none of these kids will want to be my friend* page: Combine clues from the words and illustrations to infer how he's feeling here. Share your inference and clues with a friend; ask them to share theirs.

Learning Targets:

- I use details to describe characters' traits.

- I explain how characters react to events and challenges.

- I connect characters' actions to their traits.

- *If we look on the bright side* page: Notice what's happening on this page. [They're making pizza toast and doing a shadow puppet show.] Where did he get these ideas? [From the time he spent living on the school bus.]

After Reading

- What did you learn about the boy from noticing how he reacted to the events in the story?

- On the back flap there is a picture of Chad Otis and his family. It says, "Chad Otis lived on a school bus for about four years and didn't go to school with other kids until the third grade!" Talk about that with a classmate.

Extend the Experience

- Select a memorable event from the story. On one side of a blank piece of paper write and/or draw the event. Then, flip the paper over and show how the boy reacted to that event. Think about what you learned about the boy's character traits from his reaction.

- It's healthy for your brain to be optimistic or look for the bright side. Let's help each other remember to think positive thoughts when disappointing or unexpected things happen.

Similar Titles

 ***Saturday* (Mora, 2019) [Spanish Edition: *Sábado*]**

About the Book: Every Saturday, Ava and her mother spend the day together. They go to story time at the library, get new hairdos, picnic on the grass, and do something else special. This Saturday, they are planning to see a one-night-only puppet show. Even though everything that could go wrong does, Ava's mom reassures her that it will still be a splendid day. When her mom realizes that she's left the puppet show tickets at home, it's Ava who reminds her mom that the most important thing about Saturdays is that they spend them together. Scan the QR code for a bonus read-aloud experience for *Saturday*.

Bonus Read-Aloud Experience for *Saturday*

https://qrs.ly/hhfn8p6

 ***Yenebi's Drive to School* (Santamaria, 2023) [Spanish Edition: *El viaje de Yenebi a la escuela*]**

About the Book: Up at four o'clock in the morning, Yenebi wakes her little sister Melanie for their drive to school with Mami—a drive that includes waiting in what Yenebi describes as her "archenemy . . . La Línea." The line is packed with lanes of cars waiting to cross the border into the United States. During their multihour wait, they see vendors selling their wares and carts rolling by with mouth-watering food. The trio enjoys their breakfast together and soon the vendors are replaced by border agents as they inch forward for their turn. Passing through customs, it's now seven o'clock and they're on schedule to make it to school on time. In the author's note, Sendy shares a bit about her lived experience as a Mexican American living in a border city.

Key Vocabulary and Kid-Friendly Definitions:

- antsy: not able to relax, sit still, or stay quiet

- jumbled: mixed up or confused

Upper Elementary Extension:

Initiate a micro-inquiry project to discover unique kinds of houses. Give students 15–20 minutes to locate a photo and write a fun fact or two about the most unique dwelling they can find. Post their findings and do a gallery walk to see them all.

Wacky House Article
https://qrs.ly/22fn8p5

Event and Reaction Work Sample

My Favorite Read Alouds for Facing Challenges

Learning Targets:

- I notice how characters' words and actions affect people around them.
- I think about how my words and actions affect people around me.
- I look for ways to reach out to people.

Reach Out

Book Title: *The Together Tree* (Saeed, 2023)

About the Book: It's springtime when Rumi joins his new class. During recess, Rumi sits under a shady old willow tree twirling a stick while the other kids play. Later, Asher and Ella make fun of Rumi's colorful, decorated shoes, but Han doesn't say anything. When Asher's bullying escalates to pebble throwing, Han reaches out and asks Rumi to play. Han notices that Rumi has created beautiful drawings in the dirt under the tree. Eventually, after a written apology from Asher, all of the kids play together under the tree.

To find a book like this one, look for the following:

- Characters who navigate relationships at school
- Stories that highlight relationship building

Comprehension Conversation

Before Reading

Notice the Cover Illustration

Looking at the cover of a book gives you a sneak peek and little clues about the story inside. In this book, LeUyen Pham combined different art tools and techniques to make her illustrations unique and interesting. This type of art is called *mixed media.* Tell a neighbor something you noticed on the cover of *The Together Tree.* Share any predictions you have after studying the cover.

Set a Purpose: It looks like these four friends are having a nice time underneath the tree. Let's read to find out more about them and see if we learn any lessons about being together.

During Reading

- Title page: Look at this page carefully. Share something you notice. [The boy with the green shirt is off by himself.] Hmmm! I wonder why.
- *Rumi joined Ms. Garza's class on the first warm day of spring* page: Put yourself in Rumi's shoes. How might it feel to join a class in the spring? Can you infer how he's feeling by his facial expression and body language?
- *When he heard a laugh, he looked up* page: What could Han have done instead of staying quiet?
- *Then Asher picked up a pebble* page: Describe Asher to your partner. [Discuss the fact that Asher is a bully because he is being unkind on purpose and keeps trying different things to make Rumi feel scared, sad, and unsafe.] How should Ella and Han handle this situation?
- *"Rumi!" Han called out* page: What changed? Why do you suppose Asher is illustrated in black and white now? Let's turn to the next page to see what Rumi was doing with his twig.

After Reading

- Why do you think this book is called *The Together Tree*? What should you do when someone new joins a group?

- In the author's note, Aisha Saeed explains that this story was based on her son's experience of being bullied in kindergarten. Why do you think she wrote this book?

Extend the Experience

- Let's make our own *Together Tree* like the one on the back cover of this book. On this heart-shaped piece of paper, draw and/or write one way you could reach out to someone who looks like they're feeling lonely or left out. Then, we'll put the "leaves" together on our tree.

- Write, draw, or talk to finish this sentence: A lesson I learned from reading *The Together Tree* is . . .

Similar Titles

The Day You Begin (Woodson, 2018)

About the Book: Based on a poem about her great-grandfather's experience titled "It'll Be Scary Sometimes," Woodson's book shares the heart-wrenching stories of children starting the school year feeling different from their classmates. In the end, when a girl decides to speak up and share her story, she finds that she has something in common with one of her classmates and a friendship begins.

The Proudest Blue: The Story of Hijab and Family (I. Muhammad & Ali, 2019)

About the Book: It's the first day of sixth grade and Asiya's first day of wearing hijab. Her younger sister Faizah, who is the narrator, thinks Asiya looks like a princess in her bright blue hijab. Asiya expresses her faith with strength and pride even when faced with bullies. According to the author's note, Olympic gold medalist Ibtihaj Muhammad wrote this story so that readers "can see two sisters taking pride in hijab." Fun fact: The sisters in the story are named after Muhammad's sisters.

Key Vocabulary and Kid-Friendly Definitions:

- sputtered: moved with jerky action

- wandered: walked somewhere without a plan

Upper Elementary Extension:

Pose and discuss this prompt—Ponder what the tree symbolizes in the story. Explain using evidence from the text and illustrations.

Learning Targets:

- I notice how characters' words and actions impact people around them.

- I think about how my words and actions impact people around me.

- I look for ways to compromise.

Compromise

Book Title: *The Only Astronaut* (Jain, 2023)

About the Book: Space enthusiast Avni builds a movable spaceship out of cardboard boxes and other found materials. After an imaginary asteroid crash, she decides that space travel is a bit too challenging alone and makes it her mission to find an assistant. Following a few failed attempts to recruit a helpful assistant, Aquanaut Aya volunteers to join Anvi but has her own ideas about their shared adventures. Finally, Avni realizes that having a creative copilot makes the mission much more rewarding.

To find a book like this one, look for the following:

- Characters who compromise
- Characters who engage in imaginative play

 ## Comprehension Conversation

Before Reading

Notice the Cover Illustration

- When you look at this cover, what's the first thing that catches your eye? Are there any other small details that might be important? Think about the title *The Only Astronaut.* Why do you suppose one girl takes up most of the cover and the other girl is peeking out of the corner?

- Front endpapers: What can you infer about Anvi by looking at her room?

- Back endpapers: Where have we seen this girl before? [On the cover.] What can you learn about her by looking at her room?

Set a Purpose: We've already learned a little about Avni and the other girl in this book by studying the endpapers. Let's find out more about the girls and their relationship.

During Reading

- *My house is a space station, and every day is launch day* page: Do you recognize any of the materials Avni used to make her space ship? Trade ideas with a friend.

- *Phew* page: What is Avni's mission? [find an assistant] Do you think it will be easy to find one? Why or why not?

- *Kai didn't work out, but astronauts never give up* page: Why does she keep adding to her astronaut's log? [Because she is learning more about the kind of assistant she wants.]

- *We climb into the rocket ship* page: Why do you suppose the illustration where they're taking off has blue and orange speech bubbles and drawings? [Blue shows Aya's words and imaginary world, orange stands for Avni's.] Look at Avni's face. Can you infer how she's feeling about Aya's ideas?

- *The ship jerks* page: Look carefully at the illustration. What happened? [Part of Avni's rocket ship got caught on the girl's bike and Aya saved her.] Predict what you think will happen next.

After Reading

- What's the difference between a copilot and an assistant? When you're playing with your friends, which would you rather be?

- In this story Avni had to *compromise,* or give up a little bit of what she wanted to make both she and Aya happy. Compromising is a friendly way to solve problems. Can you think of a time when you had to compromise with a friend or family member/caregiver?

Extend the Experience

- Let's practice four things we can do to help us when we need to compromise:
  - Talk: Calmly tell your friend what you want and listen to what they want.
  - Empathize: Think about how your friend is feeling about the situation.
  - Problem Solve: Brainstorm creative solutions together.
  - Be Flexible: Understand that there is more than one right answer or way to do something. Be willing to try your friend's solution.

- Get ready for a box challenge! [To pose a box challenge, create a schedule that allows enough time for each student to have a week to complete the challenge. When it is that child's week, send home the book *What to Do With a Box* (Yolen, 2016) with the *Box Challenge Family/Caregiver Letter Printable* located on the companion website (resources.corwin.com/more-rampedup-readalouds). Enjoy seeing all the creative designs!)]

Key Vocabulary and Kid-Friendly Definitions:

- assistant: a person who helps
- distracted: not able to focus or concentrate
- mission: a special job to complete

Upper Elementary Extension:

Introduce students to Dan Santat's graphic novel *The Aquanaut* (2022) (using the book trailer linked from the QR code to the left). Invite interested readers to sign up on a sticky note for their chance to read the book. Once the first reader finishes, they pass it to the next one on the list, and so on.

Similar Titles

 I Lived Inside a Whale (Li, 2024)

About the Book: The story begins on the front endpapers, where we meet a girl reading in a whale chair surrounded by books. Inspired by the book, she decides to escape her too-noisy life by hiding out inside an imaginary whale. Soon, an "intruder" in the form of a bow-tied boy breaks the silence. Annoyed, she ignores him for a while. Finally, they compromise: She'll play with him, if he's quiet first. In the end, the boy listens to her as she shares the stories she loves and encourages her to share them with others.

The Aquanaut Book Trailer

https://qrs.ly/zffn8p8

 Yuna's Cardboard Castles (Tang, 2022)

About the Book: Inspired by the author's lived experience moving from Hong Kong to the United States, newcomer Yuna tries to fit in with the kids in her American home. To do this, she uses her origami skills to create an imaginary paper and cardboard world. Eventually, Yuna and the rest of the neighborhood children connect through imagination and the language of play.

THE BOX CHALLENGE!

Dear Student,

It's your turn to get creative at home! The directions are simple:

1. Read the enclosed book with someone.

2. Find a box that is no bigger than 14 x 14 inches. Use your imagination to turn it into something unique. *You can brainstorm ideas with your family, but make sure that you do your own work.*

3. Bring your Box Creation to school on_____ to share with the class! **If it is too big to carry, you can bring a picture of your creation to school instead.**

HAPPY CREATING!
Your Teacher

_____

Dear Families and Caregivers,

This activity is OPTIONAL. PLEASE COMPLETE THE FORM AND RETURN TO SCHOOL. Provide your child with any supplies or help they may need, but please let your child do their own thinking and work. Encourage them to make mistakes and learn from those mishaps. That's part of the problem-solving process. Happy creating!

_____My child **is participating** in the box challenge this week.

_____My child **is unable to participate** in the box challenge this week.

Box Challenge Family/Caregiver Letter Printable

My Favorite Read Alouds for Nurturing Relationships

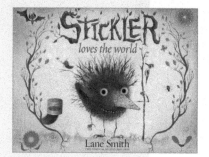

Show Appreciation

Book Title: *Stickler Loves the World* (L. Smith, 2023)

About the Book: Stickler notices and celebrates the beauty found outdoors with its multiple, ever-changing eyes. It happens upon a stranger with a pea can stuck on his head and instead of noticing it's their friend Crow, Stickler assumes it's a stranger from another planet. Stickler gives Crow the grand tour pointing out Earth's treasures. When the pea can pops off Crow's head, Crow thanks Stickler for opening his eyes to the spectacular natural sights. Fun fact: The character of Stickler first appeared in Lane Smith's book *A Gift for Nana* (2022).

To find a book like this one, look for the following:

- Characters who spread joy
- Characters with positive mindsets

Learning Targets:

- I notice how characters' mindsets and actions affect people around them.
- I think about how my mindset and actions affect people around me.
- I look for ways to spread joy.

Comprehension Conversation

Before Reading

Notice the Cover Illustration

When you look at this cover, where do your eyes go first? What other details do you notice in Lane Smith's illustration? What's your opinion so far: Do you think Stickler is a good name for this character? Why or why not? Lane Smith used a mixture of art tools, including paints and a digital pencil, to draw Stickler and the world it loves.

Set a Purpose: We're going to read to learn more about Stickler and find out why it loves its world. Notice Stickler's mindset, mood, and the way it acts with other creatures.

During Reading

- *"Three new sticks!"* page: I'm going to flip back and forth between this page and the one before it. What do you notice? [They are almost exactly the same. On the first page you only see eyes and outlines, on the second one you can see the details and creatures.] What might Stickler love more than sticks? Share with a neighbor.

- *"Elpppp!" said a voice* page: Can you figure out what the stranger is saying? [Get this off my head.] Is it really a stranger? [It might be Crow.]

- *Over here* page: How would you describe Stickler's mindset or attitude about the wonders of its planet? What is the stranger saying on this page? [Seasick—notice the swirls above its head!]

- *The colors of SUNSET* page: Can you infer what Crow means when he says, "Today you really *did* open my eyes"?

After Reading

- How did Stickler's mindset and actions impact Crow? If you were to describe Stickler to a friend, which words would you use? Start with: Stickler is _____.

- Think back to what happened in the story. What are some of the ways that Stickler spread joy?

Extend the Experience

- On the pages that begin with *Everything else* and *But Stickler tried anyway*, Stickler uses adjectives to describe its wonder-filled world. Draw a picture of your favorite outdoor space and label the things in your illustration like Stickler did. See how many different adjectives you can use.

- Stickler appreciated the spectacular sights it saw in nature and showed that appreciation by sharing them with Crow. Let's brainstorm different ways you can show appreciation.

Similar Titles

 How to Send a Hug (Rocco, 2022)

About the Book: Artie is an expert at giving in-person hugs. When she wants to send a long-distance hug to her Grandma Gertie, she knows exactly what to do. She writes her hug on a piece of paper, tucks it in a "jacket" (an envelope), and sticks a "ticket" (a stamp) in the corner. Now, the hug is ready to give to a "Hug Delivery Specialist" (aka a postal carrier). While Artie waits to get a hug back, readers see different ways mail is delivered to seven locations. Then, a two-page spread features the seven grateful hug recipients along with snippets of their letters. A heart-warming celebration of the lost art of letter writing.

 The Red Jacket (Holt, 2023)

About the Book: Bob, the seagull, is feeling left out and lonely. When a cheery, chirping bird notices Bob's glumness, he gives him his red jacket (with french fries in the pocket). Bob is so thrilled with his "swanky stylish" coat that he enthusiastically greets his fellow sea creatures. When a wave whooshes the jacket away, his new friends assist him in locating it. Bob pays the kindness forward by gifting the red jacket to a gloomy turtle.

Ways to Show Appreciate Chart

Key Vocabulary and Kid-Friendly Definitions:

- bursting: suddenly popping open or breaking out

- impressed: feeling amazed when you look at someone or something

Upper Elementary Extension:

Provide students with loose parts or art supplies to design their own imaginary character. Once completed, they can use their created character as inspiration for a narrative.

Written by
Tammi Sauer

Illustrated by
Fernando Martin

Learning Targets:

- I notice how characters' mindsets and actions affect people around them.
- I think about how my mindset and actions affect people around me.
- I look for ways to spread kindness.

Share and Care

Book Title: *All Kinds of Special* (Sauer, 2023) [Spanish Edition: Tan especial]

About the Book: Mia and her mom move into their new home. They are excited that it has a yard and a mango tree. Mia is thrilled to eat their first mango, but soon there are too many mangos. When Mia's mom asks her to come up with an idea, Mia decides they should share the mangos with their neighbors. What happens next is *All Kinds of Special*.

To find a book like this one, look for the following:

- Characters who display kindness to fellow community members
- Themes that highlight the power of community

Comprehension Conversation

Before Reading

Notice the Cover Illustration

- Does anyone recognize the fruit the girl is holding in her hands? [Pause for responses.] It looks like a mango to me, but we'll have to read to find out.
- Case Cover: Peek underneath the wraparound book jacket at the front and back of the case cover. What do you notice? [The front case cover has a girl by herself under the tree, the back case cover shows her with someone else.] Hmmm! I wonder why the book jacket and the case cover are different.

Set a Purpose: I'm so curious about why the title of this story is *All Kinds of Special*. Can you think of something you would consider "all kinds of special"? Swap ideas with a friend. Pay close attention to the special things that happen in this story.

During Reading

- *Our apartment was all kinds of special* page: Can you infer what made that one good-bye *extra* hard? Notice the word *extra* is in italics. Italics is used to read it with emphasis, like this: "One good-bye was EXTRA hard."
- *Don't get me wrong* page: What makes this mango so special? [It grew from their own tree.]
- *My knee won't stop bouncing as Mama prepares our mango* page: Why do you think the page where she's eating the mango looks different? [Because she's imagining summer.] Can you name a food that makes you imagine a certain season?
- *Side by side, we study our tree* page: Predict what Mia and her mom will do with all of the mangos. What would you do with them?
- *And another makes me think our mango tree is about to grow something extra sweet* page: Can you infer what extra-sweet something might grow? [their friendship]

After Reading

- Retell some of the special things that happened in this story. What made them special?

- How did Mia spread kindness? [by sharing the mangos] What happened because she shared the mangos? [They met people in their neighborhood, she made new friends.]

Extend the Experience

- Make a list of special things you could do for friends at school or people in your community that would show them you care. (Figure 1.24)

- Remember the page where Mia said the mango "tastes, smells, looks and feels like summer"? Think of a food that reminds you of a certain season or place. Draw a picture of yourself eating that food in that place or during that season.

Similar Titles

All Are Neighbors (Penfold, 2022)

About the Book: From the creators who gave us *All Are Welcome* (Penfold, 2018) and *Big Feelings* (Penfold, 2021) comes a rhyming glimpse into a diverse and vibrant community of folks who live, work, and play together. Ideal for illustration study as readers follow a mother, child, and infant as they are welcomed into their new home by friendly neighbors and many other community members.

Lolo's Sari-Sari Store (Lee, 2023)

About the Book: A girl shares fond memories of her time spent in the Philippines working alongside her Lolo (grandfather) at his sari-sari store, a shop with a variety of goods, similar to a convenience store. As they fulfill the needs of their neighbors, Lolo imparts his wisdom. He encourages her, through words and actions, to give back to the community, be a listening ear, make others happy, notice what people need, and share what she can. Now living with her mother in the United States, the girl struggles to feel the same sense of belonging. Guided by the example of her grandfather, she seeks out people to assist and befriend.

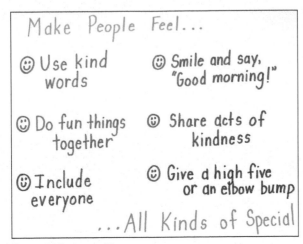

Spread Kindness Chart

Key Vocabulary and Kid-Friendly Definitions:

- nudging: gently pushing or encouraging you to do something

- prop: to rest or lean on something

- situation: all of the things happening at a certain time or place

Upper Elementary Extension:

Challenge learners to find one fact about mangos that no one else will know and turn the fact into a true or false quiz question. Quiz each other during free moments between activities.

"And, easy as that, Chester's problem was done when he

realized that playing with words should be . . . FUN!"

—*Chester van Chime Who Forgot How to Rhyme*
by Avery Monsen and Abby Hanlon

Focus on Foundational Skills

Phonological Awareness, Skillful Decoding, Vocabulary, Fluency, and Comprehension Monitoring

Unlock the Power of Written Words

Building on the knowledge base students are gaining during your systematic, structured word recognition instruction, the read-aloud experiences in this chapter nudge learners to apply the intricacies of these essential skills. These exemplar lessons serve as a bridge to help you connect the theoretical understanding of constructs found in the *Active View of Reading* (Duke & Cartwright, 2021) that you gained in the introduction to actionable classroom instruction. In fact, you can view each book experience as a template that will empower you to intentionally reinforce key skills as you read aloud other books that connect with your students. While pondering and exploring picture books together, readers gain a heightened awareness of the sounds and rhythm of language, the meaning and flow of words, and the art of comprehension. I've selected the books in Chapter 2 to help you reinforce these foundational understandings as you share delightful fiction and nonfiction texts. These evidence-guided experiences will support learners as they build word knowledge and develop bridging processes in the following ways:

- Foster phonological awareness
- Practice skillful decoding
- Use vocabulary strategies
- Read with fluency
- Attend to comprehend

As you and your students read and discuss the books in this chapter, you'll unlock the synergy between intentional instruction and the joy found within the pages of a well-chosen picture book.

Scan here to find a complete learning target chart with book-related online links, a bonus read-aloud experience, and printable resources.

https://qrs.ly/vafn8pa

Big Idea: Featured Title	Learning Targets
Tune in to Sounds: *Song in the City* (Bernstrom, 2022)	• I hear and say the sounds in words. • I notice that when you change the letters you change the way a word sounds.
Move Sounds Around: *ZAP! CLAP! ZOOM! The Story of a Thunderstorm* (Salas, 2023b)	• I hear and say the sounds in words. • I swap parts of words to make new words. • I use key details to help me predict.
Use Sound-Spelling Relationships: *It's a Sign* (Pumphrey, 2022a)	• I connect letters to sounds when I read and write. • I use word families to help me read and spell words.
Work With Word Families: *Chester van Chime Who Forgot How to Rhyme* (Monsen, 2022)	• I connect letters to sounds when I read and write. • I use word families to help me read and spell words. • I notice if rhyming words have the same spelling pattern.
Notice Shades of Meaning: *MINE!* (Fleming, 2023)	• I wonder about words. • I notice shades of meaning among similar words. • I use key details to help me predict.
Infer the Meaning From Context: *Behold the Octopus!* (Slade, 2023)	• I wonder about words. • I infer the meaning of words from context clues. • I use key ideas and details to learn about a topic.
Watch for Signals: *The Umbrella* (Ferry, 2023)	• I notice punctuation and other text signals. • I use punctuation and other text signals to read fluently with expression. • I use key details to describe characters.
Express Yourself: *Carina Felina* (Deedy, 2023)	• I join in on repeated parts of a story, song, or poem. • I notice the text pattern. • I use the text pattern to help me predict.
Think About Your Thinking: *Watercress* (Wang, 2021)	• I notice when the story is making sense. • I pause and reread when the story is not making sense. • I use strategies to improve my comprehension.
Pause and Reread: *Jumper: A Day in the Life of a Backyard Jumping Spider* (Lanan, 2023)	• I notice how the text structure helps me remember key details. • I pause and reread to better understand the topic. • I talk, write, or draw about my new learning.
Bonus Lesson (online)	• I wonder about words.
Compare and Contrast Words: *Buffalo Fluffalo* (Kalb, 2024)	• I notice the differences among similar words. • I use key details to help me predict and infer.

My Favorite Read Alouds for Highlighting Foundational Skills

Tune in to Sounds

Book Title: *Song in the City* (Bernstrom, 2022)

About the Book: Emmalene navigates the world with a National Federation for the Blind (NFB) white cane. On her way to church with Grandma Jean, she hears a busy city symphony, but her grandmother calls it a commotion. Once in church Grandma Jean enjoys the music while Emmalene pouts because Grandma Jean won't listen to her city music. Finally, she covers Grandma Jean's eyes and, together, they listen to the city song.

To find a book like this one, look for the following:

- Storylines that highlight sounds
- Texts that include onomatopoeia

Comprehension Conversation

Before Reading

Notice the Cover Illustration

- Imagine you are the girl on this wraparound cover; what sounds do you hear?
- This is illustrator Jenin Mohammed's first picture book. I see a lot of different colors in her digital illustrations. What else do you notice?

Set a Purpose: The author, Daniel Bernstrom, uses a special kind of word to help us hear the city noises. We're going to learn more about sound words, or onomatopoeia, as we listen to the *Song in the City.*

During Reading

- Title page: Zoom-in on what Emmalene is doing. What do you notice? [She is reading a book using her hands (Braille) and she has a white cane propped up on her bed. We can infer that she is blind.]
- *Sunday morning, Emmalene heard a sing-along song* page: Do you remember what the sound words on this page are called? [onomatopoeia] Onomatopoeia are words that imitate the sounds they represent. Let's reread the city sounds together!

[Continue to invite students to join you in rereading the onomatopoetic words that appear on the pages that follow.]

- *"Grandma Jean!" said Emmalene* page: Think about what Grandma Jean said and notice how she's standing and walking. Is she interested in Emmalene's pretty ditty? *Ditty* is another word for a short song.
- *In the church, in the pew* page: Look at the two characters now. How have their feelings changed? [Grandma Jean is happy and Emmalene is not.] Why do you suppose their attitudes are different?
- *And Grandma Jean tried* page: Can you figure out what Emmalene is trying to show Grandma Jean? [How to listen the way she does.] Do you think it will work?

Learning Targets:

- I hear and say the sounds in words.
- I notice that when you change the letters you change the way a word sounds.

After Reading

- This book was filled with words that imitate sounds. Do you remember what those are called?

- Let's compare some of the onomatopoeia and see how small changes in the letters make a different-sounding word. [Display a word pair. Ask learners to identify the change in letters, say the words aloud, and listen for the change in the way the word sounds.]

HONKY - HONK	drumming - humming
pitter - patter	clap - clapping
sprinkled - crinkled	singing - ringing

Extend the Experience

- Let's play with some of the words from the story. [Select a few words from the story to practice phonemic awareness skills. For the examples below, I chose the following root words from the *Then they listened to the city* page: tip, tap, bip, bop, yip, clap.]

- Close your eyes and listen to the sounds of our classroom [or playground]. Draw a picture to show what you hear when you listen carefully.

Similar Titles

Everybody in the Red Brick Building (Wynter, 2021)

About the Book: Everybody in the red brick building is asleep until Baby Izzie starts crying, "WaaaAAH!" Her wailing sets off a chain reaction of noisy nighttime fun. In a cumulative fashion, each apartment dweller's noise is added to the person before, culminating with a boisterous two-page spread. Then, in reverse, the characters quiet down and return to sleep. Pair with *The Napping House* (Wood, 1984).

The Quiet Forest (Offsay, 2024)

About the Book: The forest is quiet until a mischievous mouse lands in the rabbit's pancakes with a "Splat!" This sets off a chain reaction of rollicking events, each punctuated by an onomatopoeia. Just as a bear cub is about to join the fun, the forest whispers, "Whoosh. Swish." The animals calm each other down and enjoy some quiet time together.

Phonemic Awareness Skill Practice Examples	
Phonemic Awareness Skill	**Prompts to Target That Skill** Root words from *Then they listened to the city* page: **tip, tap, bip, bop, yip, clap**
Hearing	I'm going to say the beginning sound of two words *tip, bip*. Listen to these sounds: /b/ and /t/. Are they the same or different?
Generating	What sound does the letter *b* make? What sound does the letter *t* make?
Isolating	What sound do you hear first in the word *bop*? [repeat for middle and end]
Blending	Listen to these sounds. Blend them together and say the word. What word is this: /t/ /a/ /p/?
Segmenting	Say each sound in the word *yip*.
Manipulating	Take away the /l/ sound from the *clap*. Say the new word.

Move Sounds Around

Book Title: *ZAP! CLAP! BOOM! The Story of a Thunderstorm* (Salas, 2023b)

About the Book: Three children frolic in the sunshine and kick a bright red ball out of sight. While looking for the ball, the sky darkens and ZAP! CRASH! BOOM! a storm approaches. Page by page, the storm intensifies, producing a "pounding sounding distant crash" and "spilling splashing chilling rain." Finally, the children and a trio of goats take shelter. Once the storm has passed and the world is "dazzling, sparkling, fresher," the children recover their lost ball and befriend the baby goats. Laura Purdie Salas's poetic text rolls off the tongue and provides plenty of opportunities to explore words.

To find a book like this one, look for the following:

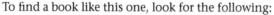

- Poetic texts with plenty of word play
- Texts that describe thunderstorms

Comprehension Conversation

Notice the Cover Illustration

ZAP! CLAP! BOOM! Would you want to be in one of the houses on the top of this hill? Why or why not? The subtitle of this book is *The Story of a Thunderstorm*. Elly MacKay used paper collage and digital paint to make these stormy illustrations.

Set a Purpose: As we learn more about thunderstorms, we are going to notice how the poet Laura Purdie Salas played with words by changing a sound here or there to make this book so much fun to read aloud.

During Reading

- *Sunny day sits warm and dry* page: Hmmm! What do you predict is going to happen next? Do you have any evidence to support your prediction?
- *Warmer air begins to rise* page: I'm going to reread the second stanza on this page starting with: *Clouds of fluffy, puffy white.* Listen to the words: *fluffy* and *puffy*. Which sounds are different? How about between the words *pillows* and *billow*?
- *ZAP! CLAP! BOOM!* page: Where is the storm now? Do you think the kids will make it back home before it rains? Trade ideas with a classmate.
- *Flicker, flitter, skitter, flash* page: Let's reread the first line of this page together. What do you notice about the sounds in these words?
- Two-page spread with no text: Where is the storm now? Make a prediction about what the kids might do next. Why do you think that?

After Reading

- What did Laura Purdie Salas do as a poet to help you make a picture in your mind of what was happening during the storm? [Used a repeated onomatopoeia, rhyme, and short phrases.]
- How did the storm change the Earth?

Extend the Experience

- The repeated line in this book *ZAP! CLAP! BOOM!* has some words that we can use to swap sounds. Let's give it a try! [Note: Phoneme manipulation is the most challenging phonemic awareness skill. Adjust this extension accordingly by changing it to segmenting or blending, if needed.]

- In the backmatter of the book, Laura Purdie Salas adds "The Science Behind Storms." We can read this when we want to learn more about thunderstorms.

Similar Titles

 Blue on Blue (D. White, 2014)

About the Book: Adjective-rich, rhyming text describes the passing of a thunderstorm over a family farm. Starting with gentle, fluffy early morning clouds, shifting to the raging midday rain, and concluding with the vivid imagery of "black on gold on silver night," Dianne White's rich text and Beth Krommes's exquisite scratchboard and watercolor illustrations skillfully capture the evolving weather conditions.

 Tap Tap Boom Boom (Bluemle, 2017)

About the Book: A storm is heading to the city. Two children peer out between the wrought iron playground railings as raindrops begin to fall and umbrellas go up. As the storm intensifies, the kids, their grown-ups, and other city dwellers head into the subway for shelter, where "the storm above makes friends of strangers." Bouncy rhymes and the repetitive refrain, "Tap Tap Boom Boom," make this a perfect rainy-day read aloud.

Phonemic Awareness Skill Practice: Swapping Sounds

Say zap. Change /z/ to /t/ and the word is _____. [tap]	Say boom. Change /b/ to /r/ and the word is _____. [room]
Say tap. Change /t/ to /l/ and the word is _____. [lap]	Say room. Change /r/ to /l/ and the word is _____. [loom]
Say lap. Change /l/ to /c/ and the word is _____. [cap]	Say loom. Change /l/ to /d/ and the word is _____. [doom]
Say cap. Change /c/ to /cl/ and the word is _____. [clap]	Say doom. Change /d/ to /z/ and the word is _____. [zoom]
	[The words *loom* and *doom* appear in the story.]

Key Vocabulary and Kid-Friendly Definitions:

- **fiercely:** in a dangerous or wild way

- **hover:** to hang in the air

- **threat:** something that makes you feel unsafe or worried

Upper Elementary Extension:

Reread the book to interpret the figurative language used throughout like *pillows billow, newborn winds, smudgy watercolor mark, electric zigzags,* and so on.

By **Jarrett Pumphrey**
and **Jerome Pumphrey**

Learning Targets:

- I connect letters to sounds when I read and write.
- I use word families to help me read and spell words.

Use Sound-Spelling Relationships

Book Title: *It's A Sign!* (Pumphrey, 2022a)

About the Book: Foxlike character Two is trying to make a sign for a club but doesn't know how to write (although Two is good at folding paper hats). One, who knows every letter, offers help by writing the letter "a." Along comes purple Kat with knowledge of longer words and word families. Kat writes "HAT." Finally, Four joins the group, gets a paper hat, and writes the word "CLUB." When they put the words together to form a HAT CLUB you would think they have the perfect club name, but One has a different idea.

To find a book like this one, look for the following:

- Plots that include word play
- Texts that offer opportunities to highlight word families

 ## Comprehension Conversation

Before Reading

 #### Notice the Cover Illustration

- This book was created by an author-illustrator team who are also brothers. To craft their illustrations, they use hand-cut foam stamps and then add color using a digital device. [You can learn more about their stamping process via the QR code.]

The Pumphrey Brothers' Stamping Process

https://qrs.ly/oifn8pc

Talk with a partner about what you notice on the cover. Why do you suppose the book is called *It's a Sign*?

Set a Purpose: As you listen and try to figure out why this book is called *It's a Sign,* the characters are going to teach us some important things to remember about letters, sounds, and words. It is important to focus on the sounds and spellings of words because knowing them helps us read and write.

During Reading

- *Hi, One! What are you making* page: The creators give you a hint to help you keep track of which character is named One and which is named Two. Look at the details in the illustrations to see if you can figure out the clue. [The number of dots on One and Two's tails matches their name.]

- *Wow! Will you join my new club* page: Predict what you think Two will write on the sign. What would you write on the sign? Share with a shoulder partner.

- *It is a letter AND a word* page: Do you know any other letters that are both a letter and a word? [I]

- *And even "HAT"* page: Reread the words Kat wrote. Tell us something you notice. [The words *bat, sat, mat, rat,* and *hat* are all part of the -at word family—and so is Kat's name!]

- *GASP! I know what we can name our club* page: What do you think One is going to name their club?

After Reading

- What was your reaction to the ending of the story (before the Elephant and Piggie pages)? Did the ending surprise you? Did it make you smile or laugh?

- Share something you learned about letters, sounds, and words that will help you as a reader and writer. [Sometimes letters are words and other times you put letters together to make words. Word families help you read and spell a lot of different words.]

Extend the Experience

- Add to Kat's word family work by making a list of other words in the -at family. On a whiteboard or piece of paper write the words *bat, sat, mat, rat,* and *hat.* Reread Kat's words and add a few more. Each time you add a word to your list, slide through the sounds, and then say the word. As an extra challenge, write a sentence or short story using a few of the words on your list.

- In this story, the characters were making a sign for their club. Let's make some signs for our classroom or school.

Similar Titles

 The Bug in the Bog **(Fenske, 2020)**

About the Book: A bug is happily sitting and singing on a log. Along comes a hungry frog. When the fog rolls in, readers hear a "CHOMP! CHEW! SLURP! SWALLOW!" What happens next may come as a surprise! Read to highlight the -og word family. This book is tailor-made for retelling because it has a simple beginning, middle, and end.

 Mouse Calls **(Pace, 2022)**

About the Book: When Mouse spots an impending storm in her spyglass, she calls for Moose. Then, Moose calls Goose, setting off a chain reaction to round up Dog, Hog, and Hare. The first group of animals huddle together in a cave as Mouse ventures out to find more of her friends. The book continues this way until all the creatures are tucked safely in the cave and, together, call out, "Thank You, Mouse!" Ideal for studying rhyming word pairs.

Upper Elementary Extension:

Provide resources for students to learn more about origami. Then learners can create a how-to video or diagram that teaches the steps to folding a paper hat or other object.

Work With Word Families

Book Title: *Chester van Chime Who Forgot How to Rhyme*
(Monsen, 2022)

About the Book: Poor Chester is baffled and queasy because rhyming is no longer easy. Even though illustrated rhyming word pairs appear everywhere in his house and around the neighborhood, he can't come up with a single rhyme. At school, his classmates try to help him, but to no avail. On his way home, he recognizes that everyone has a bad day once in a while. This realization helps him regain his joy for word play and return to his old, rhyming self (except when he sees an orange tree!). Don't miss the cameo appearances of Nursery Rhyme characters in the illustrations!

To find a book like this one, look for the following:

- Books brimming with rhyming word pairs
- Texts that invite word play

 Comprehension Conversation

Before Reading

Notice the Cover Illustration

- Meet Chester van Chime. Can you infer how he's feeling about forgetting how to rhyme?
- Abby Hanlon's gouache paint and colored pencil illustrations add rhyming fun to this story. What do you notice about the pictures on the front and back cover? [There are a lot of rhyming word pairs.] Her pictures are so bright because gouache paint is thicker and less see-through than watercolor paint.

Set a Purpose: The first time we read about Chester van Chime we're going to see if we can help Chester out when he's trying to think of rhyming words. Then, we'll reread to study the detailed illustrations.

During Reading

- *There once was a youngster name Chester van Chime* page: Where have you seen this illustration before? [on the back cover] What's the problem in this story? Let's keep reading to see how Chester solves his problem.
- *It baffled poor Chester* page: Wait a second! Do you know a word that makes sense in this sentence and rhymes with *queasy*? [easy]
- *His friends tried to help tackle Chester's complaint* page: Which art supply did they use to make rhymes? [paint] Look carefully: What is the fox in socks doing with the paint? [Pouring it on the floor.] I wonder if the teacher will notice.
- *Then they brought tons of rhymes to the room where he sat* page: What do all of these words have in common? [They all rhyme with *sat* and end in -at.]

Learning Targets:

- I connect letters to sounds when I read and write.
- I use word families to help me read and spell words.
- I notice if rhyming words have the same spelling pattern.

- *"So maybe I don't need to be quite so stressed* page: Talk with a friend about the lesson Chester learned. [It's okay to have a bad day.] What word do you predict we'll see on the next page?

- *As the sun turned to red and the moon started climbing* page: Did anything on this page make you smile? ["Orange . . . uh, never mind."] Why do you suppose the butcher, the baker, and the candlestick maker are pictured in a tub? [Because they were in a tub in the nursery rhyme "Rub a Dub Dub."]

After Reading

- How was the problem in the story solved or resolved?

- Have you ever had a day when you're not feeling your best? What did you do to change your attitude?

Extend the Experience

- [Print or project the *Rhyming Word Pairs Printable* located on the companion website (resources.corwin.com/more-rampedup-readalouds). To model decoding and help students make the letter–sound connections, revisit the word pairs and use Cunningham's (2017) *Rounding Up the Rhymes* strategy:

  o Display rhyming word pairs.

  o Demonstrate how to do sound-by-sound decoding by sliding through sounds of each word. Notice whether the two words have the same spelling pattern or two different spelling patterns.

  o If they have the same spelling pattern, keep them displayed.

  o If they don't have the same spelling, tear up the cards (kids love this!) or delete if doing this electronically.

  o Wrap up the lesson by pointing out that similar spelling patterns and word families are helpful to learn because they will help children read and spell a lot of words!]

- Project the *He tried not to panic* page. Work with a partner. See how many rhyming word pairs you can find. Write them down on a whiteboard or piece of paper. Once you think you've found all of the rhymes, look again for characters from traditional tales like the troll under the bridge, Old King Cole, and so on.

Key Vocabulary and Kid-Friendly Definitions:

- complaint: a statement that you are not happy with something

- panic: to suddenly feel afraid

- queasy: feeling sick to your stomach

Upper Elementary Extension:

Teach students how to write fractured nursery rhymes by changing the character, setting, problem, or solution.

Similar Titles

 Bros (Weatherford, 2024)

About the Book: The sun is up and a playful group of five Black boys embark on an adventure-filled day. With boundless energy, they play, create, read, care for the community garden, and support one another. Inspired by Danielle Young's #BlackBoyJoy movement, Carole Boston Weatherford's perfectly paced rhyming text captures the essence of childhood wonder and camaraderie. Bursting with energy, Reggie Brown's vibrant illustrations make the pages come alive with the enthusiasm of these young friends.

Catside Up, Catside Down: A Book of Prepositions (Hrachovec, 2023)

About the Book: Whether they appear inside a sock or between two flamingos, Anna Hrachovec's adorable knitted cats make this concept book featuring prepositions irresistible. The witty descriptions of classic cat behavior are written in rhyming couplets, with each preposition highlighted in a bold font. The author has also upped the ante on the vocabulary, including words like *lolling*, *configure*, and *affixed* among others.

Rhyming Word Pairs

queasy

easy

song

wrong

Rhyming Word Pairs Printable

My Favorite Read Alouds for Practicing Skillful Decoding

Learning Targets:

- I wonder about words.
- I notice shades of meaning among similar words.
- I use key details to help me predict.

Notice Shades of Meaning

Book Title: *MINE!* (Fleming, 2023)

About the Book: A single red apple dangles from the "tip-tippy top" of a tall, tall tree. One by one, animals come along and spot the tasty treat, each one imagining it is theirs. Then, the wind blows the apple down, a scuffle ensues, and the apple rolls right into the hands of an opossum who kindly shares the apple with its resident worm. Candace Fleming's expertly crafted repetitive pattern, playful language, and repetition of the word "MINE!" make this book ripe for reading aloud and reader's theater. Compare it to *Mine!* (Mack, 2017), a one-word tale about two mice who are fighting over what they think is a big rock.

To find a book like this one, look for the following:

- Playful language
- Repetitive pattern

Comprehension Conversation

Before Reading

Notice the Cover Illustration

- Look at Eric Rohmann's cover illustration. Tell your classmate a quick story about what you think is happening. Listen to your classmate's story. [All of the animals are saying, "MINE!" because they want to eat the apple.]
- Make a prediction. Which animal will get to eat the apple? Why do you think that?

Set a Purpose: Readers use clues from the words and illustrations to make predictions. Predictions aren't "right" or "wrong." Sometimes predictions match the author's thinking, other times predictions take the story in a different direction. What's important is that you can share the reasons behind your predictions. We'll do that as we read *MINE!*

During Reading

- *And he hoppity-boinged into the tall grass to wait* page: I notice the word "MINE!" is repeated. Join in and read it as if you were the rabbit! [Continue in the same fashion with the other animals.]
- *Along padded fox* page: What do you think fox means when he says he'll be eating supper with patience and a breeze? [He just has to wait until the wind knocks the apple to the ground.]
- *Along trotted deer* page: First we saw the mouse, then the hare, fox, and now a deer. Do you notice anything about the animals? [They keep getting bigger.] Which animal do you predict will come along next? [Bear, because it was the biggest animal on the cover.]
- *Along whooshed the wind* page: Uh-oh! Swap your predictions with a neighbor.
- Wordless two-page spread where the apple rolls away page: Hmmm! How do you predict the story is going to end?

After Reading

- Did the ending surprise you?
- What do you think Candace Fleming wants us to ponder after reading this story?

Extend the Experience

- Candace Fleming uses a variety of words to describe how the animals move. Let's collect these words from the book and put them in order according to which one we think shows the slowest movement to the word we believe shows the speediest movement.
- Predict what the rest of the animals will do next. Draw a picture and/or write to share your prediction.

Similar Titles

 Buffalo Fluffalo (Kalb, 2024)

About the Book: Don't mess with Buffalo Fluffalo. He's surly and "tuffalo." He lets any animal who approaches him know it with this repeated refrain: "I'm the Buffalo Fluffalo—I heave and I huffalo. Leave me alone because I've had enuffalo!" When a storm blows in, Buffalo Fluffalo loses his "puffalo" and, in the process, gains some friends. (See bonus read-aloud experience on the companion website, resources.corwin.com/more-rampedup-readalouds.)

 Oh, No! (Fleming, 2012)

About the Book: When a frog, mouse, loris, sun bear, and monkey fall into a hole, the tiger is ready to pounce. Then, elephant comes along, saves the animals, and tiger falls into the hole. Will the animals help him out? "Oh no!" This book, also written by Candace Fleming, has many similarities to *MINE!* making them a well-suited pair for comparing and contrasting.

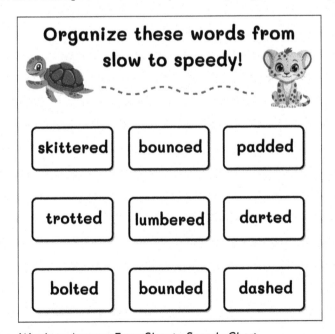

Words to Arrange From Slow to Speedy Chart

Key Vocabulary and Kid-Friendly Definitions:

- deceive: make something seem different or trick someone into believing something that isn't true
- divine: very good, beautiful, or tasty
- morsel: a small piece or a bite-size amount

Upper Elementary Extension:

Candace Fleming and Eric Rohmann are a husband-and-wife creator team who have written many books both together and separately. Gather some of their other fiction and nonfiction titles for students to enjoy.

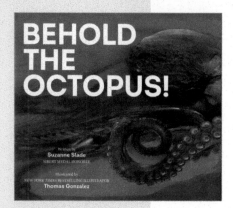

Infer the Meaning From Context

Book Title: *Behold the Octopus!* (Slade, 2023)

About the Book: Learn fascinating facts about 11 different species of octopus. Thomas Gonzalez's vivid, lifelike illustrations enhance Suzanne Slade's two-tiered text. The first tier of text is sparse, usually one word per spread, and uses mainly verbs and adjectives to describe each octopus's behavior. The second tier is an accompanying paragraph adding interesting details. The two different levels of text make this an ideal read aloud in both primary and upper elementary grades.

To find a book like this one, look for the following:

- Informational texts about kid-appealing topics
- Informational texts written in unique and engaging ways

Comprehension Conversation

Before Reading

Notice the Cover Illustration

The title of this book is *Behold the Octopus!* In this title, the word *behold* means that the author wants you to pay attention, look carefully, and learn something about octopuses. Doesn't the illustration of the octopus look real? Thomas Gonzalez uses pastels, colored pencils, and an airbrush to make these lifelike illustrations. An *airbrush* is a tiny, paint-spraying pen that artists use to make pictures with smooth, blended colors. I can't wait for you to see the octopuses inside the book!

Set a Purpose: There is so much to learn in this book that we're going to read it three different ways. First, we're going to enjoy the main text by reading the whole book without stopping. Then, we'll go back and add details to what you've learned by inferring the meaning of some key words. [Read-Aloud Experience 1] At another time, we'll reread the main text and learn even more from the detailed paragraphs. [Read-Aloud Experience 2] Show me you're ready to *Behold the Octopus!*

During Reading

Read-Aloud Experience 1—Focus: Vocabulary Strategies

- *Amazing octopus* page: [Read the large text of the book straight through without pausing to ask any questions until the last page. You might consider playing some underwater sounds or relaxing underwater music (easily found on YouTube) as you read.]

Lesearning Targets:

- I wonder about words.
- I infer the meaning of words from context clues.
- I use key ideas and details to learn about a topic.

- *Behold, the marvelous octopus only lives a short time* page: Wow! I have so many questions about the different kinds of octopuses we saw on those pages, I'm also wondering about a few of the words. First, let's flip back a few pages to see if we can use context clues to figure out what the words mean.

- *Luminous* page: *Luminous* is the first puzzling word. Let's read this paragraph to see if we can find any context clues to help us define the word *luminous*. [Notice the phrase *glowing lights*.] I'm inferring from the phrase *glowing lights* in the paragraph that luminous has something to do with light. If this octopus is luminous, it must have glowing lights. Do you see how the context clues helped us figure that out?

- *and utterly tenacious* page: On this page, I'm wondering about the word *tenacious*. What can we do? [Read the paragraph, find context clues, and infer the meaning.] This octopus guards her eggs by staying near them for months or years. What do you infer *tenacious* means? [never gives up, determined, persistent]

Read Aloud Experience 2—Focus: Key Ideas and Details

- *Amazing octopus* page: We already learned a little about the luminous glowing sucker octopus and the tenacious deep-sea octopus. Let's see what we can discover about the other octopuses in this book.

- *gliding* page: Tell a friend something you learned about how octopuses glide.

- *changing* page: Explain some of the ways octopuses change. [Some can change their color, pattern, texture, appearance, and even their behavior.] Why do they change? [To fool predators.]

- *adventurous* page: What is unique about the algae octopus? [It is able to walk on land.]

After Reading

- Suzanne Slade used verbs and adjectives to describe octopuses' behavior and traits. Did this technique help you learn more about these creatures? Why or why not?

- How does using context clues help you to infer the meaning of words?

Extend the Experience

- Write and/or draw a diagram showing the steps readers can take when they come to a word they don't know.

- There are 11 octopuses highlighted in this book. Pick the octopus you found the most interesting and explain why. Use this sentence stem to help you: I think the _____ octopus is interesting because _____.

Key Vocabulary and Kid-Friendly Definitions:

- adventurous: ready to explore new places and try new things

- amazing: something really special that makes you feel happy and excited

- precious: something special, valuable, and important

Upper Elementary Extension:

Help learners select an accessible resource from the *Learn More About the Octopus* page in the backmatter and create an infographic to share new facts they discover about the octopus.

Similar Titles

 Behold the Hummingbird (Slade, 2024)

About the Book: Learn fascinating facts about 12 different species of hummingbirds. Thomas Gonzalez's vivid, lifelike illustrations enhance Suzanne Slade's two-tiered text. The first tier of text is sparse, usually one word per spread, and uses mainly verbs and adjectives to describe each hummingbird's characteristics and behavior. The second tier is an accompanying paragraph adding interesting details. The two different levels of text make this an ideal read aloud in both primary and middle grades.

 Not a Monster (Martínez, 2023) [Spanish Edition: No es un monstruo]

About the Book: An egg hatches in the murky waters of a canal, but it is "Not a Monster." Trace the life cycle of an axolotl from egg to adult and learn the stories the abuelos (grandparents) tell about these strange creatures. Martínez skillfully weaves Spanish words throughout so readers can either infer their meaning or consult the glossary in the backmatter. While sharing the backmatter, check out the author's note, complete with photographs of her pet axolotls!

My Favorite Read Alouds for Building Vocabulary

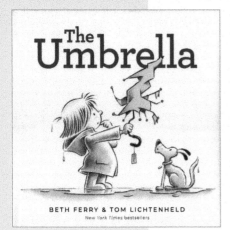

Watch for Signals

Book Title: *The Umbrella* (Ferry, 2023)

About the Book: When a little girl takes her dog for a rainy-day walk, they happen upon a curio shop. They find a tattered yellow umbrella hidden inside a steamer trunk. As they run back home with their free umbrella, the tatters scatter across a field. On their next walk, they discover a field of bright yellow umbrellas and share them with the townspeople, chasing the rain away. *The Umbrella* was written in memory of the late Amy Krouse Rosenthal, whose signature symbol is a bright yellow umbrella.

Learning Targets:

- I notice punctuation and other text signals.
- I use punctuation and other text signals to read fluently with expression.
- I use key details to describe characters.

To find a book like this one, look for the following:

- Punctuation and other text clues that signal readers to adjust their phrasing, emphasis, and intonation to convey meaning and emotion
- Stories with interesting characters

Comprehension Conversation

Before Reading

Notice the Cover Illustration

This book is called *The Umbrella*. What might the girl be wondering as she looks at the umbrella? Which colors do you see in Tom Lichtenheld's pencil and watercolor illustrations? Let's notice if he uses the same colors on the inside pages.

Set a Purpose: As we're reading about this girl and the umbrella, we're going to notice the punctuation or signals the author includes to give us clues as to how to read them with meaning and emotion.

During Reading

- Copyright page: Do you notice anything unique about the text on the copyright page? [It looks like rain!]
- *Drip. Drop. Nonstop* page: I'm going to reread the first few pages. Listen carefully as I reread. Which punctuation mark appears after each word? [a period] Beth Ferry is signaling us to stop after we read each word. What's the tone or mood of the beginning of the story?
- *Gotta wonder* page: Wow! There are a few new signals on this page! Which punctuation marks do you see? [Discuss the purpose of an ellipsis, question marks, and italics.]
- *Trail of tatters* page: Oh no! What is happening to the umbrella?

- *Come on, pup. Hurry up* page: Tell your neighbor what you think they might be seeing.

- *Come on, pup. Dig them up* page: Listen as I reread this page. What do you notice? [As the text gets bigger, my voice gets louder.]

After Reading

- If you were going to rate this book using zero to five stars, five stars being the best book ever, show us your rating with your fingers. Share the reasons behind your opinion.

- How did the mood change from the beginning to the end of this story? Let's compare the first page to the last; what do you notice about the colors in the illustrations? Notice the front and back endpapers.

Extend the Experience

- As we were reading, we noticed how an author's use of punctuation marks helps us to read fluently with expression. How might you use what you've learned when you're writing a story?

- Which adjectives would you use to describe the girl in this story? Use clues from the text or illustrations to explain. Here are a few examples:

  She is energetic because she likes to walk her dog.

  She is curious because she went into the shop.

  She is kind because she shared the umbrellas with the townspeople.

Similar Titles

 Mole Is Not Alone (Tatsukawa, 2023)

About the Book: When Mole receives an invitation to Rabbit's party, it debates to itself, "Hmm . . . should I actually go this time?" The doubts and self-talk continue as Mole gets ready and ventures through its elaborate underground tunnel system. Once outside Rabbit's home, Mole meets Skunk, who is equally hesitant. They both decide to skip the party and spend some quiet time together. Was that Rabbit's plan all along? Observant readers will spot animals preparing for the party above ground. The author marks Mole's inner monologue in interesting ways. Notice and reread Mole's thoughts using those signals.

 Stick and Stone (Ferry, 2015)

About the Book: Stick and Stone become buddies when Stick stands up to Pinecone, who is bullying Stone. This friendship story is written by the same author-illustrator duo as *The Umbrella* and is filled with opportunities to read expressively.

Key Vocabulary and Kid-Friendly Definitions:

- grim: sad, dull, and/ or gloomy

- splendid: something wonderful that makes you feel happy and excited

- weary: bored or unhappy with something

Upper Elementary Extension:

Pair students up to retell or rewrite this story in first-person point of view from the girl's perspective.

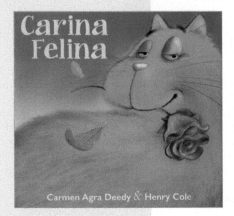

Express Yourself

Book Title: *Carina Felina* (Deedy, 2023) [Spanish Edition: El cuento de Carina Felina]

About the Book: Carmen Agra Deedy's Caribbean spin on the folktale "The Cat and the Parrot" introduces readers to Carina Felina, who is always looking for her next dish. The tale begins when Pepe the Parrot falls in love with Carina and she swallows him whole. "With a gobble and a gulp," fellow villagers succumb to the same fate until two land crabs come up with a plan to stop Carina. The backmatter includes the story behind this version of the folktale, a recipe for Cuban Crackers, and a glossary with pronunciation guides for the Spanish words.

To find a book like this one, look for the following:

- Repetitive text that invites readers to join in
- Cumulative or add-on story

 Comprehension Conversation

Before Reading

Notice the Cover Illustration

- Get ready, story sleuths! There are some important details in Henry Cole's cover illustration that I don't want you to miss. I'll open the wraparound cover so that you can meet Carina Felina. What else do you see? [Feathers flying around near her mouth, crabs hanging from the tree.] Think about these details as you share a prediction with a classmate.

- Now I'll read the back cover blurb. Do you want to revise your prediction?

Set a Purpose: As we read *Carina Felina*, we'll find out if our predictions match Carmen Agra Deedy's thinking or go in a different direction. Remember that readers revise predictions as they learn new information.

During Reading

- *"Why, I'm Carina Felina!"* page: We've heard this phrase before on the back cover. Join in with me as I reread it. Use your best cat voice!

  [Continue to encourage listeners to join you on the repeated refrain; point out that each time they repeat it their fluency improves because they're practicing.]

- *Feeling quite full of herself, and the parrot* page: Use your eagle eyes. Do you spot anything in this illustration that appeared on the cover? [The two land crabs are hiding under the table of books.] Hmmm! I wonder what they're doing and if we'll see them again.

  [Learners will enjoy spotting the land crabs on the pages that follow!]

Learning Targets:

- I join in on repeated parts of a story, song, or poem.
- I notice the text pattern.
- I use the text pattern to help me predict.

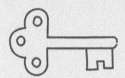
- *"Who are you?" piped a young voice* page: What do you notice about the pattern of this story? [It's a cumulative or add-on story.] Can you predict what is going to happen next?

- *But all laughter stopped when they saw You Know Who* page: Look at the land crab. If it had a speech bubble above its head, what would it say? What do you predict will happen next? How did the pattern of the story help you make your prediction?

- *After that big family dinner, Carina took a catnap* page: It sounds like the crabs have a plan. What do you think they'll do? What would you do?

After Reading

- Were there any surprises in this book? What was your favorite part? Why?

- Cumulative or add-on stories with repeated parts are fun to read together because we can join in and act like the characters. When we read with expression as if the character is talking, we're reading fluently!

 ## Extend the Experience

- Let's record ourselves rereading this book. I'll upload the recording to our shared classroom drive so you can listen to it while rereading the book.

- The crabs saved the day in this version of the folktale. Rewrite the ending to create your own version of *Carina Felina*.

Similar Titles

 ### *City Beet* (Cohen, 2023)

About the Book: Victoria and her neighbor, Mrs. Kosta, decide to make raw beet and garlic salad for the midsummer potluck block party. Together, they plant a beet in the community garden in their city neighborhood. Similar to all of the other versions of the Russian folktale "The Enormous Turnip," the beet grows too big to harvest. According to the city workers who offer a helping hand, Victoria is too small to help. So, she busies herself making the salad while the taxi driver, police officers, street sweeper, recycler, and bus driver lend a helping hand. Just in the nick of time, Victoria saves the day. The cumulative pattern and repeated lines will invite readers to join in. [Find a read-aloud experience for comparing turnip tales in *The Ramped-Up Read Aloud*.]

 ### *Wombat Said Come In* (Deedy, 2022)

About the Book: Wombat is prepared to snuggle in his burrow under his crazy quilt and wait out the wildfire raging above, until Wallaby comes a-knocking. With only the slightest hesitation, Wombat welcomes him in with a catchy refrain. Wallaby is followed by Kookaburra, Platypus, Koala, and finally, Sugar Glider. Wombat invites all of them in with the same repeated, rhyming phrase. When the smoke clears, Wombat decides it's time for his friends to go home . . . or is it? The book jacket contains a detailed look at the rooms in Wombat's burrow.

Key Vocabulary and Kid-Friendly Definitions:

- devoured: ate or swallowed something quickly

- disbelief: finding it hard to believe something

- slumber: a nice, peaceful sleep

Upper Elementary Extension:

Carmen Agra Deedy marked the dialogue in *Carina Felina* using creative synonyms for the word *said*. Students can collect the synonyms and use them when they are writing.

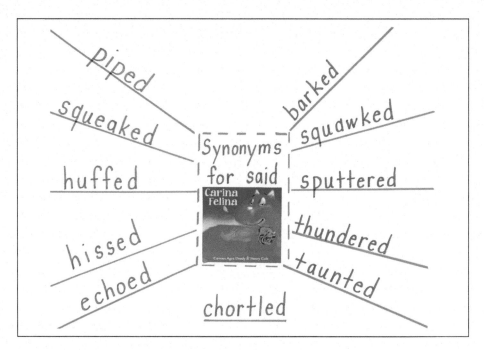

Synonyms for Said Chart

My Favorite Read Alouds for Fostering Fluency

_____
_____
_____
_____
_____
_____
_____
_____
_____
_____
_____
_____
_____
_____
_____
_____
_____
_____
_____
_____
_____
_____
_____
_____
_____
_____
_____
_____

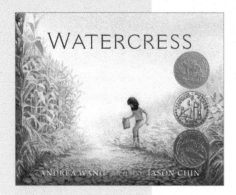

Learning Targets:

- I notice when the story is making sense.
- I pause and reread when the story is not making sense.
- I use strategies to improve my comprehension.

Think About Your Thinking

Book Title: *Watercress* (Wang, 2021)

About the Book: This moving story shows how a young girl's embarrassment evolves into understanding when her mother shares a story of loss from her childhood in China. Andrea Wang's author's note explains, "This story is both an apology and a love letter to my parents."

To find a book like this one, look for the following:

- Plots with opportunities to predict, infer, and question
- Family stories

Comprehension Conversation

Before Reading

Notice the Cover Illustration

- As I open the book so that you can see Jason Chin's Caldecott Award–winning watercolor illustrations, talk with a friend about what you notice.

- Compare and contrast the front and back covers. Do you think the two illustrations are set in the same time and place? What other questions do you have? If you can peek under the book jacket of the hardcover book, you'll see a close-up illustration of watercress.

Set a Purpose: The questions you came up with while looking at the cover give you a clear purpose for reading this book. I'm guessing that one of the reasons you want to read this book is to find the answers to your questions. Previewing a book and thinking about your goal for reading it are two smart ways to get your brain ready to read.

During Reading

- *The tops of the cornstalks make lines that zigzag across the horizon* page: When I'm reading and I come to a word or phrase that I don't quite understand, I pause and try to figure it out. On this page it reads, "Mom's eyes are as sharp as the tip of a dragon's claw." I know she spotted the watercress from a moving car, so I'm inferring that in this sentence *sharp* means able to see small things from far away. Does that make sense to you? Now, it's your turn; talk with a friend about the phrase "two voices heavy with memories."

- *From the depths of the trunk* page: Where have you seen a picture like this before? [on the cover] Now that we've learned a little more about this family, we might be able to answer some of the questions we had before we started reading. Is there anything you're still wondering?

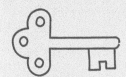

- *On the dinner table that night is a dish of watercress* page: Who is telling the story? [the girl] Why do you suppose she is acting this way? How does the scene on this page connect to what happened so far in the story?

- *"During the great famine"* page: A *famine* is a time when there isn't enough food for people in an area or even a whole country to eat. Can you infer what happened to the uncle? How do you think the girl feels after hearing this story?

- *I take a bite of the watercress* page: Talk with a partner about why you think Mom's memories of home are "delicate and slightly bitter."

After Reading

- Sit quietly for a moment. Think about how this book made you feel.

- Suppose someone asked you to describe the book *Watercress* using only two words. What would those two words be?

Extend the Experience

- As readers, we stopped along the way to make sure we were understanding what was happening in the story. When we do this, we are monitoring our comprehension by taking the time we need to think about our reading. Let's record some of the comprehension monitoring strategies we tried so that you can continue to use them as you read on your own.

- Now that you've heard *Watercress,* I'm going to read aloud the author and artist's notes. After listening to them we'll discuss how their stories add to the book's meaning. We can also ponder whether you would have preferred learning more from their notes before reading the book rather than after.

Similar Titles

 Finding Papa (Krans, 2023)

About the Book: As a toddler, Mai loves playing the game crocodile chomp, "CHOMP! CHOMP!" with her papa. One morning, after giving Mai an extra-long hug, Papa walks away down the dirt road of their village. Mama explains that Papa is trying to find a new home for both of them. After many letters from Papa, Mai and Mama leave in the middle of the night to find him. During their perilous journey across land and sea, Mai's memories of their game give her comfort. Finally, with the help of aid workers, they reunite with Papa in a big city.

 Water Day (Engle, 2023b) [Spanish Edition: El día del agua]

About the Book: It's water day in this vibrant Cuban community. A young girl narrates the excitement she and her family experience as they eagerly await the delivery of water to their neighborhood. Olivia Sua's cut-paper illustrations enhance Margarita Engle's lyrical narrative that emphasizes the joy and significance of this essential commodity.

Key Vocabulary and Kid-Friendly Definitions:

- abrupt: when something happens suddenly or when you don't expect it

- ashamed: feeling embarrassed or uncomfortable because of something you said or did

- glistening: when something looks shiny or sparkly

Upper Elementary Extension:

If students were to interview the main character, what would they ask her? Ask them to write down three questions, then share and compare with classmates.

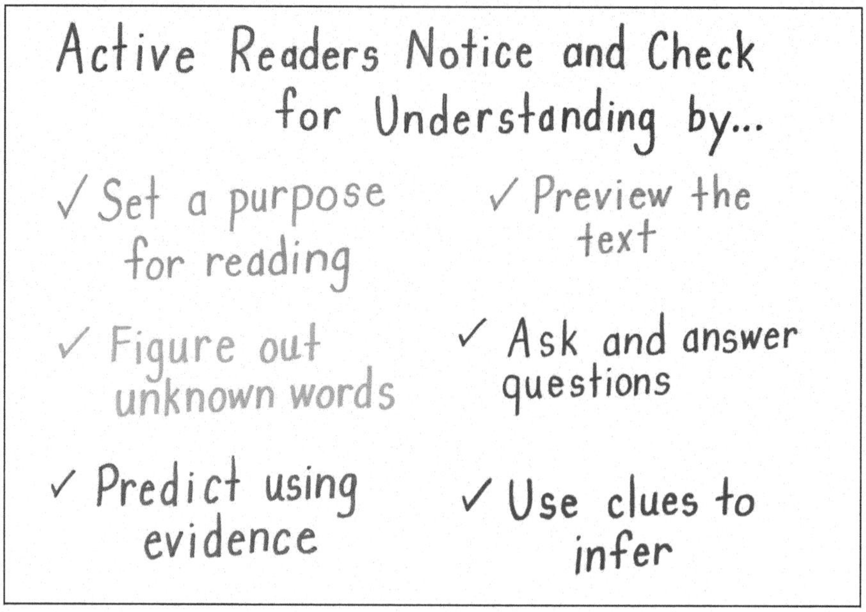

Active Readers Notice and Check
for Understanding by...

✓ Set a purpose for reading

✓ Preview the text

✓ Figure out unknown words

✓ Ask and answer questions

✓ Predict using evidence

✓ Use clues to infer

Comprehension Monitoring Strategy Chart

My Favorite Read Alouds for Monitoring Comprehension

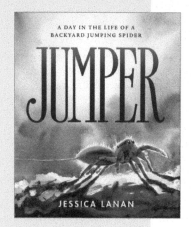

A DAY IN THE LIFE OF A
BACKYARD JUMPING SPIDER

JUMPER

JESSICA LANAN

Learning Targets:

- I notice how the text structure helps me remember key details.

- I pause and reread to better understand the topic.

- I talk, write, or draw about my new learning.

Pause and Reread

Book Title: *Jumper: A Day in the Life of a Backyard Jumping Spider* (Lanan, 2023)

About the Book: This creatively crafted nonfiction book gives readers an up-close look at the daily life of a jumping spider aptly named Jumper. Set in a community garden, a pig-tailed girl's actions often mirror the spider's behaviors. Declarative sentences like, "This is how Jumper moves" summarize each aspect of Jumper's behavior. The backmatter, which includes diagrams and a glossary, provides more details about the ways jumping spiders use various body parts to help them survive and grow. *Jumper* was a 2024 Robert F. Sibert Honor book.

To find a book like this one, look for the following:

- Informational texts about kid-appealing topics
- Informational texts written in unique and engaging ways

Comprehension Conversation

Before Reading

Notice the Cover Illustration

Wow! That spider looks like it is going to jump right off the page. Show me with a facial expression how you feel about spiders. [If you have the hardcover version, display the case cover underneath the book jacket that shows a close-up of the spider's face!] The creator, Jessica Lanan, used ink, watercolor, and gouache paint to make these realistic-looking pictures. Gouache paint is thicker and less see-through than watercolor paint; it has a creamy texture, like melted ice cream.

Set a Purpose: The title of this nonfiction book is *Jumper* and the subtitle is *A Day in the Life of a Backyard Jumping Spider.* What are you expecting to discover as we read this book? When you read a nonfiction text to find out more about a topic, it is helpful to pause and check in with yourself to see if you are remembering the important details. Let's notice how the structure or organization of this book helps us learn more about spiders.

During Reading

- Title page: What do you suppose the girl sees on the sidewalk? Whisper your answer to a friend. Let's turn the page to find out!

- *What if you were very small* page: Oh! This page surprised me! I thought she might find a spider. What did she find? [a lima bean] What do you notice about the text on this page? [It gradually gets smaller.] Why do you think Jessica Lanan did that?

- *That is how Jumper feels* page: This is the third time we read a sentence like this. First, we read, "That is Jumper's world." Then, "That is how Jumper moves." You can turn these sentences into questions to check for understanding. What could you do if you don't remember how Jumper's sense of touch works? [reread]

[Continue to point out and demonstrate how to monitor for meaning by turning the summary sentences into questions.]

- *Jumper climbs among the beans* page: Have you noticed anything about the girl? [She's often doing something similar to what Jumper is doing.] How does this comparison help you better understand how jumping spiders move?

- *Footsteps fade away* page: Based on the information you just read, what do you predict Jumper will do next?

After Reading

- Share the most interesting fact you learned about jumping spiders.

- Once we discovered the format of this book, we paused at the summary sentences to check for understanding. Did you find those sentences helpful? Why do you suppose Jessica Lanan chose that format to organize this nonfiction book?

Extend the Experience

- Reading a nonfiction book like this one helps us better understand a topic. Oftentimes, authors of nonfiction books include *backmatter,* or additional information at the end of the book that teaches even more. In the first page of backmatter, Jessica Lanan adds details to explain more about a jumping spider's paws, silk, senses, and ability to jump. What are you still curious about?

- Remember the summary sentences in the book? You can use them to write about your new learning about jumping spiders:

  Jumping spiders move by _____.

  Jumping spiders feel with their _____.

  Jumping spiders jump by _____.

  Jumping spiders hear by _____.

  Jumping spiders see with _____.

Similar Titles

 Bears Are Best (Holub, 2023) ⭐

About the Book: Laugh while discovering the distinguishing features of the eight different species of bears. In this fast-paced, witty blend of fact and fantasy, readers hear right from each bear's mouth what makes its species unique. Because this tale is told mainly though speech bubbles, readers have to monitor their comprehension by honing-in on the facts while at the same time enjoying the humorous bear banter. The book wraps up with a summary paragraph about each bear, written in first-bear point of view, along with books and websites to extend the learning.

 Stranded! A MOSTLY True Story from Iceland (Benediktsson, 2023) [Based on True Events]

About the Book: Based on the true story of the author's grandfather, this lively picture book blends the folklore and magic of Iceland with a recounting of the adventures of two men stranded on a newly formed volcanic island named Surtsey, off the coast of Iceland. The author keeps readers guessing until the end about the one detail of the story that isn't true. This book is sure to spark interest in Iceland, Surtsey, and volcanoes. Readers can start their inquiry process by consulting the engaging backmatter.

Key Vocabulary and Kid-Friendly Definitions:

- detects: notices or discovers something

- stealthy: sneaky

- ventures: moves in a brave or daring way

Upper Elementary Extension:

Jessica Lanan includes a variety of features in the backmatter of this book. Students can select one feature to study as a mentor text, then use what they've discovered to add a similar feature to their own nonfiction text.

"*I LOVE all kinds of books . . . books that teach me unbelievable facts, books that take me on adventures, and books about great people who changed the world.*"

—*Rocket Says Speak Up*
by Nathan Bryon and Dapo Adeola

Strengthen Listening Comprehension

Develop Strategic Readers

Picture book read alouds are immersive opportunities to nurture thoughtful readers capable of connecting the text to their broader understanding of the world. As you facilitate the comprehension conversations in this chapter, you'll guide learners to apply key strategies such as, among others, inferring, questioning, and determining importance. Discussing how these strategies help students as readers builds metacognition, or an awareness of their thought processes. In addition, they have the opportunity to listen in as you think aloud and demonstrate how proficient readers puzzle their way through a text. With each read-aloud experience, learners will further develop language comprehension, build reading-specific background knowledge, and engage with both fiction and nonfiction texts with confidence and curiosity as they:

- Analyze characters
- Notice story structure
- Ask and answer questions
- Ponder point of view
- Infer

In these read-aloud experiences, research meets reality and picture books become a cornerstone for developing strategic, reflective, and enthusiastic readers.

Scan here to find a complete learning target chart with book-related online links, a bonus read-aloud experience, and printable resources.

https://qrs.ly/hyfn8pg

Big Idea: Featured Title	Learning Targets
Notice How Characters Feel: *Abuela's Super Capa* (Siqueira, 2023)	• I use key details to infer characters' feelings. • I notice how characters' feelings change. • I think about how I might feel in the same situations.
Notice How Characters Change: *The Wilderness* (McCarthy, 2023)	• I use key details to learn about characters. • I notice how characters change. • I think about the events that caused the change.
Use Story Elements to Retell: *Rocket Says Speak Up!* (Bryon, 2023)	• I identify the characters, setting, problem, and solutions in a story. • I use what I know about story elements to understand the events. • I retell using story elements.
Use Story Elements to Predict and Infer: *Down the Hole* (Slater, 2023)	• I identify the characters, setting, problem, and solutions in a story. • I use what I know about story elements to predict. • I use what I know about story elements to infer.
Find Answers: *Finding Family: The Duckling Raised by Loons* (Salas, 2023a)	• I ask and answer questions to help me better understand a topic. • I notice where questions lead. • I find answers to my questions.
Imagine Possibilities: *Twenty Questions* (Barnett, 2023)	• I ask and answer questions to help me better understand an image or text. • I notice that questions can have different answers. • I ponder where questions lead.
Notice Who's Talking: *I Am a Tornado* (Beckmeyer, 2023)	• I identify who is telling the story at different points. • I think about how knowing who is talking helps me better understand the story. • I infer big ideas or themes.
Notice Who's Sharing Facts: *We Are Branches* (Sidman, 2023)	• I notice the author's choice of point of view. • I think about how noticing point of view helps me better understand the information. • I identify the main purpose of the text.
Connect Text and Pictures: *Something, Someday* (Gorman, 2023)	• I use what I already know to help me infer. • I connect details in the words and illustrations. • I put what I learn together to make an inference.
Link Details Across a Text: *Every Dog in the Neighborhood* (Stead, 2022)	• I connect details in the words and illustrations. • I link key details across a text to infer. • I talk, write, or draw about the themes or big ideas in a story.
Bonus Lesson (online) Use Story Elements to Infer Big Ideas: *How This Book Got Red* (Greanias, 2023)	• I identify the characters, setting, problem, and solutions in a story. • I use what I learned to infer the theme or big ideas.

My Favorite Read Alouds for Strengthening Listening Comprehension

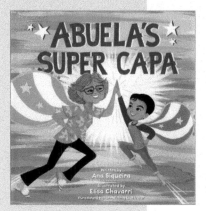

Notice How Characters Feel

Book Title: *Abuela's Super Capa* (Siqueira, 2023) [Spanish Edition: La supercapa de Abuela]

About the Book: Every Saturday, Luis and his abuela (grandmother) don their capes and joyfully imagine they are superheroes. One Saturday, Abuela can't come over because she's in the hospital. Luis uses his superpowers to try and help her get better—he even lets his little sister, who he usually calls "the intruder," join in the hugging. After a while, Abuela comes home, but she is still not well enough to play superhero. Eventually, Abuela gives her cape to Luis and he lets his little sister be his new sidekick.

To find a book like this one, look for the following:

- First-person accounts of intergenerational relationships
- Stories that highlight the realities of aging

Comprehension Conversation

Before Reading

Notice the Cover Illustration

- How would you describe the mood of the illustration on this cover? Elisa Chavarri used cut paper and paint to make her *vibrant* illustrations. Vibrant means colorful, lively, and full of energy.

- *Abuela* means grandmother in Spanish. Can you figure out what the word *capa* means?

Set a Purpose:

During Reading

- *Abuela's eyes shine like estrellas* page: I notice there is a mix of English and Spanish words in this book. If I don't have the asset of speaking Spanish, I can either use context and picture clues to help me figure out the words or I can look in the glossary in the back of the book. [If you and your students speak Spanish an alternative question might be: I know some/a lot of/you also speak Spanish. Do you speak Spanish and English at home, or do you speak mainly just one language?] Are there any words we should work on together to figure out? Why do you suppose Luis thinks his little sister is an "intruder"?

- *Rest* page: Describe how Luis is feeling on this page. [sad] Share the clues that helped you to infer his mood. [he's crying, he's sitting hunched over by himself, the background color is blue instead of bright] How would you react?

- *Abuela doesn't get better* page: What does Mami mean when she says, "Luis, Abuela needs to hang up her capa"? [Discuss the figurative meaning of that saying.] What is making Luis's super vision go cloudy? [tears]

Learning Targets:

- I use key details to infer characters' feelings.
- I notice how characters' feelings change.
- I think about how I might feel in the same situations.

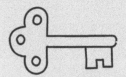

- *Papi brings me my capa* page: At this point in the story, Luis's feelings have changed. How would you describe them, now? [angry, upset, mad]

- *"This capa is perfecta for you"* page: What does Luis realize here? [That his sister can be his sidekick, just like he was Abuela's sidekick.]

After Reading

- Let's go back and look at the pages where Luis was sad and angry. How did the illustrations change on those pages? [The illustrator added background colors.] Were the colors she chose helpful in figuring out his mood?

- How did this story make you feel? Would you recommend it to a friend? Why or why not?

Extend the Experience

- Think about a family member or caregiver who is special to you. Draw a picture of that person that shows your mood when you are with them.

- Luis and his abuela loved pretending they were superheroes. If you could become your own unique superhero, what would your name be? What would be some of your superpowers? Draw a picture of yourself as a superhero and label it with your superhero name and superpowers.

Similar Titles

 My Baba's Garden (Scott, 2023)

About the Book: As explained in the author's note, this is the story of Jordan Scott's grandmother. Told from the point of view of young Jordan, readers experience the quiet daily routines the two of them shared each day before and after school. The morning begins with a swimming-pool-sized bowl of oatmeal in the kitchen of Baba's chicken coop home. Then, a slow walk through the rain to and from school, where Baba collects worms to enrich her garden. When Baba is no longer able to live on her own, she joins the family in their home and the roles of child and caregiver are reversed.

 Zora, the Story Keeper (Wilkins, 2023)

About the Book: When she grows up, Zora wants to be a gifted storyteller just like her Aunt Bea. But right now, her happy place is spending time with Aunt Bea after school as she regales her with stories from the family book. Zora begins to notice that Aunt Bea is not feeling well and she is eventually taken to the hospital. When Uncle Ralph comes home without Aunt Bea, the stories stop. But not for long, because the family book and all of the stories are passed on to Zora. Have a box of tissues nearby when reading this one!

Key Vocabulary and Kid-Friendly Definitions:

- intruder: someone who is not supposed to be there

- rescue: to help someone or something that is in trouble or danger

- sidekick: a partner who helps you

Upper Elementary Extension:

Book talk the first book in one of these engaging series that feature cape-wearing superheroes: *The Princess in Black* (Hale & Hale, 2014); *Zita the Spacegirl* (Hatke, 2010); and *Stuntboy, in the Meantime* (Reynolds, 2021).

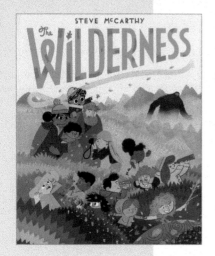

Notice How Characters Change

Book Title: *The Wilderness* (McCarthy, 2023)

About the Book: Oktober Vasylenko is one of 12 children, each named for a month of the year. Although Oktober wants to be a great adventurer, he prefers the experiences found safely inside the covers of a book. When his parents coax him out into the wilderness where the creature called the Wilderness lives, Oktober gets lost and meets the Wilderness face-to-face. Realizing the Wilderness is as scared as he is, Oktober bravely waves. The Wilderness then helps Oktober find his way back home, where he writes his own adventure book.

To find a book like this one, look for the following:

- Characters who change over the course of the story
- Characters who face fears

Comprehension Conversation

Before Reading

Notice the Cover Illustration

- Wow! There are a lot of kids on this book cover. How many do you count? [12]
- Look at the facial expressions. Most of them seem to be enjoying the wilderness. Do you see any who aren't? [The girl surrounded by bees and the boy on the man's shoulders.]

Set a Purpose: Sometimes in stories an event happens and characters learn new ways of thinking that cause them to change. These events are called *turning points*. As you trek through *The Wilderness*, notice any turning points in the story.

During Reading

- *Much like his brothers and sisters, Oktober dreamed of being a great adventurer* page: How is Oktober different from his brothers and sisters? [He prefers reading about adventures rather than having them outside.] Why do you suppose he feels this way?

- *"What if the Wilderness is down there . . . ?" said Oktober* page: Let's talk about the wise advice Oktober's parents give him. ["Scared is how you *feel*, but bravery is what you do."] ["Not knowing things can be scary."] Do you agree with their advice?

- *"Whooft!" said Mom, which was a noise that meant* page: Even though Mom was *wonderstruck* or amazed by the beauty around them, Oktober doesn't react in the same way. Tell a neighbor how you think Oktober is feeling right now.

- *With the Wilderness by his side* page: How did meeting the Wilderness help Oktober overcome his fears? Identify an event or turning point that had the most to do with his change of heart.

Learning Targets:

- I use key details to learn about characters.
- I notice how characters change.
- I think about the events that caused the change.

After Reading

- Share some of the lessons Oktober learned about courage, curiosity, and the magic of the outdoors.

- Can you predict what Oktober will write about in his book called *The Wilderness*?

Extend the Experience

- Draw and/or write about Oktober at the beginning of the story, the turning point, and the end of the story using the *Pondering When Characters Change Printable*. (Located on the companion website, resources.corwin.com/more-rampedup-readalouds.)

- Steve McCarthy added details to the illustrations to give you clues about the different personalities of Oktober's sisters and brothers. I'm going to put this book in a special place so that you can study the illustrations to learn more about the kids in the Vasylenko family.

Similar Titles

 Desert Jungle (J. Baker, 2023)

About the Book: A boy from a tiny village in the Valley of the Cirios in Baja, California, prefers his tablet over nature. During a visit to his grandpa's remote desert home, a coyote steals his bag and tablet. Desperate to find it, he sets out and loses his way in the desert jungle. He eventually finds his way back to Grandpa's ranch house and shares his fear of the natural world. His grandpa helps him discover the beauty of nature through exploration. Jeannie Baker was inspired to write this book when she learned that many children suffer from "nature-deficit-disorder," or a lack of familiarity with the natural world. Backmatter includes details about the setting.

 Lawrence & Sophia (Cronin, 2023)

About the Book: A boy named Lawrence is afraid to go "out there" where it's too big, too loud, and too crowded. Meanwhile, a bird named Sophia avoids going "down there" because it's dark, bumpy, and dangerous. The two meet and invent creative (and hilarious) ways to play together, all while staying in their respective safety zones. When a storm forces each of them to take a risk to find the other, they realize the value of their friendship and, together, wonder what's "over there."

Key Vocabulary and Kid-Friendly Definitions:

- **adventurer:** a brave and curious person who likes to explore

- **impressive:** something you remember because it is special

- **lurks:** hides or waits quietly to do something sneaky or surprising

Upper Elementary Extension:

Use the end papers, where Steve McCarthy has created a humorous glossary of fictional plants and animals, as inspiration for students to invent their own imaginary dangers of the wild.

Name _____

Pondering When Characters Change

Beginning	Turning Point	End

Pondering When Characters Change Printable

My Favorite Read Alouds for Studying Characters

by **Nathan Bryon** · illustrated by **Dapo Adeola**

Learning Targets:

- I identify the characters, setting, problem, and solutions in a story.

- I use what I know about story elements to understand the events.

- I retell using story elements.

Use Story Elements to Retell

Book Title: *Rocket Says Speak Up!* (Bryon, 2023)

About the Book: In the third installment of the *Rocket* series, Rocket learns that her beloved public library is in danger of closing. Inspired by Rosa Parks, she rallies her classmates and the community and they join together in a peaceful protest, with Rocket dressed in her favorite outfit (an orange space suit). Eventually, generous donors save and renovate the library.

To find a book like this one, look for the following:

- Straightforward plots with clearly identifiable story elements
- Human characters who are relatable to your students

Comprehension Conversation

Before Reading

Notice the Cover Illustration

- Zoom-in on the details on the cover of this book. Talk with a neighbor about something you see.

- Let's flip the book over and read the back cover blurb to get a preview about what is going to happen in this story. How does previewing a book help you as a reader?

Set a Purpose: As we join Rocket in trying to save the town library, we're going to pay attention to the parts or elements of the story. Noticing the character, setting, problem, and solution helps you better understand the story. You can also use these elements to tell your friends or family/caregivers about the book.

During Reading

- *Every Friday after school . . .* page: Who is telling the story? [Rocket] Would you say she's the main character? Why or why not?

- *Today, Layla the librarian hands me a book she thinks I'll love* page: What's the problem in the story? Remember what we learned in the preview? How do you predict Rocket is going to solve the problem?

- *On Monday at school* page: How did Rocket let her classmates know about the problem? [She spoke up and shared interesting facts.] Do you think that was a good strategy?

- *And it's the mayor of our town* page: Did Rocket's peaceful protest work? What is the solution to the problem? [People from all over the world gave money to save the library.]

- *The library celebration is AWESOME* page: Wow! They had enough money to *refurbish,* or make the library look and feel brand new. What do you predict the loud, beeping noise might be?

After Reading

- Think of three adjectives to describe Rocket, using clues from the book. Share your adjectives with a partner. Start by saying: Rocket is _____, _____, and _____ because . . .

- Have you ever seen a traveling library or bookmobile? Where do you think the traveling library might go?

Extend the Experience

- Let's review and write down the elements of this story.

- The book *Rocket Says Speak Up!* is part of a series. We can compare the story elements in *Rocket Says Speak Up!* to those in one of the other two books in the series, *Rocket Says Look Up!* (Bryon, 2019) and *Rocket Says Clean Up!* (Bryon, 2020), to see how they are similar and different.

Similar Titles

 ### *Rocket Says Clean Up!* (Bryon, 2020)

About the Book: Rocket and her family are traveling to a tropical island to visit her grandparents, who give whale-watching tours and run an animal sanctuary. When Rocket finds a young turtle tangled in plastic, she enlists the help of fellow beachgoers to clean up the trash. Rocket's emotions and energy jump off every page, unlike her brother, who is glued to his smartphone. [Find book experiences for this book in *Shake Up Shared Reading*.]

 ### *Rocket Says Look Up!* (Bryon, 2019)

About the Book: Rocket is fascinated by space and dreams of becoming an astronaut. When she finds out that the Phoenix meteor shower is coming, she encourages her neighbors, and especially her phone-obsessed teenage brother, to appreciate the beauty and wonder of the night sky.

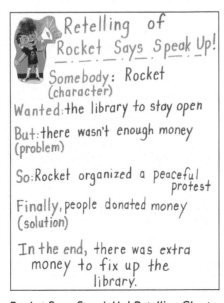

Rocket Says Speak Up! Retelling Chart

Key Vocabulary and Kid-Friendly Definitions:

- inspired: feeling really excited or brave enough to do something

- prepared: ready

- protest: when people get together to show they don't agree with something and want it to change

Upper Elementary Extension:

Rocket shares three interesting facts about libraries. Divide the class into three groups. Give each group time and resources to research one of the facts and share their findings with the class.

Use Story Elements to Predict and Infer

Book Title: *Down the Hole* (Slater, 2023)

About the Book: A hungry, scarf-wearing fox sits outside Rabbit's burrow trying to coax him out of the hole. Meanwhile, below the ground, the bunnies have hatched a plan to avoid becoming Fox's next meal. Readers will be rooting for the bunnies as they observe their underground antics. Will their idea work? Readers will have to infer Fox's fate.

To find a book like this one, look for the following:

- Straightforward plots with clearly identifiable story elements
- Opportunities to predict and infer

Comprehension Conversation

Before Reading

Notice the Cover Illustration

I'll open this wraparound cover so that you can take in everything that's going on. Pick a character on this cover, imagine a thinking bubble above its head. What thoughts would be in that bubble? Notice the setting. Adam Ming created the characters and setting by combining hand-painted paper with digital tools.

Set a Purpose: We can expect that a story will have certain elements like characters, setting, problem, and solutions. We're going to use what we already know about these elements to help us make predictions and infer. Get ready to go *Down the Hole!*

During Reading

- *Fox sat down next to the hole* page: Think about other stories you've read with foxes in them. What do you already know about fox characters? Combine that schema with what it says on this page to infer why there are fewer bunnies in the hole.

- *Rabbit was waiting inside the hole* page: On this page, you can use the details in illustrations to help you infer what Rabbit and his friends have planned for Fox.

- *"You think a bunny in your tummy sounds yummy?"* page: Why is Fox trying to coax Rabbit out of the hole? [So he can eat him.] What does Fox mean when he says, "You have my word"? Do you think Rabbit should believe him? Why or why not?

- *". . . aaaaaand STOP."* page: Think about everything we've read so far in this story as you look at this illustration. Turn and talk about your predictions with a friend.

- *The bunnies played outside of their hole without a care* page: How can the bunnies be certain that Fox would not be stopping by again?

Learning Targets:

- I identify the characters, setting, problem, and solutions in a story.
- I use what I know about story elements to predict.
- I use what I know about story elements to infer.

After Reading

- The last page in this book is a picture of a bear. What detail in this illustration helps you infer the ending of the story? [The purple scarf that Fox was wearing is now around Bear's neck.]

- Would you recommend this story to a friend? Why or why not?

Extend the Experience

- Draw and/or write about the elements of this story using the *Story Elements Printable*. (Located on the companion website, resources .corwin.com/more-rampedup-readalouds.)

- What are some other ways Rabbit and the bunnies could have solved the problem? Work with a partner to come up with a different plan.

Similar Titles

 ***How This Book Got Red* (Greanias, 2023)**

About the Book: Red, a red panda, and Gee, a giant panda, are reading a book called *Pandas Everywhere*. By the end of the book, Red is fuming because there is no mention of red pandas. To solve the problem, Red sets out to write her own red panda book. When she's faced with writer's block, the two go for a walk. Red shows Gee that they live in a giant panda–obsessed world and, feeling "like the smallest speck of dust," she tosses her unfinished book into a trash can. Fortunately, it is discovered by a group of red pandas (and one giant panda) who implore her to finish it. (See bonus read-aloud experience on the companion website, resources.corwin. com/more-rampedup-readalouds.)

 ***Lucky Duck* (Pizzoli, 2024)**

About the Book: Susan the duck is feeling unlucky. The nonrefundable roller skates she ordered are too big. Luckily, a wolf appears at her door with a prize—a giant cooking pot. As the day continues, whenever Susan encounters more bad luck, the wolf brings another "prize" like onions, celery, and carrots. You can predict where this story is heading, but an unexpected and humorous turn of events culminates in a satisfying ending. Readers will enjoy keeping track of the little yellow bug's antics. *Lucky Duck* pairs perfectly with *My Lucky Day* (Kasza, 2003).

Key Vocabulary and Kid-Friendly Definitions:

- certain: being very sure about something

- inquired: asked a question

- smirked: had a sly or sneaky smile on their face

Upper Elementary Extension:

Ponder these questions with your learners—"Why do you think foxes are often portrayed as sly or tricky in stories?" "Are real-life foxes tricky?"

Title _____

Characters:	Setting:
Problem:	**Solution:**

Reader _____

Story Elements Printable

My Favorite Read Alouds for Noticing Story Structure

Find Answers

Book Title: *Finding Family: The Duckling Raised by Loons* (Salas, 2023a)

About the Book: Part science journal, part lyrical narrative, Laura Purdie Salas transports readers to a Wisconsin lake to witness the touching true story of a loon couple who adopt and care for a mallard duckling. According to the backmatter, this is only one of two documented cases of this unlikely family forming. Perhaps because loons and mallards are typically enemies! This section also includes a detailed Venn diagram comparing loons and mallards.

To find a book like this one, look for the following:

- Books that lead to more questions
- Informational books based on true events

Learning Targets:

- I ask and answer questions to help me better understand a topic.
- I notice where questions lead.
- I find answers to my questions.

Comprehension Conversation

Before Reading

Notice the Cover Illustration

- The first time I looked at this cover, I had some before-reading questions like, "Why is the duckling sitting on the loon's back?" Are you wondering anything else about these two birds? [Record students' before-reading questions digitally or on chart paper divided into three sections: **B**efore Reading, **D**uring Reading, **A**fter Reading.]
- The title of this true story is *Finding Family* and the subtitle is *The Duckling Raised by Loons*. Now that you know a little bit more, do you have any other questions?

Set a Purpose: Readers ask questions to help them focus on what is happening in a book and to clear up anything they don't understand. Sometimes you can find the answers to your questions in the book and other times you need to research to learn the answers. It's also possible that there will be questions that no one can answer. Let's continue to wonder as we learn about this loon and duckling family.

During Reading

- *Mother and Father loon guard the nest* page: The nest they're guarding rests in the shadow of the *tamarack*. If I'm not sure what a *tamarack* is, what strategies might I use to figure it out? [Context clues: What is making a shadow? Picture clues: I see that the loons are under a tree. Do a quick online search: It's a type of tree.]
- *June 23* page: On this page, the author asks many questions. What is her answer to those questions? [Nobody knows.] Did you find anything surprising? Would you add any other questions to the ones she's asked? Turn and talk about your questions with a partner. [Add students' during-reading questions to During Reading section of the chart.]

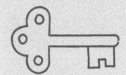
- *July 9* page: Why do you suppose Duckling is doing things that loons do? What do you think the author means when she writes, "Mallard bones are not loon-heavy, pulling them into the deep"?

- *Duckling is practically full-grown* page: Again, this page has many unanswered questions. What are you wondering, thinking, or feeling as you listen to all of the unanswered questions?

After Reading

- As you keep thinking about this book, what has left you curious?

- Why do you suppose Laura Purdie Salas included dates on some of the pages? What time of the year did this event happen?

Extend the Experience

- Write any after-reading questions on a sticky note and add them to our chart.

- In this book, we can find some answers in the backmatter, or information the author adds at the back of the book. How else can we find the answers to our questions?

Similar Titles

 ***Steve the Dung Beetle: On a Roll* (Stoltz, 2022)**

About the Book: Grab a colleague and read this book together with two voices. One person can read the questions like, "Why are you rolling that ball of poo?" that Steve is asked by the African animals he meets on his way home. The other can share Steve's informative answers. An entertaining and educational read aloud rolled into one (ball of dung!). This book pairs perfectly with the story *More Dung! A Beetle Tale* (Weber, 2024).

 ***Why Do Elephants Have Big Ears?* (S. Jenkins & Page, 2023)**

About the Book: Collaborators Robin Page and the late Steve Jenkins give readers the inside scoop on an intriguing collection of 19 creatures. High-interest questions coupled with economical and conversational answers make this a must-read addition to any animal unit. Read this book aloud like you would a chapter book, answering a few questions each day. Learn more details about each creature in the backmatter.

Find Answers to Question Chart

Key Vocabulary and Kid-Friendly Definitions:

- emerge: to show itself or come out from somewhere

- hover: to float or stay up without touching the ground

- snatches: quickly grabs something

Upper Elementary Extension:

Use the popular *Who Would Win?* Series, by Jerry Pallotta, as a mentor text for students to design a loon versus mallard infographic with the facts found in the Venn diagram in the backmatter.

MAC BARNETT CHRISTIAN ROBINSON

Learning Targets:

- I ask and answer questions to help me better understand an image or text.
- I notice that questions can have different answers.
- I ponder where questions lead.

Imagine Possibilities

Book Title: *Twenty Questions* (Barnett, 2023)

About the Book: You'll find questions and illustrations that prompt imagination, interpretation, creativity, and play wrapped between the covers of *Twenty Questions*. The book begins in a familiar way with the question, "How many animals can you see in this picture?" Then, it shifts on the next page to, "How many animals can you not see in this one, because they're hiding from the tiger?" After that, readers are invited to interpret Christian Robinson's distinctive illustrations using Mac Barnett's questions as their guide.

To find a book like this one, look for the following:

- A text that invites multiple interpretations.
- Books that spark more questions.

Comprehension Conversation

Before Reading

Notice the Cover Illustration:

I'll bet you recognize Christian Robinson's mixed media illustrations from other books he's worked on like *Last Stop on Market Street* (2015) and *Milo Imagines the World* (2021). Mixed media means he uses a variety of art tools to make each picture. If you were to ask a question about the cover illustration, what would it be? Share your question with a friend, and then listen to their question.

Set a Purpose: I heard you wondering a lot of different things about the cover, from "Why is the snake in the sneaker?" to "Whose sneaker is it?" Why do you suppose we have different questions when we're all looking at the same illustration? [Perhaps because we all see it in our own way.] We'll explore this idea further as we enjoy *Twenty Questions* together. [To provide ample time for the collaborative conversations, you may want to split the book in half and read it in two separate read-aloud experiences.]

During Reading

- *How many animals can you see in this picture* page: [10] What was your counting strategy? Share with a friend. Did any animal make counting tricky? [The snake because it's on both sides of the page.]

- *How many animals can you not see in this one* page: What is the difference between this question and the one on the first page? [The question on pages 1–2 had one answer; this one could have a lot of answers.] Which type of question do you prefer?

[This book is ideal for stressing the importance of thinking and talking together with a partner to ask and answer questions. As you continue reading, encourage listeners

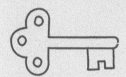

to discuss their answers and the reasons behind them. Remember, they don't always have to share their answers with you; it's the partner conversation that will help their thinking grow.]

After Reading

- Now that we've had time to think through this book together, I want to come back to the question I asked you before we started: Why do you suppose we have different answers when we're all looking at the same illustration? [Discuss and record students' responses.]

- Why do you think Mac Barnett and Christian Robinson wrote this book? Do you like answering questions that have more than one possible answer? Where did the questions lead us?

Extend the Experience

- [Display one or more pages from the book and provide students with a blank sheet of paper.] We came up with a lot of different answers as we read this book. Study this illustration while I reread the question. Think of a creative answer that you haven't already heard. Something unique. Draw and/or write your response on the page. Once we're done, we'll share our ideas and see how they compare.

- Mac Barnett and Christian Robinson worked as a team on this book. Work with a partner or small team. Begin by finding or creating an image. Then, trade images with your teammates so they can write a question to match your image. After they're done, we'll post our images and questions so people can ponder them.

Similar Titles

 ***Time to Make Art* (Mack, 2024)**

With paint palette and brush in hand, a young creator has questions . . . lots of them. "What if I can only draw stick figures? Are smiley faces art?" Artists from around the globe and throughout history offer possible answers related to their unique type of art. As you're reading aloud, invite listeners to add their own answers, sparking a rich discussion about visual expression. Read a snippet of kid-friendly information about each featured creator and their art in the backmatter. This book also pairs nicely with the read-aloud experience on page 164.

 ***The Wordy Book* (Paschkis, 2021)** ☆

About the Book: In this thought-provoking book, Julie Paschkis has compiled, as she says in the author's note, a collection of "wordy paintings." Each painting is paired with a question like, "What lies beyond beyond?" and "When does where become here?" Word-filled illustrations are a vocabulary lesson waiting to happen.

Key Vocabulary and Kid-Friendly Definitions:

- bandits: a group of robbers or thieves that steal from people who are traveling

- noggin: another word for your head

- upset: a feeling you have when you are hurt or uncomfortable

Upper Elementary Extension:

Integrate this book into a content-area unit from your curriculum, and then have students create 10 questions about a topic related to that content area.

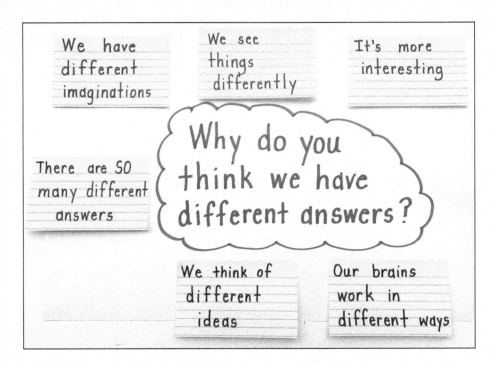

Why Do We Have Different Answers? Chart

My Favorite Read Alouds for Questioning

I AM A
TORNADO

DREW BECKMEYER

Learning Targets:

- I identify who is telling the story at different points.
- I think about how knowing who is talking helps me better understand the story.
- I infer big ideas or themes.

Notice Who's Talking

Book Title: *I Am a Tornado* (Beckmeyer, 2023)

About the Book: Tornado is spinning out of control. A caring cow caught up in the funnel cloud questions the reason behind Tornado's explosive behavior. With gentle nudging from Cow, Tornado loses steam. In the end, Tornado asks Cow to stay by its side while it blows away. Tornado's dialogue is represented in all capital letters with black or white fonts while Cow's words appear in mainly a brown upper- and lowercase font. Readers learn a little about tornadoes while at the same time exploring emotional meltdowns.

To find a book like this one, look for the following:

- Plots where two different characters' points of view are clearly portrayed
- Texts where speakers' words are differentiated by font appearance

Comprehension Conversation

Before Reading

Notice the Cover Illustration

- I'll open this book so that you can study the picture on the wraparound cover. I bet you can tell by looking at the cover that Drew Beckmeyer made the illustrations using cut paper. What is happening in this scene? [Tornado has knocked over some houses. It has eyes, and they seem to be looking at the cow.]
- This story is called *I Am a Tornado*. Do you predict this will be realistic fiction or make-believe? What are the clues? [If you are able peek under the book jacket to see the case cover, discuss why readers think there are only pictures of Tornado and Cow.]

Set a Purpose: When readers pay attention to who is talking in the story, it helps them to better understand the plot, or what is happening. Let's see if we can figure out who's talking as we spin around with Tornado and Cow.

During Reading

- *I AM A TORNADO* page: Uh-oh! What is happening as Tornado blows through? What do you notice about the words *I AM A TORNADO*? [They appear in all capital letters and the font color is black.]
- *Look out* page: What do you predict is going to happen to Cow? Turn and swap predictions with a friend. Do Cow's words look different than Tornado's? How? [They appear in upper- and lowercase letters and the font is brown.]
- *Could you put me down* page: Who is saying, "Could you put me down?" How can you tell? Make a prediction about what Tornado is going to do next.
- *Nothing* page: Can you figure out what is bothering Tornado? Why do you suppose it's choosing not to tell Cow?
- *Wait* page: Have you ever felt like you need more space? When this happens, what do you do?

- *IF I DID DECIDE TO PUT YOU DOWN* page: Notice what's happening to Tornado. [It's getting smaller.] What are the illustrations showing you about its mood?

After Reading

- In this story, Drew Beckmeyer uses a tornado as an *analogy* for something. An *analogy* is like a bridge between two things that helps us understand one thing by comparing it to something else. In this book, what would you say Tornado is an analogy for? Share your thoughts with a classmate.

- How did paying attention to who's talking help you to better understand this story?

Extend the Experience

- Writers, when you are creating a story with two characters, you might decide to put the words they say, their dialogue, in two different colors to help your readers better understand who is talking.

- Cow helped Tornado calm down. Let's make a list of strategies you could use or things you could say to help yourself or someone else calm down.

- Mistakes are like stepping stones. They show you the way and help you grow and learn.
- Kindness is like a boomerang. When you toss it out into the world, it comes back and makes everyone happier.
- Imagination is like a superpower. It helps you create worlds, adventures, and much more in your mind.
- Your brain is like a muscle. The more your exercise it by reading, learning, and problem solving, the stronger and smarter it becomes.

Simple Analogies to Share With Students

Similar Titles

 Do You Remember? (Smith, 2023)

About the Book: A mother and son snuggle on a bed in their new home and take turns reminiscing about past events and the senses they evoke. You can infer that for some reason they've left the boy's dad behind to start a new life together. The mom's memories appear in a red font and the boy's in blue, making it an ideal book for pondering point of view.

 The Real Story (Ruzzier, 2023)

About the Book: When Cat discovers a broken cookie jar, he asks a book-reading mouse to explain what happened. Mouse is more than happy to oblige by telling a fantastical story about how the cookies came to life and escaped. Cat asks him to "tell me the real story." Mouse continues by spinning tales about slimy monsters, aliens, and a parade of cookie-loving bugs. In the end, Mouse tells Cat the true story, Cat thinks it's boring, and asks for another cookie story! Each character's dialogue appears in a different font. Read this book to identify point of view, as inspiration for kids to write their own cookie stories, or to perform in a reader's theater fashion.

Key Vocabulary and Kid-Friendly Definitions:

- irritable: feeling grumpy or easily bothered
- rage: feeling really, really angry
- rapidly: doing something quickly or in a short time

Upper Elementary Extension:

Share a few simple analogies with students. Divide students into pairs or small groups. Invite them to create an analogy or two to share with their classmates.

Notice Who's Sharing Facts

Book Title: *We Are Branches* (Sidman, 2023)

About the Book: Told from the point of view of the branches themselves, the creators take readers on a scavenger hunt to find occurrences of branching in the natural world. From tree branches to the arteries, veins, and nerves that branch out throughout our bodies, once you start looking, branching is everywhere! Beth Krommes's scratchboard and watercolor masterpieces enhance Joyce Sidman's lyrical look at this unique and intriguing topic.

To find a book like this one, look for the following:

- Informational texts told from interesting points of view
- Informational texts about kid-friendly topics

Comprehension Conversation

Before Reading

Notice the Cover Illustration

- Take a moment to appreciate Beth Krommes's cover illustration. She made these pictures using a special kind of paper called scratchboard. The scratchboard starts out all black, then she scratches white lines with a sharp tool. After doing this, she adds color with watercolor paint. Can you see all of the tiny lines she had to make just to create this one illustration?
- The title of this book is *We Are Branches*. Tell someone nearby any branches you notice on the front or back cover.

Set a Purpose: I'm excited to share this nonfiction book with you. I think you'll be surprised by what you learn about branches. As we're adding to our schema about branches, notice who is sharing the facts.

During Reading

- *Look how we sing deep in the soil to drink and grasp and steady* page: Which part of a tree drinks, grasps, and steadies? What do the roots look like? [branches]
- *Feel our soft strength stretching to sail the wind* page: I don't see tree branches or roots on this page. Where are the branches? [bee wings, butterfly wings, bird wings, flower petals] Who is teaching us about branches? [the branches] How can you tell? [The author uses words like *we* and *our.*]
- *finding paths* page: What kind of branches do you see on this page? [water branches] Let's read the labels to find out what they're called.

Learning Targets:

- I notice the author's choice of point of view.
- I think about how noticing point of view helps me better understand the information.
- I identify the main purpose of the text.

- *We splinter rock and mud* page: Have you ever seen splinters or cracks in rocks, the dirt, sidewalks, or the blacktop? Talk with a partner about where you've seen things splinter.

- *We are inside you, too* page: Wait a minute! What kind of branches are inside of us? [veins, arteries, nerves]

After Reading

- This book was told from the point of view of the branches. What did you think about this approach? Did it help you remember facts about branching?

- Let's revisit the cover. Do you notice any branches that you didn't see the first time we looked at it? How did this book make you see the world differently?

Extend the Experience

- In the backmatter, Joyce Sidman teaches us even more about branches. Let's learn all of the different things branches do. [If students have been listening for an extended period of time, you might choose to read the backmatter during another read-aloud experience.]

- [Give each student a piece of brown construction paper that resembles a branch. See the tree on the title page for inspiration.] Let's record our new learning on this branch. Use this sentence stem: The most surprising thing I learned about branches is _____. Then, we'll put all of our branches together to make a tree.

Similar Titles

 I Ship: A Container Ship's Colossal Journey (Schmitt, 2023)

About the Book: Float along with a massive container ship as it narrates the journey from port to port. Readers get a first-hand look at the goods that are transported via intermodal container shipping. They also experience the challenges of a blocked canal and a storm at sea. Extensive backmatter explains the reasons, benefits, and challenges of intermodal container shipping. It also includes a glossary and details about jobs in shipping and trading.

 KABOOM! A Volcano Erupts (Kulekjian, 2023)

About the Book: Told from the point of view of an expressive cartoony volcano, junior vulcanologists will laugh and learn as it transforms from dormant to explosive. The volcano's description of its inner workings is accompanied by additional scientific details and explanations that appear in the speech bubbles of a little red bird. Curious readers will enjoy learning more by reading the backmatter that includes a diagram and short paragraphs about the phases and types of volcanoes.

Key Vocabulary and Kid-Friendly Definitions:

- crackle: to make small, snapping noises

- splinter: when a small piece is broken off of a larger piece

- unfurling: to unroll or spread out

Upper Elementary Extension:

Incorporate this book into a science unit and encourage learners to write about a natural phenomenon from a first-person point of view.

Amanda Gorman · **Christian Robinson**
#1 New York Times Bestselling Author · Caldecott Honor-Winning Illustrator

Learning Targets:

- I use what I already know to help me infer.
- I connect details in the words and illustrations.
- I put what I learn together to make an inference.

Connect Text and Pictures

Book Title: *Something, Someday* (Gorman, 2023)

About the Book: In this poetic picture book, written by Amanda Gorman, a boy and his mother walk past a pile of trash in their neighborhood. Even though the boy has been told that it's not a problem and that he's too small to do anything about it, he decides to try and make a difference. With the help of fellow community members, the boy eventually replaces the garbage with a raised bed garden. Christian Robinson's signature illustrations bring Gorman's hopeful text to life.

To find a book like this one, look for the following:

- Illustration and text clues that support inferences
- Poetic narratives

Comprehension Conversation

Before Reading

Notice the Cover Illustration

What is the boy on this cover doing? What do you notice about this illustration? Christian Robinson digitally blends paint and collage together to make his unique artwork. To make a *collage*, artists arrange different materials like a puzzle to make a finished picture.

Set a Purpose: An important strategy readers use is making inferences. When we infer, we use clues from the book to figure out what is happening. As we're reading, we say to ourselves, "I hear this happening in the words and see this happening in the pictures, I can put these together to infer." Let's make some inferences as we read *Something, Someday*.

During Reading

- *You are told that this is not a problem* page: Let me show you how I make an inference. The words say "this is not a problem." The picture shows the boy looking at a pile of trash. When I put these two ideas together, I can infer that the boy thinks the trash is a problem even though someone told him it wasn't. Do you notice anything about the grown-up with him? [She looks like she's going to have a baby.]

- *You're told that what's going on is very, very sad* page: Now it's your turn; can you connect the words and pictures to infer what is making the boy angry? [People are still littering even after he cleaned up.]

- *You make a promise to each other* page: Can you infer how they are going to try to fix the problem? Talk with a friend about the clues you used to make your inference.

- *You make another friend* page: What do the words say? ["It's okay to be sad."] What does the picture show? [The plants are not growing.] Put these two ideas together to infer what happened in this part of the book.

- *Suddenly, there's something* page: What is making the boy feel "hopeful, happy, and loved"? Remember to use the pictures and words to infer.

After Reading

- Look at the front and back endpapers. What do they show? [The front endpapers show the trash pile, the back endpapers show the garden.]

- How did inferring help you to better understand what was happening in this book?

Extend the Experience

- Today you practiced inferring as we read *Something, Someday*. Now we're going to do a different kind of inferring. We're going to infer the lessons or big ideas that you learned from reading this book. Write or draw the big ideas on a sticky note or on the *Big Idea Printable*. (Located on the companion website, resources.corwin.com/more-rampedup-readalouds.)

- The two words in this title are compound words that start with the word *some*. Let's see if we can find others in the book.

Similar Titles

 Every Dreaming Creature (Wenzel, 2023) [Poetic narrative]

About the Book: One by one, creatures dance across the pages and into the dreams of a child. On the page before each animal appears, Wenzel gives clues in both his award-winning mixed-media illustrations and in the repetitive, poetic text. These hints support readers as they infer and predict which animal will wake the child from that dream and lead them to the next one.

 In the Dark (Hoefler, 2023)

About the Book: There is so much to notice, infer, ponder, and unravel in this first-of-its-kind picture book that shines a light on the darkness that stems from assumptions and misconceptions. The book is designed to be read in a vertical format and features two voices. The first voice is that of the townspeople who suspect the forest dwellers are witches. The townspeople's thoughts appear in a regular font while the words of the folks in the forest, who are really flying bird kites, appear in italics. The color palette of Corinna Luyken's illustrations also parallels the perspective and tone of each group. When kindness and truth overcome suspicion, the pages brighten to reflect the metaphorical light in the dark.

Key Vocabulary and Kid-Friendly Definitions:

- confused: having trouble understanding

- hopeful: believing that something you wanted to happen will happen

Upper Elementary Extension:

Amanda Gorman recited her spoken-word poem "A Hill We Climb" at the presidential inauguration of Joe Biden in 2021. Watch or read her poem and ask students to compare it with *Something, Someday*.

Big Idea Printable

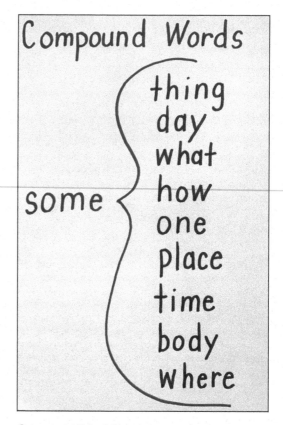

Compound Word Chart

My Favorite Read Alouds for Inferring

Book Title: *Every Dog in the Neighborhood* (Stead, 2022)

About the Book: In reply to Louis's request for a dog, Grandma says, "Nonsense! There are enough dogs in the neighborhood already." Surprisingly, she doesn't know exactly how many dogs, so Louis writes a letter to City Hall to find out. Meanwhile, Grandma composes her own letter to City Hall about an unkept, vacant lot. When neither get the response they want, they take matters into their own hands—Louis conducts a neighborhood dog survey and Grandma spruces up the lot for a dog park.

To find a book like this one, look for the following:

- Illustration and text clues that support inferences
- Characters enjoying intergenerational relationships

Comprehension Conversation

Before Reading

Notice the Cover Illustration

- Did you know that the illustrator of this book, Matthew Cordell, won the Caldecott Medal for his signature pen, ink, and watercolor illustrations in *Wolf in the Snow* (2017)? It's easy to spot a book he's illustrated.

- If you were sitting on the steps in this neighborhood, what might it sound like? Do you notice anything on the wraparound cover besides dogs?

Learning Targets:

- I connect details in the words and illustrations.
- I link key details across a text to infer.
- I talk, write, or draw about the themes or big ideas in a story.

Set a Purpose: Reading is kind of like being a detective. Sometimes we have to use clues from the pictures and words to understand more about what is happening in the story. When we do this, we are inferring. I'll show you what I mean as we read *Every Dog in the Neighborhood*.

During Reading

- *But Grandma doesn't answer my question* page: Can you use clues to infer why Grandma needs to write a letter to City Hall? [Perhaps it has something to do with the empty lot.]

- *Grandma takes off her reading glasses and tosses her letter in the trash* page: Can you infer how Grandma is feeling about the letter she got from City Hall? What do you think the letter said? Whisper your answer to a neighbor. What do you predict Grandma will do next?

- *"And what lesson is that?" asks Grandma* page: Connect the details you see on this page to what you learned earlier. Is it getting easier to infer what Grandma is doing?

- The last two-page spread at Grandma's Dog Park: Can you infer what Grandma is thinking as she looks at the city bus? [She's worried about the exhaust polluting the air.]

After Reading

- Louis learned there are 19 dogs in his neighborhood. Did he discover anything else?

- There are a lot of interesting visual details and dog names that we might have missed while we were reading this book for the first time. Let's go back and find a few; then I'll put this book in a special place so you can discover more on your own.

On page with these dogs . . .	Notice . . .
6. Aesop 7. Fable	Aesop's fables are stories with a moral that teach readers lessons.
8. Wilbur 9. Orville	They were the Wright Brothers and the first to fly a power-driven, heavier-than-air plane. Notice the owner and one of the dogs is wearing old-fashioned flying gear.
10. E. B.	E. B. White is the author of a story called *Charlotte's Web* (1952/1980) about a pig named Wilbur, and the dog owner looks like this author.

Extend the Experience

- Fold a blank piece of paper into thirds. Label each section with one adjective to describe Louis's grandmother's personality. Draw a picture or write about what she did or said that showed you that particular trait.

- Write Grandma's next letter to City Hall. Share the problem and persuade the people reading the letter of the reasons why they need to solve it.

Similar Titles

 This Story Is Not About a Kitten **(de Sève, 2022)**

About the Book: If this story is not about a kitten, then what is it about? It's about community, working together, and problem solving. When a girl and her mother find a scared, unhoused kitten under a car, the neighbors pitch in to rescue and find the kitten a home. Written in a cumulative fashion that echoes "The House That Jack Built," readers will be trying to infer what the book is about until it is revealed at the end.

 The Walk **(Bingham, 2023)**

About the Book: Join Granny and her granddaughter on THE WALK. Told from the granddaughter's point of view, we learn that this isn't an ordinary stroll. The duo prepares with water, sandwiches, and Granny's trusty cane. Along the way, they gather neighbors, creating a vibrant procession toward their unknown destination. Together, this group of "treasured souls" arrives at the school, where they all cast their votes "for hope." This book invites inferring because you don't know where the group is going until they reach their destination. Pair *The Walk* with *Last Stop on Market Street* (de la Peña, 2015) and *Milo Imagines the World* (de la Peña, 2021).

Key Vocabulary and Kid-Friendly Definitions:

- concerned: to care a lot about something

- stern: serious, strict, or determined

- thorough: finishing something completely and pay attention to details

Upper Elementary Extension:

Ask students to brainstorm a list of possible survey questions for their classmates, family/caregivers, or trusted neighbors. Then, give them time to conduct their survey and share the results.

I will use my art to tell the stories of hardworking, passionate people who make the world more beautiful. I will tell their stories. I will tell my story."

—Growing an Artist: The Story of a Landscaper and His Son
by John Parra

Build Content Knowledge

Blend Literacy With STEAM

Link Literature and Learning

In this chapter, readers will meet passionate individuals and characters who are making a positive impact through study, innovation, and creation. The read-aloud experiences merge English-Language Arts (ELA) standards and the foundational principles of science, technology, engineering, arts, and mathematics, or STEAM education. Carefully designed book experiences seamlessly weave science, engineering, and math practices into the comprehension conversations. So you're not only saving instructional time but, more importantly, building content knowledge that is essential for comprehension. Learners unravel the mysteries of the scientific practices, develop an appreciation for the technological world, witness engineering solutions, meet artistic characters, and discover the storytelling potential of numbers as they:

- Think like a scientist
- Notice how technology helps
- Solve problems through engineering
- Create art
- Be a mathematician

The books in this chapter build content and background knowledge, fostering readers who are not only literate, but also critically engaged citizens of the world.

Scan here to find a complete learning target chart with book-related online links, a bonus read-aloud experience, and printable resources.

https://qrs.ly/9dfn8pi

Big Idea: Featured Title	Learning Targets
Investigate: *Night Owl Night* (Richmond, 2023)	• I use details in the text and illustrations to better understand the main idea. • I notice how scientists investigate and use tools. • I talk, write, or draw about my new learning.
Solve Problems: *Destiny Finds Her Way: How a Rescued Baby Sloth Learned to Be Wild* (Engle, 2023a)	• I use details in the text and illustrations to better understand a topic. • I notice the ways scientists solve problems. • I talk, write, or draw about my new learning.
Understand the Power of Personal Devices: *A Day With No Words* (T. Hammond, 2023)	• I use details in the text and illustrations to better understand a character. • I notice how technology helps people. • I talk, write, or draw about how technology helps people.
Learn About Machines and Systems: *Special Delivery: A Book's Journey Around the World* (Faber, 2022)	• I use details in the text and illustrations to better understand how things are connected. • I notice how machines and systems make our lives better. • I talk, write, or draw about how machines help people.
Protect Our Environment: *Flipflopi: How a Boat Made from Flip-Flops Is Helping to Save the Ocean* (Lodding & Pabari, 2023)	• I use details in the text and illustrations to better understand the topic. • I notice how engineering helps solve problems.
Make Improvements: *Railroad Engineer Olive Dennis* (Baillie, 2022)	• I use details in the text and illustrations to better understand the person. • I notice how engineers investigate and make improvements.
Sketch What You Experience: *Growing an Artist: The Story of a Landscaper and His Son* (Parra, 2022)	• I notice who is telling the story. • I ponder the author's purpose for writing this text. • I create art to tell my stories.
Make Art Full of Heart: *The Artist* (Vere, 2023)	• I ponder the author's purpose for writing this text. • I infer themes or big ideas. • I use what I learned when I create art.
Tell a Story in Numbers: *One Boy Watching* (Snider, 2022)	• I use details from the text and pictures to better understand how the author uses numbers. • I notice and wonder about the numbers found in the text. • I talk, write, or draw about details using numbers.
Depict Details Using an Infographic: *Friends Beyond Measure: A Story Told With Infographics* (L. Fisher, 2023)	• I use details from the text and illustrations to better understand information and/or characters. • I notice and wonder about the infographics found in the text. • I create infographics to clearly explain details.
Bonus Lesson (online) Investigate: *The Ocean Gardener* (Anganuzzi, 2023)	• I use details in the text and illustrations to better understand the main idea. • I notice how scientists investigate and use tools. • I talk, write, or draw about my new learning.

My Favorite Read Alouds for Building Content Knowledge

Investigate

Book Title: *Night Owl Night* (Richmond, 2023)

About the Book: We learn from Sova that her mama is a scientist who studies birds. Each October, Mama heads to a Massachusetts wildlife sanctuary at night to investigate owl migration. When Sova is finally old enough, she joins Mama to learn more about the waiting, work, and rewards of tracking migrating owls. Backmatter includes QR codes that lead readers to the owl calls mentioned in the text along with a note from the author about Saw-Whet owl banding.

To find a book like this one, look for the following:

- Highlights the investigative practices of scientists
- Features scientists who study living creatures

Comprehension Conversation

Before Reading

Notice the Cover Illustration

The title of this book is *Night Owl Night*. Do you know what it means to be a *night owl*? A night owl is someone who likes to stay up late at night. Ask your friend if they know any people who are night owls. Look at the details in the cover illustration. Do you think this title might have another meaning?

Set a Purpose: Let's join the girl and her grown-up on a *Night Owl Night* to see if we can figure out the main idea of this book.

During Reading

[Because this book is lengthy, I've divided the during-reading conversation into two sections. You can decide if that makes sense for your students.]

Part 1:

- *The second time, I pleaded from the kitchen* page: Tell your partner something you've learned about Sova and Mama so far. [Mama is a scientist who studies owls and other birds, Sova really wants to go with her to study owls.] Are there any details in the illustrations that tell you more about these two characters?

- *Tonight, I'm finally old enough* page: Did you notice any changes each time Sova asks to join her mother? [Mama tells her she sounds like a different kind of owl. She is growing older.] Why do you think the author wrote they *swoop* out the door together? On this page, they are driving to a *sanctuary*. A wildlife sanctuary is a safe place for animals to live.

- *When we arrive at the woods* page: Have you ever seen any of the tools Sova's Mama is going to use to help them investigate owls? [headlamps, mist net, audio lure] A *lure* is used to attract an animal to come closer. Fishers use lures to attract fish.

Learning Targets:

- I use details in the text and illustrations to better understand the main idea.

- I notice how scientists investigate and use tools.

- I talk, write, or draw about my new learning.

- *We walk to the wildlife sanctuary's cabin* page: Here we learn about more of the scientific tools Mama and Sova are planning to use. Can you figure out which tool is for weighing, which is for measuring, and which they will use to mark the owl for its journey?

- *Back in the cabin, we set the timer for thirty more minutes* page: We're going to pause here and leave you in suspense. Do you predict they will find an owl in the mist net? Why or why not? What have you learned so far about being a scientist?

Part 2:

Before we continue reading, let's retell what happened so far. Who wants to start us out? [Invite students to take turns retelling key details until they reach this point in the book.]

- *Mama sets a time for one last check* page: It's been a long night! Tell someone nearby whether you would have enough patience to wait this long to see an owl.

- *Then we hear a swish through darkness* page: Think about what you've already learned about their investigation. Predict what they might do with this owl.

- *Mama carefully closes a small metal bracelet around the owl's leg* page: Sova says that she wants to learn more about owls. Do you have any unanswered questions? Scientists, like Sova's Mama, investigate to try to find answers to questions.

After Reading

- Would you say you learned more about owls or about scientists who study owls? Which was the main idea? Use evidence from the text to support your thinking. Why do you think the author wrote this book?

- Share something you learned about being a scientist who studies owls.

Extend the Experience

- Sova's Mama is an ornithologist, or a scientist who studies birds. What are some of the tools she used to investigate owls? Draw and label the tools you remember on a blank sheet of paper or in the *Scientist's Backpack Printable*. (Located on the companion website, resources.corwin.com/more-rampedup-readalouds.)

- If you were a scientist, what would you study? Research to find out what that type of scientist is called and use these sentence stems to teach us about what you learned: If I were a scientist, I would study _____. I would be called a _____.

Similar Titles

The Girl Who Built an Ocean: An Artist, an Argonaut, and the True Story of the World's First Aquarium (Keating, 2022)

About the Book: From an early age, Jeanne enjoyed creating things with her hands. She fashioned "wearable works of art" first in Paris and later in Sicily. It was in Sicily that she fell in love with the sea and its creatures while observing, collecting, and sketching them. But there was a problem—the animals ran away too quickly. So Jeanne designed a solution: a small

---

Key Vocabulary and Kid-Friendly Definitions:

- disappointment: feeling sad when something didn't happen the way you wanted

- journey: a long trip

- pleaded: asked for something you really wanted

Upper Elementary Extension:

Provide students with a device so that they can use QR codes in the backmatter to listen to the owl calls.

aquarium to house and study them. Her story highlights the science and engineering practices of curiosity, investigation, and innovation.

 The Ocean Gardener (Anganuzzi, 2023)

Ayla loves her island home and its precious coral reef. When she and her marine biologist mother discover the coral is fading due to rising temperatures, they work together to rescue and regrow the coral, creating their own ocean garden. As they plan and carry out their investigation, they carefully gather data. In the backmatter, readers meet the inspiration for the story: Chloé Pozas, a marine biologist who has set up coral nurseries on islands in the Seychelles, the setting for the story. (See bonus read-aloud experience on the companion website, resources.corwin.com/more-rampedup-readalouds.)

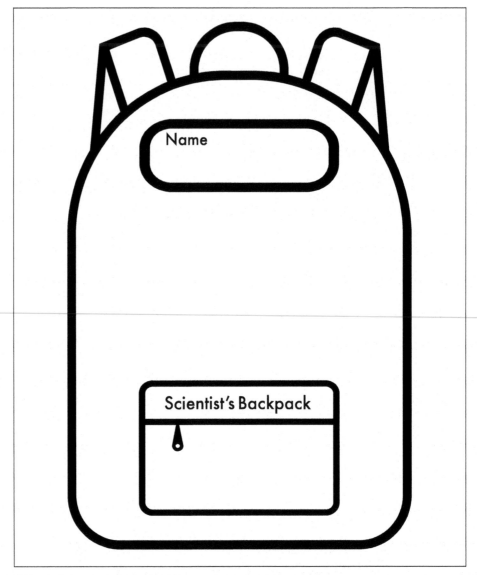

Scientist's Backpack Printable

My Favorite Read Alouds for Thinking Like a Scientist

_____

_____

_____

_____

_____

_____

_____

_____

_____

_____

_____

_____

_____

_____

_____

_____

_____

_____

_____

_____

_____

_____

_____

_____

_____

_____

_____

_____

Learning Targets:

- I use details in the text and illustrations to better understand a topic.

- I notice the ways scientists solve problems.

- I talk, write, or draw about my new learning.

Solve Problems

Book Title: *Destiny Finds Her Way: How a Rescued Baby Sloth Learned to Be Wild* (Engle, 2023a)

About the Book: Who can resist the adorable face of a three-fingered sloth? Fortunately, the scientists at The Sloth Institute (TSI) in Costa Rica can't. They are committed to rescuing and releasing these slow-moving creatures back into the wild. In this narrative nonfiction book, Margarita Engle introduces readers to Destiny, one of the nearly 400 sloths that TSI has helped. Backmatter expands on the text with author and photographer notes, a map, and a list of sloth facts.

To find a book like this one, look for the following:

- Highlights the inquiry-based practices of scientists
- Features scientists who study animals

Comprehension Conversation

Before Reading

Notice the Cover Illustration

- Share something you notice about the cover illustration. [It's a photograph of a sloth.] Notice that instead of the word *illustrator* on the cover, it reads "Photographs by Sam Trull."

- The title of this book is *Destiny Finds Her Way* and the subtitle is *How a Rescued Baby Sloth Learned to Be Wild*. How does reading the subtitle help when you're previewing a book? [It gives more details about the topic of the book.]

Set a Purpose: Author and poet Margarita Engle uses some interesting writing techniques as she teaches us about Destiny. Let's see what you can learn from her as a writer and also what you discover about this baby sloth named Destiny.

During Reading

- Page 5: Which sense are you using to imagine this tropical rainforest? [The sense of hearing.] Notice the technique the author uses to help you imagine the rainforest sounds. [She adds sound words called onomatopoeia.] I bet you could add onomatopoeia when you're writing an informational piece!

- Page 7: What does the scientist want to do? [Rescue the sloth, help it get better, and let it go.] How might they go about doing that?

- Page 11: Can you infer why the scientist gave Destiny the same foods her mother would have? [To get her used to eating what she will eat in the wild.]

- Page 18: Tell a neighbor which words the author uses to help you imagine the smells Destiny is experiencing. [fragrant, stink, stench] Would you rather smell something *fragrant* (like cookies baking) or something that has a *stench* (like a skunk)?

- Page 23: Wow! It took a whole year to get Destiny ready to be released. That's longer than you will be in *this* grade. Think of adjectives to describe the scientists in this book. Start this way: The scientists were _____ because . . .

After Reading

- Did you learn any new information about sloths?
- Would you like to be a scientist who works to rescue and release animals? Why or why not?

Extend the Experience

- To share your new learning about sloths, you're going to write a sloth acrostic poem. First, we'll work together to look through the book to find facts we learned that begin with the letters in the word *sloth*. Then, you can use these facts or others you've learned about sloths to write your own acrostic poem.

- The scientists in this book needed to solve a problem. What was the problem? Brainstorm a list of questions that these scientists might have asked as they were trying to rescue and return Destiny to the wild.

Similar Titles

 ***One Turtle's Last Straw: The Real-Life Rescue That Sparked a Sea Change** (Boxer, 2022)*

About the Book: Based on a true story that was captured on video, this book recounts the discovery by marine biologists of an olive ridley sea turtle in the waters of Costa Rica. When they brought him on board their boat, they found something stuck in his nostril. As they tried to pull it out, they realized it was a plastic straw. Fortunately, they were able to get the whole straw out and save the turtle. Extensive backmatter enhances the impactful story with an afterword, author's note, information about young activists, and resources for further exploration.

 ***Yoshi, Sea Turtle Genius: A True Story About an Amazing Swimmer** (Cox, 2023)*

About the Book: A five-year-old loggerhead turtle gets trapped in a net and is saved by a fisherman. He cares for her and names her Yoshi, meaning good luck in Japanese. Before heading back to Japan, he brings Yoshi to an aquarium in Cape Town, South Africa, where she lives for over 20 years. Then, scientists figure out a way to release her back into the sea. Fitted with a tracking device, the world watches as Yoshi swims 22,998 miles and, after 25 years, returns to the beach where she was born.

Key Vocabulary and Kid-Friendly Definitions:

- hesitate: to stop or pause when you're not feeling sure
- injured: hurt
- recover: to get better or healthier again

Upper Elementary Extension:

Show students how to use the data found on the map on page 30 to create a bar graph that represents the three-fingered sloths living in North American countries versus South American countries.

S	L	O	T	H
• Slow • Scientists save them	• Love leaves • Live alone • Long arms	• Orphans • Only three fingers	• Tropical rainforest • Treetops	• Home is disappearing • High climbers • Hide from predators

Sloth Facts Chart

Slow Sloths

Slow movers

Live alone

Only three fingers

Treetop homes

High climbers

Sloth Acrostic Poem Demonstration Text

My Favorite Read Alouds for Thinking Like a Scientist

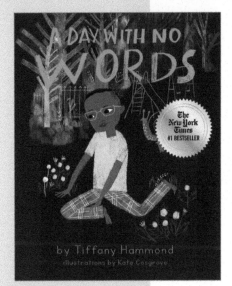

Understand the Power of Personal Devices

Book Title: *A Day With No Words* (T. Hammond, 2023)

About the Book: The book is told from the point of view of an autistic boy who uses a tablet to communicate. Aidan and his mother spend the day together engaging with each other and their community through their respective devices. This story is based on the lived experience of the author, Tiffany Hammond, who is an autistic writer, advocate, and mother of two autistic boys.

To find a book like this one, look for the following:

- Characters using technology tools to help themselves or others
- Books that feature neurodiverse characters

Comprehension Conversation

Before Reading

Learning Targets:

- I use details in the text and illustrations to better understand a character.
- I notice how technology helps people.
- I talk, write, or draw about how technology helps people.

Notice the Cover Illustration

- Share what you notice in the cover illustration. Kate Cosgrove created the illustrations using a pencil and a digital illustration app. What are your favorite drawing tools?

- If we read the back cover blurb, we learn that the boy on the cover is named Aidan. What did you imagine this story might be about when you read the title *A Day Without Words*? Turn and trade ideas with a neighbor.

Set a Purpose: People use words to communicate their thoughts and feelings. What are some of the ways you share your ideas? Today, as we read the author's written story and study the illustrator's pictures, we'll learn more about Aidan and his day without words.

During Reading

- *My eyes squeeze shut, I'm not ready to get up* page: Aidan uses his tablet to tell his mama that he's ready to get up. Brainstorm other ways people communicate without using spoken words. Share your ideas with a friend.

- *Some people have big voices that feel like storms in my head* page: Do you know people with big voices and other people who speak quietly? Which kind of voice do you prefer?

- *I was born like this* page: Who is telling you the story? [Aidan] What have you learned about Aidan so far? [He doesn't speak, he likes his mama and daddy's voices, he uses a tablet to talk.]

- *Mama taps, "park . . . now . . . no . . . crowd?"* page: We know Mama can speak; why do you suppose she's using a tablet too? Think back to the title of the book, *A Day With No Words*.

- *"My son does not speak, but his ears work just fine"* page: Infer how people might feel after reading Mama's words. What should they do differently next time?

After Reading

- Which specific details in the words and illustrations helped you get to know Aidan as a character?

- How did technology help Aidan? Think of other ways you use technology to help you in your daily life.

Extend the Experience:

- Create a collage of images to represent Aidan; do not add any words. When we're done, we'll do a gallery walk to tell each other about the reasons we chose the different images.

- People invent technological tools and machines, like Aidan's tablet, to solve problems or make their lives better. Imagine a device that could help you do something. Show us how it works using the *Design a Device Printable*. (Located on the companion website, resources.corwin.com/more-rampedup-readalouds.)

Similar Titles

 Bitsy Bat, School Star (Windness, 2023) [Neurodivergent character]

About the Book: It's Bitsy Bat's first night at her new school. Although she's been practicing with her family, she still does things differently than her classmates. After she gets overwhelmed and has a meltdown, her family encourages her to try again the next night. Bitsy heads back to school with her sunglasses, headphones, and a "Big Star idea!" Written by an autistic creator who shares more about herself and about autism in the backmatter.

 More Than Words: So Many Ways to Say What We Mean (MacLean, 2023)

About the Book: The book begins with Nathan, who prefers listening to talking and is happy pondering the world outside his window. Many of Nathan's classmates express themselves using spoken words. Alternatively, we meet a variety of children sharing ideas their own unique ways, a few using "Augmentative and Alternative Communication" (learn more about ACC in the backmatter). In the end, Nathan communicates through his love of nature and his classmates learn to listen in a new way. A bit more about communication and ideas for improving communication access appear in the backmatter.

Key Vocabulary and Kid-Friendly Definitions:

- anxiety: feeling scared or worried about something

- chattering: talking a lot and really fast

- sneer: an unfriendly face that means a person is unhappy or making fun of something

Upper Elementary Extension:

In the author's note, Tiffany Hammond invites readers to have a day with no spoken words. Offer students the opportunity to do this for a set amount of time. Discuss their observations and insights.

Name

My device is called _____

_____.

It helps people _____

_____.

Design a Device Printable

My Favorite Read Alouds for Noticing How Technology Helps

Learn About Machines and Systems

Book Title: *Special Delivery: A Book's Journey Around the World* (Faber, 2022)

About the Book: Jay's birthday is just around the corner. On the other side of the world, factory workers are gearing up for a busy day manufacturing the book *Special Delivery.* Follow the book's step-by-step journey through an interconnected system of workers and their machines until it arrives at a local bookstore. There it is spotted by Jay's grandmother who, in turn, mails it to Jay as a birthday gift.

To find a book like this one, look for the following:

- A book that features machines and/or systems that enhance our daily lives
- A plot that highlights essential workers

Comprehension Conversation

Before Reading

Notice the Cover Illustration

- The title *Special Delivery* is painted on the side of this truck. That truck and all of the other details that you see on this cover were created using digital tools. Tell someone nearby what else you notice on the cover. Most of the things on this cover fit into a category. How would you label that category? [things that move, transportation]

- The subtitle of this book is *A Book's Journey Around the World.* Can you spot the book on the cover? [It's in the boy's hand.]

Set a Purpose: Software that helps artists create pictures is one example of *technology*. Technology is when people use their knowledge and creativity to design, build, and use tools, machines, and systems to make their lives better, solve problems, and have fun. As we follow this book's journey, we'll see if we can spot any machines or systems that help the book on its way.

During Reading

- *It's forty more sleeps until Jay's birthday* page: What can you learn about Jay by looking at the details in his room? Do you see any machines that he uses to help him or to have fun?

- *Something's being printed, cut, pressed* page: Which book are they manufacturing or making in this factory? [The book we're reading!] Wow! I see a lot of machines working together to create the book. People designed and helped build all of these machines.

Learning Targets:

- I use details in the text and illustrations to better understand how things are connected.

- I notice how machines and systems make our lives better.

- I talk, write, or draw about how machines help people.

[Continue to notice the people, machines, and systems that move the book along its journey.]

- *Hannah scans everything to see where it goes next* page: Have you even seen a scanner like the one Hannah is using? A scanner usually scans a *barcode,* like the one on the back cover of this book. A barcode is like a high-tech language that machines speak to communicate information quickly and accurately. How do you think the barcode helps the book get where it's going?

- *Molly pushes her mail cart down Jay's street* page: What do you notice about this page? [It shows the entire journey so far.] Where do you predict the book will end up?

After Reading

- Talk with a partner about some of the machines or systems that helped get the book from the factory to Jay's home.

- Do you think the book would have been delivered as quickly without the role of technology?

Extend the Experience

- Ponder some of the ways machines help you. Draw a picture of a machine that helps you do something or just have fun. Write a sentence that explains how the machine helps you.

- We met a lot of workers in this book. Let's go back to the page that begins with: *Molly pushes her mail cart down Jay's street.* If you were going to try out one of these jobs, which one would you choose? Explain your reasons.

Similar Titles

 Not Just the Driver! (Ackerman, 2024)

About the Book: Readers take a peek behind-the-scenes to learn about the workforce that keeps transportation systems moving smoothly. From harbormasters coordinating busy harbors to dispatchers ensuring safe routes, the book emphasizes the teamwork found in the transportation industry. With vivid illustrations and lively rhymes, it expands readers' awareness and appreciation of the machines and essential roles workers play in shuttling people and goods.

 Thank a Farmer (Gianferrari, 2023)

About the Book: "If you like the food on your table, THANK A FARMER." So begins this book of gratitude to the people, machines, and animals that bring milk, bread, mushrooms, berries, and more to our tables. Learn more about farming methods in the backmatter. Read aloud to build content knowledge about food, farms, machines, and systems.

Key Vocabulary and Kid-Friendly Definitions:

- arriving: reaching a place

- enormous: very big, huge

- hoisted: lifted something high in the air

Upper Elementary Extension:

Invite interested students to do a micro-inquiry into the origin and inner workings of the barcode. Who invented the barcode? How does it work?

Protect Our Environment

Book Title: *Flipflopi: How a Boat Made from Flip-Flops Is Helping to Save the Ocean* (Lodding & Pabari, 2023)

About the Book: Juma and his grandfather, Babu Ali, are walking to the coast of Lamu, Kenya, to fish when they find the beach covered in flip-flops and other plastic *takataka* (trash). Juma comes from a family of master boat builders, so he and Babu Ali make a plan to design and build a boat made of recycled materials. The islanders pitch in and collect enough washed-up plastic to build their boat—10 metric tons. As explained in the backmatter, this book is based on the true story of a dhow boat made entirely of plastic waste, including a colorful skin engineered from 30,000 recycled flip-flops.

To find a book like this one, look for the following:

- Features people who design solutions
- Highlights creative ways to protect our environment

Comprehension Conversation

Before Reading

Notice the Cover Illustration

We can learn a lot by using the cover to preview this book. The title is *Flipflopi* and the subtitle is *How a Boat Made from Flip-Flops Is Helping to Save the Ocean*. With that information in mind, look at the wraparound illustration. What do you see happening?

Set a Purpose: What do you already know about plastic pollution? In this book, we're going to learn about one creative solution to the plastic trash problem. Let's notice what steps they take to solve the problem.

During Reading

- *Today Juma was going fishing with Babu Ali* page: We can look in the glossary in the back of the book to learn that *Babu* means grandfather. Let me show you on this map where Lamu, Kenya, is located. [Locate Lamu, Kenya, on a digital map and show students where it is in relation to their school or home and/or how long it would take to travel there.]

- *The sea was the life of their Kenyan coastal community* page: Put together facts you already know about oceans with the text we read on this page to infer what the author means by "the sea was the life." What's the problem in their community?

- *"Yes!" yelled Juma* page: How are they planning to solve the problem? [build a boat] What are they drawing in the sand? [a sketch of their design] Why is drawing a design helpful?

Learning Targets:

- I use details in the text and illustrations to better understand the topic.
- I notice how engineering helps solve problems.

- *By the time they were done with their sketch, a small crowd had gathered* page: Infer what the word *takataka* means. Let's check the glossary to see if we're right.

- *When the cheers faded, Juma turned to Babu and said, "We did it. We're done!"* page: Why do you suppose Babu said they've just started?

After Reading

- Juma, his grandfather, and their community took steps to solve the problem. Let's talk about the steps they took.

- What might they do next?

Extend the Experience

- To learn more about the real Flipflopi we can read the backmatter and/or watch the videoclip. [If learners are curious to see what 10 tonnes of plastic trash look like, check out the videoclip of a boat extracting that amount of plastic from the Great Pacific Garbage Patch on the companion website, resources.corwin.com/more-rampedup-readalouds.]

Learn more about Flipflopi Project

https://qrs.ly/s4fn8pm

- Make a poster or slide to teach people one creative way to reduce plastic.

Similar Titles

 ***Great Carrier Reef* (Stremer, 2023)**

About the Book: A retired aircraft carrier named USS *Oriskany* or the "Mighty O" is chosen by scientists and engineers to become the world's largest artificial reef. Follow along as the Mighty O is meticulously transformed and precisely sunk off the coast of Pensacola, Florida, where it is quickly inhabited by sea life. The backmatter expands the narrative informational text by adding details about reefs, the Mighty O's transformation, and its past history.

 ***If the Rivers Run Free* (Debbink, 2023)**

About the Book: Written in rhyming text, this book narrates the story of "daylighting," or restoring buried rivers. Although it doesn't specifically highlight the role of engineers, it does show how, beginning in the late 19th century, "thinkers and tinkers" tried to solve the problem of polluted rivers by burying them, causing a new set of issues. Then, in the 1980s, "thinkers and tinkers" decided to restore some rivers' natural courses. Read more details about the history and future of rivers in the backmatter.

Key Vocabulary and Kid-Friendly Definitions:

- hauled: carried from one place to another

- surveyed: took a close look at an area or object

- threatened: something that may not last into the future [in this context]

Upper Elementary Extension:

Collect clean plastic objects and challenge students to plan, design, and create a protype for another type of vehicle using recycled plastics.

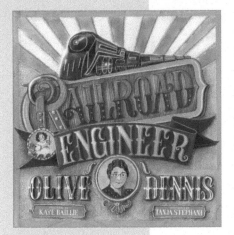

Make Improvements

Book Title: *Railroad Engineer Olive Dennis* (Baillie, 2022)

About the Book: Climb aboard and embark on a journey to learn about Olive Dennis, a trailblazing railroad engineer whose love for building things propels her into the world of engineering. Undeterred by the gender bias that denies her job opportunities, she secures a historic position as the first female engineer at the Baltimore & Ohio Railroad. During her tenure in this position, Olive revolutionizes the travel experience for women, especially. Backmatter offers additional insights into Olive's life with a detailed timeline and bibliography.

To find a book like this one, look for the following:

- Biographies about engineers
- Events that highlight engineering practices

Learning Targets:

- I use details in the text and illustrations to better understand the person.

- I notice how engineers investigate and make improvements.

Comprehension Conversation

Before Reading

Notice the Cover Illustration

When you hear the title *Railroad Engineer Olive Dennis,* what comes to mind? Based on the cover illustration, do you think this biography is about a modern-day person or someone who lived long ago? Share your reasons.

Set a Purpose: Did you know that there are two kinds of railroad engineers? One is the person who drives the train and the other is the person who comes up with the ideas about how the train should look and work. Let's read to discover which of these jobs Olive Dennis performed.

During Reading

- *SHIFTING* page: Which kind of engineer would be able to answer Olive's questions? Based on what we've read so far, do you think Olive wants to drive trains or design them?

- *When her brother started studying civil engineering* page: A *civil engineer* designs buildings, roads, bridges, and systems to safely house and move people and resources, like water, around our cities and towns. The phrase *back then* gives us a clue that the events of this biography happened a long time ago. Do you think Olive can be an engineer? Why or why not?

- *She studied fluid dynamics* page: The author gives us clues in the text and pictures to help us figure out what Olive studied. Use the clues and tell a neighbor about what Olive was learning.

- *BREATHING* page: Wow! Olive suggested so many improvements. Tell a friend one way Olive made trains more comfortable for passengers.

- *One day, the president of the B & O railroad called an urgent meeting* page: How do you think it made Olive feel when they asked her to design the luxury daytime train?

After Reading

- As a railroad engineer, what were some of Olive's accomplishments?

- What did you learn about engineering that you didn't know before?

Extend the Experience

- Make a list of words that best describe Olive Dennis.

- Throughout the story, the author included verbs to help us understand what Olive was seeing or doing. Some of those verbs describe processes or actions engineers use in their jobs. Let's reread and record those verbs.

Similar Titles

The Brilliant Calculator: How Mathematician Edith Clarke Helped Electrify America (Lower, 2023)

About the Book: "Math + Girls = Electrical Engineers." Meet Edith Clarke, the United States' first female electrical engineer. Learn how Edith's love for math and ambition to be an engineer propel her to defy her family and spend her inheritance on college. After a serious illness, she recommits to pursuing a career in engineering, invents the Clarke Calculator, and is hired by General Electric. Quotes from Edith are sprinkled throughout the biography. Extensive backmatter is included.

Jerry Changed the Game: How Engineer Jerry Lawson Revolutionized Video Games Forever (Tate, 2023)

About the Book: This biography follows Jerry Lawson's journey from his childhood fascination with simple machines in 1940s Queens, New York, to becoming a pioneering engineer in the realm of arcade games and home entertainment. Despite facing challenges as one of the few Black engineers in his field, Jerry's passion for technology drove him to innovate. His breakthrough creation, the removable cartridge for video games, revolutionized home gaming systems. This engaging narrative highlights the importance of curiosity and perseverance.

Key Vocabulary and Kid-Friendly Definitions:

- ambitious: putting hard work toward a challenging task

- improvements: changing things to make something better

- urgent: when something needs to be done quickly or right away

Upper Elementary Extension:

Task students with redesigning and making improvements to a school bus.

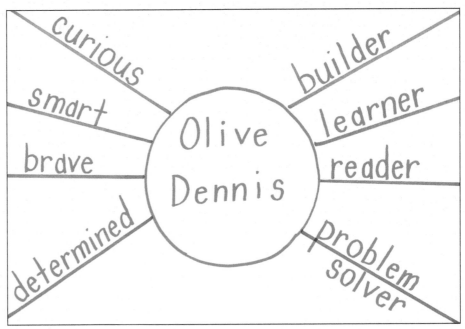

Olive Dennis Chart

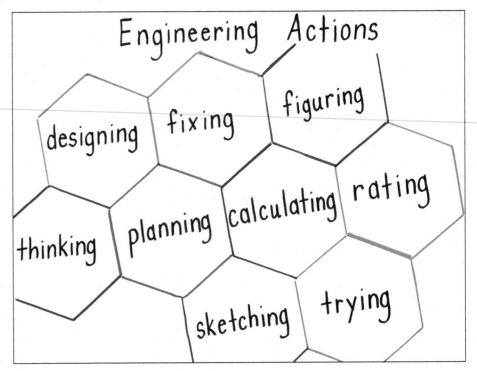

Engineering Actions Chart

My Favorite Read Alouds for Solving Problems Through Engineering

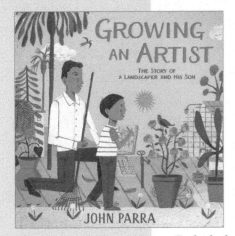

Sketch What You Experience

Book Title: *Growing an Artist: The Story of a Landscaper and His Son* (Parra, 2022)

About the Book: "The story of the little landscaper is the story of my childhood," says John Parra in the author's note. With sketchbook and tools in hand, a young boy is ready for his first day helping his father with his landscaping business. While tending to lawns and gardens, the elder Parra encourages the boy's creativity and even lets him help with a landscape design. In his debut picture book as both author and illustrator, Parra uses a first-person voice to give readers a glimpse into the life of a landscape contractor.

To find a book like this one, look for the following:

- A book written by a creator about their journey into art
- Inspiring books for budding artists

Comprehension Conversation

Before Reading

Notice the Cover Illustration

- The creator of this book, John Parra, is an award-winning illustrator. He used acrylic paints on illustration board (a thick, sturdy paper that doesn't bend or wrinkle) to create these pictures. Tell someone nearby some of the details you notice on the cover.

- This book is called *Growing an Artist*. The subtitle is *The Story of a Landscaper and His Son*. A *landscaper* uses their creativity and skills to design, plant, and take care of outdoor spaces like yards and gardens. They are outdoor artists.

Learning Targets:

- I notice who is telling the story.
- I ponder the author's purpose for writing this text.
- I create art to tell my stories.

Set a Purpose: Now that you know what a landscaper does, pause and think about the meaning of the title. As we read about the landscaper and his son, we'll be thinking about who is telling the story and the reasons why John Parra wrote this book.

During Reading

- *"Are you ready, mijo?" Papi asks* page: Are there any clues on this page that help you figure out who is telling the story? [The use of the word *I*.] Why do you suppose John Parra decided to tell this story from the boy's point of view?

- *At Mrs. Tarbe's house* page: What do you think the boy means when he says "my heart sinks"? [He's sad and disappointed because Alex pretended not to see him.]

- *The next stop is the nursery* page: Notice what the boy is doing as they are working. [sketching] Think back to the title of the book, *Growing an Artist*. How do artists grow? Tell a friend what you do to get better at something.

- *With our purchases, we head to Mr. Sardisco's house* page: Can you infer how the boy feels when Mr. Sardisco says his dad knows more about plants than anyone?

- *A few weeks later Papi, Javier, and I work to plant the last shrubs* page: Remember how the boy helped with the design? If we flip to the endpapers, you can see what a landscape design drawing would look like for this yard.

After Reading

- Who do you think this story is about? If we turn to the author's note, we can read to find out. [If you are running short on time or students' attention spans are waning, read the first line and then the third and fourth paragraphs of the author's note.]

- How would this story be different if it were told from Papi's point of view?

Extend the Experience

- Let's flip back to the end of the story and reread the page that begins with "I grab my sketchbook and turn the pages." John Parra shares his goals as an artist. Do you think this book met those goals?

- Imagine something you want to do when you get older. Create a piece of art with the title "Growing a _____" to show you doing that job or activity. Add details to give us clues as to what you are doing.

Similar Titles

 The Artivist (N. Smith, 2023)

About the Book: As the author's note explains, this book is the story of Nikkolas Smith's journey as an Artivist. Told from the point of view of a young Nikkolas, readers follow along as he makes the decision to paint the problems he sees to inspire people to work on the solutions together. Readers can infer from Nikkolas Smith's vibrant digital paintings the contemporary issues that, together, we need to address through action, allyship, healing, and hope. The book concludes with a call to action to fellow Artivists to find their own way to create positive change.

 El cuarto turquesa/The Turquoise Room (Brown, 2022)

About the Book: This bilingual picture book is an intergenerational story of dreams, imagination, and creativity. It begins with Monica Brown's grandmother Esther who, as a young girl growing up in Peru, paints a special map of South America that she eventually hangs up in her daughter Isabel's turquoise room. When Isabel grows up, she moves to the United States and fills her daughter Monica's home with paintings the color of the sea and books. With imaginations "as big as the sky," the women in Monica Brown's family pass down inspiration, stories, and memories. The author's note includes a photograph of Esther's map.

Key Vocabulary and Kid-Friendly Definitions:

- awkward: unsure of how to act or what to say

- debris: little pieces or parts that are left behind

- potential: a special ability that you can work on and use in the future

Upper Elementary Extension:

Invite students to research different careers in the arts and create a piece of art to share their discoveries.

Make Art Full of Heart

Book Title: *The Artist* (Vere, 2023)

About the Book: Author Ed Vere's creative answer to the question, "What is an artist?" Readers journey with a rainbow-colored dinosaur as she travels to the bustling city, shares her art with the world, and imparts a few lessons for budding artists.

To find a book like this one, look for the following:

- A book that celebrates the artistic process
- Art-related themes or big ideas

Comprehension Conversation

Before Reading

Notice the Cover Illustration

Let's open the book and look at the wraparound cover for details that show you this creature is an artist. What do you see? [paint brushes, paint splatter near the buildings that is the same color as the building, people taking photos on their phones]

Set a Purpose: As you find out more about this artist, see if you learn any lessons to use when making your own art. Afterward, we'll talk about why you think Ed Vere might have written this book.

During Reading

- Title page: Can you figure out who the "me" is on this page? [the author, Ed Vere] Why do you think that?

- *Here is an artist* page: Name some of the things artists do. [See wonder, joy, and beauty and make it into art.]

- *The Artist's head is full* page: Close your eyes and picture all of the ideas bumping around in your brain. Could any of those thoughts turn into art?

- *The Artist paints more* page: Predict what might happen next. Turn and share your predictions with someone nearby. Explain your reasons.

- *And then the busy city people come from all over town* page: What did the artist learn? [people love her pictures, mistakes are how you learn, her art is full of heart] Do you think she will keep painting? Would you keep painting?

After Reading

- Compare the text on the last page to the text on the title page. What do you notice? [They are the same font.] Who do you think is talking on the last page? [the author, Ed Vere]

- Why do you suppose Ed Vere wrote this book? What did you learn about being an artist from reading this book?

Learning Targets:

- I ponder the author's purpose for writing this text.
- I infer themes or big ideas.
- I use what I learned when I create art.

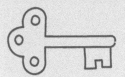

Extend the Experience

- The little girl tells the artist that her art is full of heart. Let's go back and record what else we learned about making art.

- If you had to draw all the things "fizzing, buzzing, and bumping together" inside your head, what would it look like? [Help students trace a silhouette of their head and have them draw images inside it to represent the colors, feelings, moods, and dreams that they've seen or imagined.]

Key Vocabulary and Kid-Friendly Definitions:

- bustling: full of activity and energy

- embarrassed: feeling funny or uncomfortable about something that happened

- journey: a long trip

Similar Titles

 ***The Concrete Garden* (Graham, 2023)**

About the Book: Amanda, her mom, and an apartment building full of children rush outside after a long winter. Amanda brings a cardboard box full of chalk. She begins by drawing what looks like a virus molecule. Then, Jackson adds a stem and turns it into a dandelion. From there, the children create a colorful chalk garden. Their masterpiece is photographed from above by Nasrin, who sends it to her mom in Iran. The photo goes viral and the children are celebrated. When rain washes the drawings away, the kids use remnants of Amada's box to race cardboard boats in the rainbow-colored gutters. This post-pandemic story celebrates the power of positivity after a dark spell.

 ***Oh, Olive!* (Cho, 2023)**

About the Book: Olive's parents are serious artists; her father paints squares and her mother paints triangles. Olive, on the other hand, joyfully smears, licks, and spatters paint everywhere. Olive's parents and classmates live in a monochrome world while everything Olive creates is an explosion of color. Olive's irresistible enthusiasm for art captures the attention of her classmates and, together, they paint their way through the town. Their final stop is Olive's parents' art museum, where Olive surprises everyone with her masterpiece.

Upper Elementary Extension:

Make a slide deck or print out a collection of eye-catching paintings. Ask students to identify the painting that speaks to their heart and write a caption for that painting.

Make Art With Heart Chart

one boy watching

Grant Snider

Learning Targets:

- I use details from the text and pictures to better understand how the author uses numbers.

- I notice and wonder about the numbers found in the text.

- I talk, write, or draw about details using numbers.

Tell a Story in Numbers

Book Title: *One Boy Watching* (Snider, 2022)

About the Book: A boy boards the school bus at dawn and readers travel along with him, enjoying the sights and sounds he experiences on the route. This adjective-filled story is based on Grant Snider's childhood experience of riding Bus Number Four to and from school in Mulvane, Kansas.

To find a book like this one, look for the following:

- Narrative enhanced with numbers
- Opportunities to apply mathematical thinking

Comprehension Conversation

Before Reading

Notice the Cover Illustration

I'm going to open the book so that you can see how the cover illustration wraps around from the front to the back. This is called a *wraparound cover*. Grant Snider drew the beautiful illustrations in this book using colored pencil and marker. Tell a friend one thing you notice on the cover. Ask them what they see. Are there any clues to the location, or setting, of this story?

Set a Purpose: We often use numbers to describe things in our world. For instance, "Our classroom has three windows." Look around and describe something you see using a number. Did you know that number words are adjectives? The title of this story includes a number; it's called *One Boy Watching*. Hmmm! What might capture the boy's attention? Let's read to find out what the boy is watching.

During Reading

- *Seven a.m.* page: Is seven a.m. in the morning or evening? How do you know? [a.m. stands for a Latin word, *ante meridiem*, that means before midday] Do you spot anything else that helps you figure out where the story takes place? [horses, a barn]

- *Bus Number Four* page: So far we read about *one* boy watching, *two* bright headlights, but something isn't following the pattern on this page. What do you notice? [The number *four* comes before the number *three*; usually in a counting book the numbers go in order.] What number do you predict we'll see on the next page?

- *Twenty-eight empty seats* page: Wait a second! Did Grant Snider surprise you? I thought this page would have the number *five*. Hmmm!

[As you enjoy the bus trip with your students, invite them to notice the variety and randomness of the numbers.]

- *One bus ride at sunrise under an infinite sky* page: Do you recognize this page? [It is the same illustration as the cover.] Think about what the boy has seen so far. Where do you think the story is set? [in the country, in a rural area] Why do you think that? [There are no big buildings, we haven't seen any other cars on the road.]

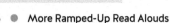

- *Ten till eight* page: Remember that the boy got on the bus at seven a.m. How long has he been on the bus? [50 minutes] Do you know another way to say *ten till eight*?

After Reading

- How many things do you think the boy will discover on his way home?
- Ponder how the setting impacts the story. How would this story be different if it took place in the city?

Extend the Experience

- Fold a blank sheet of paper into four sections. Think of four things you did today that you can describe using numbers. Let's brainstorm some sentence stems to help us as you're writing.
- As I reread the story, record all of the numbers that appear in the text. Is there a number between *one* and *10* that does not appear in the text? [*nine*] Are you curious to find out why?

Similar Titles:

 ***9 Kilometers* (Aguilera, 2020)**

About the Book: Up before sunrise, a Chilean boy sets off on his 9 kilometer (5.59 mile) walk to school scooting under barbed wire fences, hopping across river rocks, and traversing a cow pasture. Filled with musings about math, this book could lead to investigations about the distance children travel to school. The path of the boy's trek is visually represented on front and back endpapers. The backmatter includes brief stories about children around the world who also have arduous walks to school and information about the birds pictured in the book.

 ***One Sweet Song* (Gopal, 2024)**

About the Book: One by one, from balcony to balcony, community members join together to create *One Sweet Song*. Playing everything from pots and pans to violins, the tunes carry across the neighborhood. Musicians young and old join in until, "Ten notes swirl and whirl and wing, sparkling, glittering, a living thing." Then, readers count backwards from 10 to one until, "A hush, a silence, blankets all." Written by a kindergarten teacher who was inspired by the balcony-singing in Italy during the pandemic.

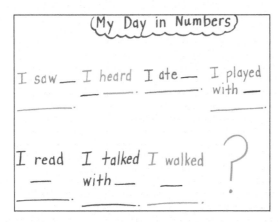

A Day in Number Sentence Stems Chart

Upper Elementary Extension:

Provide time for math-minded students to reread the book, add up the total number of items that the boy saw on his way to and from school, and then share their problem-solving strategy with the class.

Learning Targets:

- I use details from the text and illustrations to better understand the information and/or characters.

- I notice and wonder about the infographics found in the text.

- I create infographics to clearly explain details.

Depict Details Using Infographics

Book Title: *Friends Beyond Measure: A Story Told With Infographics* (L. Fisher, 2023)

About the Book: In her debut picture book as both author and illustrator, Lalena Fisher details the ups and downs of a long-standing friendship using infographics. Read aloud the first time to focus on the story. Then, return to the book during math lessons to study and discuss the different types of infographics. The backmatter explains and gives examples of useful charts students can make or combine to share information in a visually appealing way.

To find a book like this one, look for the following:

- Narrative or informational text enhanced with infographics
- Opportunities to apply mathematical thinking

Comprehension Conversation:

Before Reading

Notice the Cover Illustration

The title of this book is *Friends Beyond Measure* and the subtitle is *A Story Told With Infographics*. An infographic is like a picture that tells a story or shows facts and numbers. Can you spot any infographics on the wraparound cover? [bar graph, pie chart] Lalena Fisher created the illustrations and infographics with pencil, marker, and a digital tool.

Set a Purpose: Today we're going to read the story and focus mostly on what we can learn about the characters and why they are *Friends Beyond Measure*. We'll reread the book at another time to look more closely at some of the infographics.

During Reading

Pages 6–7: Let's pause here and learn a little more about the two characters in this book. Look at the Venn diagram. How is each girl unique? What do the two friends have in common? Can you figure out who is telling the story? [Notice that the text reads "me" under the dark-haired girl's picture. That is a clue that she is telling the story from a first-person point of view.]

Page 13: Look at the chart. Does it help you to figure out the girls' names and confirm who is telling the story? [Ana has dark hair. Remember, we learned in the Venn diagram that she likes charting. Harwin has blonde hair, and she likes horses.]

Pages 20–21: Try to imagine how you might feel if one of your friends was moving far away. Show me one of your emotions using your facial expressions.

Pages 22–23: Would you add any feelings to Ana's bar graph? Tell a friend which emotions you would add; ask them if there are any they would add.

Pages 34–35: Use the illustrations to help you list some of the ways that Ana and Harwin are going to stay in touch.

After Reading

- Think of a detail you remember about Ana or Harwin. Pretend you are introducing one of the girls to a friend. Say something like, "This is my friend Ana/Harwin. She _____."

- Why do you think the title of this story is *Friends Beyond Measure*?

Extend the Experience

- On pages 22–23, Ana finds out that Harwin is moving and uses a bar graph to show the intensity of each of her feelings. Think about an event or experience where you had mixed emotions. It could be something that happened to you personally, how you felt while reading a book, or even your emotions while watching a movie. Create a bar graph to represent your mixed feelings about that event. Remember to give your graph a title.

- There are so many interesting infographics in this book. Let's pick one to study. As we're studying one of Ana's infographics, keep the following questions in mind:

  o What is the big idea that Ana is trying to communicate?

  o Does the infographic include text? If so, how does the text help you understand the big idea?

  o Are there numbers included in the infographic? If so, are they important?

Similar Titles:

 365: How to Count a Year (Paul, 2023) [Opportunities to apply mathematical thinking.]

About the Book: What are the different systems we use to measure time? A boy and his king-of-the-jungle companion answer this question by grouping 365 days into weeks, months, and finally a year. After the boy celebrates a year on Earth, they divide the year into hours, minutes, and seconds. With humorous anecdotes (like making sure you wear 365 clean pairs of underwear) and visual representations of 365 moon phases, students will be looking at the clock and calendar with a new appreciation.

 One Day by the Numbers (S. Jenkins, 2022)

About the Book: One of the books in the late Steve Jenkins's *By the Numbers* series. This book is a fascinating exploration of the world's activities within the span of just 24 hours. Through colorful infographics and brief informational paragraphs, Steve Jenkins delves into a myriad of subjects, ranging from human behavior to animal migrations and more. Display and read this book one infographic at a time.

Key Vocabulary and Kid-Friendly Definitions:

- **adventures:** exciting, or sometimes dangerous, trips or experiences

- **agreements:** understandings between people about what they are going to do

- **disagreements:** angry discussions by people who have different ideas or opinions

Upper Elementary Extension:

Display and discuss the backmatter of the book. Prompt students to select and design one or more of the charts that the author describes to enhance an informational writing piece.

"I'm from notebooks, stubby pencils, drawing my own heroes, writing my own stories."

—*I'm From*
by Gary R. Gray Jr. and Oge Mora

Inspire Writers!

Learn From Creators

Each time you read a picture book aloud, you have the opportunity to highlight a tip, technique, or craft move of the creator. Showing children that writers and illustrators make intentional choices helps them to internalize the fact that writing is a thoughtful, decision-making process. The books in this chapter introduce your writers to characters who learn the importance of sharing their own stories. You can spotlight creative approaches authors use in informational texts to make acquiring knowledge exciting and memorable. During comprehension conversations, prompt students to notice how writers use nonfiction text structures to effectively organize and convey information. As they learn about notable figures from biographies, students gain insights into the importance of understanding the author's purpose and point of view. The poetry anthologies highlighted here are examples of diverse poetry techniques and forms. In sum, the read-aloud experiences in Chapter 5 aim to develop adept and inspired writers as students explore the following big ideas:

- Tell your story
- Detail the facts
- Be a biographer
- Prompt action
- Pen a poem

When we take the time to unpack the subtle craft moves of picture book creators, we cultivate confident, imaginative, and skilled writers.

Scan here to find a complete learning target chart with online links, a bonus read-aloud experience, and printable resources.

https://qrs.ly/uhfn8pp

Big Idea: Featured Title	Learning Targets
Write From Experience: *Abdul's Story* (Thompkins-Bigelow, 2022)	• I notice where writers get ideas. • I understand that writing is a messy process. • I think about what it means to be a writer.
Relive Memories: *A Letter for Bob* (Rogers, 2023)	• I notice where writers get ideas. • I pay attention to how writers tell their stories. • I tell stories that are important to me.
Share Facts in Innovative Ways: *One Tiny Treefrog: A Countdown to Survival* (Piedra & Joy, 2023)	• I ask and answer questions to better understand key details. • I notice ways to organize nonfiction texts. • I try out different nonfiction text structures in my own writing.
Ask and Answer Questions: *Butt or Face?* (Lavelle, 2023)	• I ask and answer questions to better understand key details. • I notice the question-answer pattern or structure of the text. • I borrow the question-answer structure when creating my own text.
Connect Events: *Ketanji Brown Jackson: A Justice for All* (Charles, 2023)	• I notice connections among ideas and events in a biography. • I remember important details about a person's life. • I talk, write, or draw about the person's character traits.
Engage the Reader: *Tomfoolery! Randolph Caldecott and the Rambunctious Coming-of-Age of Children's Books* (Markel, 2023)	• I notice the techniques the author uses. • I remember important details about a person's life. • I use what I've learned when writing biographies.
Show the Impact: *To Change a Planet* (Soontornvat, 2022)	• I notice techniques authors use to persuade. • I ponder the author's purpose. • I use what I've learned to persuade people to act.
Be Persuasive: *Autumn Peltier, Water Warrior* (Lindstrom, 2023)	• I notice techniques people use to persuade. • I ponder the point of view and author's purpose. • I use what I've learned to persuade people to act.
Notice, Wonder, and Write: *Welcome to the Wonder House* (Dotlich & Heard, 2023)	• I notice different kinds of poems. • I think about how poems are organized. • I use what I learn about poetry to write my own poems.
Ponder Your Purpose: *Champion Chompers, Super Stinkers and Other Poems by Extraordinary Animals* (Ashman, 2023)	• I ponder purposes for writing poetry. • I think about how poems are organized. • I use what I learn about poetry to write my own poems.
Bonus Lesson (online) Relive Memories: *The Blue Pickup* (Tripplett, 2024)	• I notice how characters share their memories. • I think about why storytelling is important. • I tell stories that are important to me.

My Favorite Read Alouds for Inspiring Writers

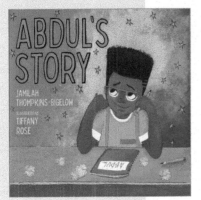

Write From Experience

Book Title: *Abdul's Story* (Thompkins-Bigelow, 2022)

About the Book: Abdul enjoys telling stories, but writing them is a challenge. Consequently, he spends more time erasing than writing. One day, a writer named Mr. Muhammad visits his class and encourages the kids to "write new stories with new superheroes." After Mr. Muhammad shows Abdul his messy writer's notebook, Abdul snaps off his eraser and begins putting his thoughts down on paper.

To find a book like this one, look for the following:

- Books that inspire writers to trust their own stories
- Books that highlight individuality

Learning Targets:

- I notice where writers get ideas.
- I understand that writing is a messy process.
- I think about what it means to be a writer.

Comprehension Conversation

Before Reading

Notice the Cover Illustration

Take a close look at the front cover. If you were going to add a thinking bubble above Abdul's head, what would be in it? Compare this picture to the one on the back cover. What do you notice? How are they different?

Set a Purpose: As you listen to *Abdul's Story*, notice what he learns about being a writer and think about how what he learns might help you when you write your own stories.

During Reading

- *Writing these stories was hard, though* page: Can you empathize with Abdul? Which do you prefer: telling stories or writing them? Trade answers with a partner.

- *Abdul tried writing neatly* page: Share some of the details that help you understand Abdul's mood. Have you ever felt like Abdul when you were trying to write?

- *"Nice sneaks! Can I see your story?"* page: Talk with a partner about the advice Mr. Muhammad gave Abdul. Predict what Abdul might do in his writer's notebook.

- *Over the next few days, Abdul rewrote a less messy mess* page: Think about how Jayda and Kwame made Abdul feel. What should they have said instead?

- *Mr. Muhammad started reading the story in a loud, clear voice* page: How are Abdul's feelings about writing changing? Which events in the story led to the change?

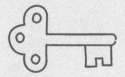

After Reading

- Where did Abdul's ideas come from? [The stories he told about his neighborhood.] Yes! He got ideas from his everyday life. That's what writers do!

- What are some of the lessons Abdul learned about being a writer? [Everyone has stories; get the messy words out and fix them up later; tell your story; writers make mistakes.]

Extend the Experience

- Let's try what Abdul learned. I'm going to set the timer for __ minutes. [Pick a time that makes sense for your kids.] Get all of your messy ideas out, no erasing. Then, you can look at your ideas and see if you can find a story to tell. Afterwards, you can decide if this strategy is helpful to you.

- [Take a noticing walk around the school/playground/neighborhood.] Abdul's stories came from noticing people in his neighborhood. Grab your writer's notebooks; let's go on a noticing walk. We'll pause every now and then so that you can sketch or jot notes about what you see. Later, you can use those ideas to start a story.

Similar Titles

 I'm From (Gray, 2023)

About the Book: Follow a boy from his "early morning wake-up" to his "moon as a night-light soft pecks on the cheeks" and listen to discover what makes him unique. Oge Mora's distinctive collage illustrations mix-in pages from the boy's composition notebook, where he can be found "drawing my own heroes, writing my own stories." Notice that she has also cleverly designed the case cover to resemble a composition book.

 You Are a Story (Raczka, 2023)

About the Book: An unseen narrator reminds young readers of all the things they are and the possibilities that lie ahead. Raczka begins with scientific examples like "you are a living thing" and "you are an animal." He then addresses metaphysical ideas such as "you are a mystery" and "you are one-of-a-kind." The final musing, "you are a story," is the seamless segue into writing narratives.

Key Vocabulary and Kid-Friendly Definitions:

- clacking: when two hard objects hit together and make short, sharp sounds
- watchful: watching closely or carefully
- wondrous: something amazing that fills you with wonder

Upper Elementary Extension:

Students can create a writing tip sheet to offer advice to writers in the younger grades. Remind them to make it age appropriate by choosing their words carefully and adding illustrations.

Relive Memories

Book Title: *A Letter for Bob* (Rogers, 2023)

About the Book: From the day Katie's family bring Bob home from the car dealership, the reliable car absorbs their spills and ferries them near and far. In this love letter to a family vehicle, Katie shares memories of Bob at the Wichita Annual Dance, after the too much fry bread at Indian Hills Powwow, on vacations to Grand Teton and Yellowstone, and to visit Aka:h (Grandma) in the Smoky Mountains. When baby Jenna is born and the family needs a bigger car, Katie says So:ti:c?a (thank you) and good-bye to their dependable companion. *A Letter for Bob* won the 2024 American Indian Youth Literature Award.

To find a book like this one, look for the following:

- Slice of life stories
- Books that celebrate memories

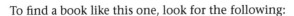

Comprehension Conversation

Before Reading

Notice the Cover Illustration

- When you see Jonathan Nelson's digitally created illustration on the cover of this book, does it make you think this story will be realistic fiction or make-believe? Why do you think so?
- Which character do you think is Bob?
- Let's read the back cover blurb to learn more about this book.

Set a Purpose: After studying the cover and reading the back cover blurb, we're predicting that this is a realistic story about a trustworthy car named Bob. Let's see what else we learn about Bob and notice how this story is told.

During Reading

- *We've made so many memories with you* page: *Regalia* is what an Indigenous dancer wears during a traditional dance. Regalia is unique to each type of dance, dancer, culture, and family. Katie is sharing a memory of her first *Tiny Tots Dance*. If we look in the glossary at the end of the book, we learn that a Tiny Tots Dance is a powwow dance for children up to six years old. I wonder what other memories her family has shared with Bob.

- *And a few years later* page: Can you infer what happened because Katie ate too much fry bread?! [She threw up in the car.] Has something like this ever happened to you? Share with a neighbor.

- *You drove us to visit Aka:h in the Smoky Mountains* page: Combine the details you learned from the words with the person you see in the picture to infer who Aka:h might be. Let's check to see if we're right by reading the definition of Aka:h in the glossary.

Learning Targets:

- I notice where writers get ideas.
- I pay attention to how writers tell their stories.
- I tell stories that are important to me.

- *You were there when we walked down to Looking Glass Falls* page: Describe the tone or mood of this page. What can you infer about Grandma? [That she is losing her memory.]

- *Today is hard because it's the day we say goodbye* page: Can you put yourself in Katie's shoes and imagine how she's feeling right now?

After Reading

- If we read the author's note, we discover that this story is based on a memory from when Kim Rogers was a little girl. Writers get ideas from memories!

- Kim Rogers chose to tell this story in a unique way, as a letter from Katie to her family car Bob. What did you think about this storytelling technique? What else did you notice?

Extend the Experience

- *A Letter for Bob* is filled with memories—both happy ones and sad ones. Events that happened in the past make great stories. List some memorable events on a piece of paper or in your writer's notebook.

- This story was written like a letter to a car named Bob. Think about an item, place, or person that means a lot to you. Write a letter to that item, place, or person to share some of your favorite memories together.

Similar Titles

 The Blue Pickup (Tripplett, 2024)

About the Book: A delightful story highlighting the power of resourcefulness and preserving cherished memories. Set in Jamaica and narrated from the perspective of Ju-Girl, we step into the story to join Ju-Girl and Grandad as they spend joyful hours working side-by-side fixing cars. During their Ting break, Grandad recounts memories of the many deliveries he made over the years in the Blue Pickup. Ju-Girl nudges Grandad to restore the Blue Pickup, reminding him of "the importance of taking care of old and forgotten things." Grandad then surprises Ju-Girl with a gift that reflects their shared memories. Debut author Natasha Tripplett writes in the author's note that she's restored and now drives her grandfather's old blue pickup truck. [See bonus read-aloud experience on the companion website (http://www.resources.corwin.com/more-rampedup-readalouds).]

 How to Make a Memory (Vickers, 2023) [Celebrates memories]

About the Book: A thought-provoking guide to gathering memories of life's joys and sorrows. Each child's memory is depicted in a colorful and detailed thought bubble providing opportunities for readers to infer the memory and explain how the illustration enhances the text. Ideal for inviting learners to write about their treasured memories.

Key Vocabulary and Kid-Friendly Definitions:

- bristly: having prickly or scratchy hairs or spikes

- deserves: when someone has earned or should get something

- trustworthy: someone or something that does what it is supposed to do

Upper Elementary Extension:

Revisit the pages where Katie's family visited National Parks. Show students how to use Google Street View on Google Earth to explore the beauty of these and other National Parks.

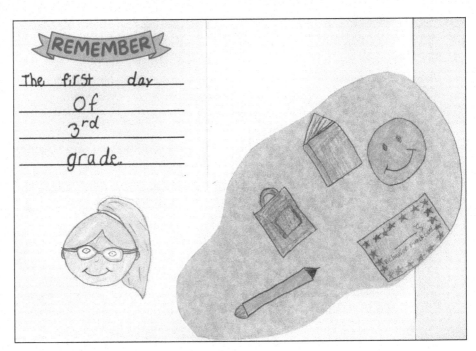

How to Make a Memory Work Sample

My Favorite Read Alouds for Teaching Narrative Writing

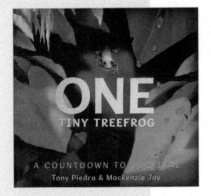

Share Facts in Innovative Ways

Book Title: *One Tiny Treefrog: A Countdown to Survival* (Piedra & Joy, 2023)

About the Book: By the creator team who call themselves Mac and Tea, readers will be on the edge of their seats as they learn about the survival strategy of the red-eyed tree frog. In the process, they'll meet a variety of species that live in the lowland rainforests of Costa Rica. This book highlights the science standard relating to how the patterns in behavior of parents help offspring survive. After reading, compare the counting back structure to *13 Ways to Eat a Fly* (Heavenrich, 2021), one of the featured books in *Shake Up Shared Reading* (Walther, 2022).

To find a book like this one, look for the following:

- Innovative nonfiction text structures
- Patterns and techniques learners can imitate in their own writing

Learning Targets:

- I ask and answer questions to better understand key details.
- I notice ways to organize nonfiction texts.
- I try out different nonfiction text structures in my own writing.

Comprehension Conversation

Before Reading

Notice the Cover Illustration

Look carefully. Can you spot any creatures on the cover of this book? [treefrog, snake, ants] I think Mackenzie Joy's digital illustrations look so realistic. I can't wait to hear what you think!

Set a Purpose: I bet you can guess from the title *One Tiny Treefrog* that this book is going to teach us more about treefrogs. Take a minute to think and talk about the subtitle *A Countdown to Survival* with a classmate. I wonder if the back cover blurb might give us a clue. [Read and discuss the details you learned by reading the back cover blurb.] Let's join the red-eyed treefrog on its epic journey.

During Reading

- *Nine alert tadpoles begin to wiggle free* page: Only nine tadpoles are *alert*. The word *alert* means watching carefully and paying close attention. Why do you suppose the tadpoles need to be alert? Zoom-in on the eggs. Can you figure out why there are only nine? [One has its eye closed. It must not be awake or alive.]

- *Eight wriggling tadpoles PLUNGE* page: Notice the details in the illustration. Why are they down to eight tadpoles? [One is being carried away by a wasp.] What is unique about this page? [You have to rotate the book to read it.]

- *Five growing tadpoles start to kick kick kick kick* page: What is happening to the tadpoles as we turn the pages? [Some are changing, others are being eaten by predators.] Is the subtitle *Countdown to Survival* starting to make more sense now?

- *One resilient tadpole sees something familiar* page: Turn and tell a friend what you think the tadpole sees.

- *SNAP* page: Oh, no! Look at the details in the illustration. Is the tadpole still alive? Can you point out what it saw?

After Reading

- How did the details in the illustrations help you to better understand the main idea of this nonfiction book?

- How might you use a countdown structure in your own nonfiction text?

Extend the Experience

- *3-2-1 Strategy* (Zygouris-Coe et al., 2004/2005). Write down three memorable details from *One Tiny Treefrog*. Then, write down two words that describe the book or the tadpoles. Finally, jot down a lingering question or connection to the text or topic. (See *3-2-1 Strategy Printable* located on the companion website, http://www.resources.corwin.com/more-rampedup-readalouds.)

- The author carefully chose adjectives to help us experience the lifecycle of a red-eyed treefrog. Let's reread to notice and record the adjectives.

Similar Titles:

 How to Find a Fox (K. Gardner, 2021)

About the Book: Written as a "how-to" guide to finding foxes, Kate Gardner details just the right amount of information about foxes in the paragraphs that accompany the brief running text. Wildlife photographer Ossi Saarinen's images of the foxes will captivate readers. Check out his Instagram account to see the rest of his stunning wildlife images.

 Tumble (Bergstrom, 2023)

About the Book: Where does a tumbleweed go when the wind blows? Journey through the desert to find out. Using mainly rhyming couplets, readers learn about the lifecycle of a tumbleweed. The backmatter includes a visual glossary of the plants and animals pictured on the pages along with some fun facts about tumbleweeds.

Key Vocabulary and Kid-Friendly Definitions:

- nimble: moves quickly and easily

- resilient: strong, tough, able to adjust to or overcome challenges

- wary: watchful around threats or danger

Upper Elementary Extension:

Project the last two pages of backmatter. Assign each student a number from 0–10. Students form a team with the people who have the same number. Each team reads the paragraph that begins with their number and shares one fact they learned that wasn't in the book.

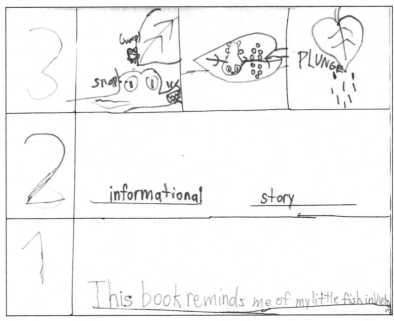

3-2-1 Work Sample

3	snap (jump) PLUNGE
2	informational story
1	This book reminds me of my little fish in Viet...

Name _____

3-2-1

Three Memorable Details:

_____

_____

_____

Two Words to Describe the Book:

_____   _____

One Question or Connection:

_____

_____

3-2-1 Strategy Printable

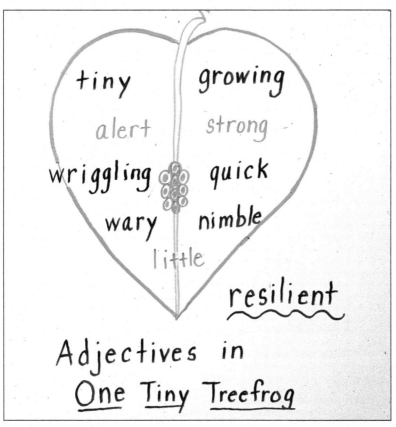

tiny   growing
alert   strong
wriggling   quick
wary   nimble
little
resilient

Adjectives in
One Tiny Treefrog

One Tiny Treefrog Adjective Chart

Ask and Answer Questions

Book Title: *Butt or Face?* (Lavelle, 2023)

About the Book: Inspired by farmers in Botswana who paint eyes on their cows' behinds to scare away predators, Kari Lavelle presents close-up photographs of 13 lesser-known creatures. On the page with the photograph, she asks readers to use their scientific observation skills to determine whether it is the creature's butt or face. The following page provides the answer along with fascinating details about that particular creature. This hilarious and informative book will keep your students guessing as they learn about animal adaptations.

To find a book like this one, look for the following:

- Informational texts with a question-answer text structure
- Humorous texts that engage learners

Comprehension Conversation

Before Reading

Notice the Cover Illustration

What do you think? Is this the animal's rear end or their face? Do you recognize this creature? Which parts of this illustration are a photograph and which details were added by an artist?

Set a Purpose: Let's learn about animals and answer the question *Butt or Face*? Notice the way that Kari Lavelle organizes this book to see if it is a pattern you might be able to use when you write nonfiction pieces.

[To allow enough time to enjoy the humor and to read the fun facts, I suggest splitting this book in half or reading a page or two a day.]

During Reading

- *From their heads to their tails, animals have evolved to thrive and survive in the wild* page: Explain what it means to use your scientific observation skills. [One way that scientists collect data or information is by observing or looking closely at what they're studying.]

- *Cuyaba dwarf frog* page: When this frog is scared it *inflates* its *posterior*. Posterior is another word for rear end. When you inflate something, you fill it with air, like a balloon. I wonder if other animals inflate themselves like this frog. That would be something interesting to research.

- *Okapi* page: Share one fact you remember about the Okapi with a partner. Start with: I remember _____. Where have you seen this photograph before? [on the cover]

Learning Targets:

- I ask and answer questions to better understand key details.

- I notice the question-answer pattern or structure of the text.

- I borrow the question-answer structure when creating my own text.

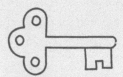
- *Star-nosed mole* page: The star-nosed mole dines on fine *delicacies*. A delicacy is a special, delicious food that is sometimes hard to find. Do worms, fish, and insects sound like a delicacy to you? Do you have any questions about this animal?

- *Promethea moth* page: I notice that Kari Lavelle used a synonym for butt on this page, *tush*. Let's pay attention to see what other synonyms she uses.

[Continue in the same fashion, defining unfamiliar, content-specific vocabulary and discussing the puns and humorous word play found on some of the pages.]

After Reading

- How is this book organized or structured? [question-answer] Have you read any other books structured this way?

- Share your opinion. Did the question-answer structure help you learn and remember facts about these creatures? Why or why not?

Extend the Experience

- Try out the question-answer pattern like the one in this book when you are writing a nonfiction text.

- In this book, we saw close-up photographs of animal parts. Scientists use magnifying glasses to look closely at objects. I've collected some interesting objects and put them out with some magnifying glasses so that you can use your scientific observation skills to see what you discover.

Similar Titles

 Creature Features: 25 Animals Explain Why They Look the Way They Do (S. Jenkins & Page, 2014)

About the Book: Discover why thorny devils are spiny and sun bears have long tongues in this distinctive nonfiction picture book. The text is written in a *Dear Animal* format, where each of the creatures is asked about one of their features and the answer is written from the creature's point of view.

 Whose Butt? (Tekiela, 2012)

About the Book: In the introduction to the book, Stan Tekiela, a wildlife photographer, explains that when you try to take pictures of animals, they often run or fly away. So he's put together these photographs of animal butts to see if readers can guess the animal by looking at its rear end. If your students love the word *butt* as much as mine do, they will enjoy this question-answer book! For a humorous pairing you could also read the book *Chicken Cheeks* (Black, 2009). [Find a read-aloud experience for this book in *The Ramped-Up Read Aloud*.]

Key Vocabulary and Kid-Friendly Definitions:

- fierce: strong and powerful
- startled: surprised or scared
- thrive: to grow strong and healthy

Upper Elementary Extension:

Discuss how our perspective changes when we view something close-up rather than far away. To illustrate your point, share the wordless picture book *Zoom* (Banyai, 1995) or digitally zoom-in on a place using Google Earth.

Connect Events

Book Title: *Ketanji Brown Jackson: A Justice for All*
(Charles, 2023)

About the Book: Introduce readers to the first Black woman to serve as Supreme Court justice, Ketanji Brown Jackson, as you trace her life through the decades. In the author's note, Tami Charles shares that her inspiration came from a photograph of Ketanji's daughter Leila proudly gazing at her mother. She wanted to spotlight the sense of pride children feel when witnessing their loved ones pursue and achieve their dreams. That connection is symbolized by the girl who appears in the illustrations and "represents the Leila Jackson within us all." Extensive backmatter expands on the key details in the narrative and includes important dates and information about influential people and historical events shown in the pictures.

To find a book like this one, look for the following:

- Biographies that chronologically connect events
- Biographies about influential women

Learning Targets:

- I notice connections among ideas and events in a biography.
- I remember important details about a person's life.
- I talk, write, or draw about the person's character traits.

Comprehension Conversation

Before Reading

Notice the Cover Illustration

Behind Ketanji Brown Jackson you see the United States Supreme Court Building. The Supreme Court is the head of the judicial branch of the U.S. government set up by the U.S. Constitution, and it currently has nine judges called justices. The justices are chosen by the president, and the U.S. Senate must agree with the choice. Once chosen, justices can keep their jobs for the rest of their lives or until they decide to retire.

Set a Purpose: The job of a Supreme Court justice is like being a referee for the rules of our country. When people have a disagreement about a law, they bring the case to the Supreme Court. Supreme Court justices listen to people's arguments, study the law and the Constitution, and then make decisions that affect the whole country. As we read about Supreme Court Justice Ketanji Brown Jackson, think about her personality and the steps she took to become *A Justice for All*.

During Reading

- *Cameras flash* page: This page explains some of the actions Ketanji took to earn her seat on the Supreme Court. [studied, pushed, prepared] What else did you learn about her?
- *1970S MIAMI* page: Share a detail you learned about Ketanji's childhood in the 1970s. How many years ago was that?
- *1980S* page: It's a decade, or 10 years, later. Do you think Ketanji is going to "set her sights low"? What have learned about her personality so far that can help you answer that question?

- *As a law clerk* page: It's another decade later and we've seen all Ketanji has accomplished so far. I'll reread this page. Listen for the words Tami Charles uses to describe her. [Optimistic, realistic, fair, dedicated, and on a mission.] Do you need me to explain what any of those words mean?

- *So as cameras flash* page: Why do you suppose Tami Charles chose to write this biography from this girl's point of view?

After Reading

- If you had the opportunity to meet Ketanji Brown Jackson, what question would you ask her?

- We talked a lot about Ketanji Brown Jackson's personality. Do you feel like that helped you remember her life story?

Extend the Experience

- It took many steps to become a Supreme Court justice. What are some of the actions Ketanji took to prepare? Record them on the *Action Steps Printable*. [Located on the companion website (http://www.resources.corwin.com/more-rampedup-readalouds).]

- Ketanji "studied, pushed, and prepared" to become a Supreme Court justice. What does this tell you about her personality? What are some words or phrases you would use to describe her? Why are traits like these important?

Similar Titles

 All Rise: The Story of Ketanji Brown Jackson (Weatherford, 2023)

About the Book: Using the repeated refrains "She rose" and "Ketanji rose," readers retrace pivotal moments in Ketanji's life. Backmatter includes a timeline and Carole Boston Weatherford's letter to her granddaughter and "all of our daughters."

The Queen of Chess: How Judit Polgár Changed the Game (Wallmark, 2023)

About the Book: At age five, Judit learned how to play chess from her mom. Her parents were training Judit and her sisters how to play "genius-level" chess. Along with other childhood activities, Judit memorized chess puzzles and played the game at least five or six hours a day. When she was nine, the family flew from Budapest to New York to compete in the New York Open. There, wearing her lucky sweater, Judit won the tournament and the "Brilliancy Prize" for the most creative and strategic game. At age 15, Judit becomes the youngest chess grandmaster. Backmatter includes a timeline and a page about the mathematics of chess.

The story that inspired the book.

https://qrs.ly/hrfn8pt

Key Vocabulary and Kid-Friendly Definitions:

- barrier: something that stops things or people from moving

- bold: being brave and not afraid

- sowed: to have planted

Upper Elementary Extension:

In her author's note, Tami Charles discusses the image that inspired the girl who appears in the illustrations. Researchers can learn about the photographer and image by watching this news clip linked from the QR code to the left.

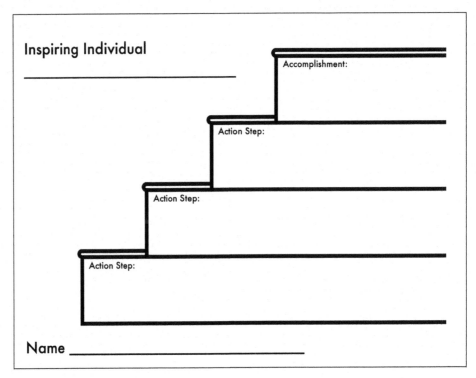

Inspiring Individual

_____

Accomplishment:

Action Step:

Action Step:

Action Step:

Name _____

Action Steps Printable

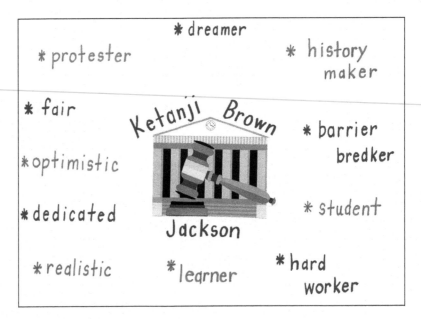

* dreamer

* protester

* history maker

* fair

Ketanji Brown

* barrier bredker

*optimistic

*dedicated

Jackson

* student

* realistic

* learner

* hard worker

Ketanji Brown Jackson Chart

My Favorite Read Alouds for Teaching Biography Writing

Engage the Reader

Book Title: *Tomfoolery! Randolph Caldecott and the Rambunctious Coming-of-Age of Children's Books* (Markel, 2023)

About the Book: Like Randolph Caldecott, this picture book biography is full of exuberant energy. The narrative, filled with vivid verbs, moves along at a perfect pace, and the metafictive devices keep listeners engaged as the narrator addresses them directly now and then. The story highlights Caldecott's transformation of picture books by infusing them with lively stories and dynamic illustrations.

To find a book like this one, look for the following:

- Biographies that are interesting to young learners
- Biographies about the history of children's books

Comprehension Conversation

Before Reading

Notice the Cover Illustration

- Notice what is happening on the cover. Can you infer what the word *tomfoolery* might mean? Tomfoolery is playful, silly, or goofy behavior. Does that make sense and match the illustration? [Notice they also define *tomfoolery* on the front flap.]

- The subtitle is *Randolph Caldecott and the Rambunctious Coming-of-Age of Children's Books*. The word *rambunctious* means full of energy and can't stop being loud and playful. Do you see any rambunctious characters on the cover?

- Would you say Barbara McClintock's ink and watercolor illustrations look modern or old-fashioned?

Set a Purpose: We know from studying the cover that this biography is about Randolph Caldecott. Have you ever heard that name before? Notice how Michelle Markel teaches us a little bit about him and what he had to do with the children's books we love to read.

During Reading

- *Come on in* page: Who is the hero of this biography? [Randolph Caldecott] *Frisky* and *sprightly* are synonyms for full of energy. Do you enjoy picture books that are full of energy?

- *Oh, there he is, strolling down the country lane* page: Why do you suppose Michelle Markel wrote all of those animal names in a different font and without any punctuation? How does she want us to read that part? Let's reread it together.

- *He tries* page: Think back to the title and to what we've learned about Randolph already. How is his artwork different than what other artists are doing? [His paintings and sculptures have people and animals in action.]

Learning Targets:

- I notice the techniques the author uses.
- I remember important details about a person's life.
- I use what I've learned when writing biographies.

- *Someone pays close attention to those pictures* page: Knowing what we know about Randolph, what will be happening in his picture books? Share your predictions with a neighbor.

- *The public is delighted* page: How did Randolph Caldecott change picture books? Aren't you glad he did?!

After Reading

- Talk about the techniques Michelle Markel uses to keep you interested and turning the pages? [Talks directly to us, asks questions, uses ellipses to quickly move us from one page to the next, and so on.]

- Which technique could you try when you're writing a biography?

Extend the Experience

- Divide a paper into thirds. Draw and label three illustrations to show three key details you remember about Randolph Caldecott.

- On pages 26–27, Barbara McClintock features Caldecott's illustration from *The Diverting Story of John Gilpin*. Compare this illustration to the one on the Caldecott Medal. What do you notice?

Similar Titles

 ***Balderdash! John Newbery and the Boisterous Birth of Children's Books* (Markel, 2017)**

About the Book: "Be glad it's not 1726" when books were not designed with children in mind, begins Markel's tribute to John Newbery. Young John began working as a printer and then became a publisher with a storefront shop in London. In those days, people thought if children read fun books, they would be wild. "Balderdash!" said John. This is a story of the namesake of the Newbery Medal, a man who changed the world of children's books.

 ***Extraordinary Magic: The Storytelling Life of Virginia Hamilton* (Crews, 2024)** ☆

About the Book: Nina Crews crafted this poetic biography to, as she shares in the author's note, "Inspire young writers to fill notebooks with stories and poems. To create extraordinary magic." Through poems with one-word titles, readers discover the impact Virginia's family and childhood had on her creative process. A stellar mentor text of a meticulously researched biography. Source notes for each poem are found on creator's website.

Key Vocabulary and Kid-Friendly Definitions:

- astonished: surprised and amazed

- frail: weak or sickly

- rambunctious: full of energy and can't stop being loud and playful

Upper Elementary Extension:

On page 29, Barbara McClintock features Caldecott-winning creators. Challenge your students to try and figure out who they are.

Show the Impact

Book Title: *To Change a Planet* (Soontornvat, 2022)

About the Book: If you are looking for a compelling book that clearly explains the big ideas related to climate change, look no further. Former science educator and Sibert Award nominee Christina Soontornvat has carefully crafted a powerful message that underscores the fact that when people join together around a cause, they can make a difference. Rahele Jomepour Bell's mixed-media illustrations, mostly two-page spreads, add eye-catching details to Soontornvat's words. Sharp-eyed readers will notice the child with the green scarf on many of the pages. Backmatter includes details about climate change and what readers can do to take action.

To find a book like this one, look for the following:

- Texts that prompt reflection and action
- Texts that highlight environmental issues

Learning Targets:

- I notice techniques authors use to persuade.
- I ponder the author's purpose.
- I use what I've learned to persuade people to act.

Comprehension Conversation

Before Reading

Notice the Cover Illustration

What do you notice on the wraparound cover? To create the illustrations in this book, Rahele Jomepour Bell made the pictures with hand-painted textured papers, and then digitally scanned them and painted another layer on top with digital brushes. I can't wait for you to see her pictures inside *How to Change a Planet*!

Set a Purpose: Take a moment to think and talk with a partner about ways you could help our planet. We're going to join this child to learn what Christina Soontornvat wants us to do to keep our planet healthy.

During Reading

- *they can change a planet* page: Point out something that is happening in this illustration that could impact our planet. Do you think these changes are helpful or harmful to our Earth?
- *But when one person, and one person* page: Compare the left side of this page to the right. Share what you think the illustrator is trying to show us. [The passage of time from long ago to today.]
- *Life. Us* page: Put together what you know about farm fields with what you see in this illustration. Infer what's happening on this farm. How might these changes affect this family?
- *become many* page: Notice all of the details in this illustration. Tell a friend something you see in this picture that can affect our planet. Ask them what they see. Do you think these changes are helpful or harmful to our Earth?

After Reading

- How did this book make you feel? What do you suppose Christina Soontornvat wants us to know and do after reading this book? Why do you think she wrote it?

- Let's flip back and notice the words and illustrations. How do they work together to encourage you to take action? [Discuss the ways that the author presents facts and uses repetition, varied sentence length, and precise word choice. Notice how the illustrations add convincing details to the text.]

Extend the Experience

- If we turn back to the page that reads, "Our planet seems tough, but it is fragile," we see on the chalkboard that the students in the class are writing letters for the planet. On the next page, we can read a few of their letters. Think about someone in your home, school, or community who might be able to do one small thing to help our planet.

  Write a letter to that person or organization. [You can either do this as a class in a shared writing format or support writers as they work in teams or individually to compose their letters.]

- Persuade your classmates to make one small, positive change to better our classroom or school. Use this sentence stem to write your idea: To improve our classroom/school you can _____ because . . .

Similar Titles

 Black Beach: A Community, an Oil Spill, and the Origin of Earth Day (Stith & Stith, 2023)

About the Book: It's January 1969. Sam is at school happily drawing a picture of her favorite place—the beach. When she gets home from school, her parents share the news of the Union Oil blowout. Sam's beloved beach is now unrecognizable. The community works together to clean up as much as they can while Sam and her classmates send oil-filled bottles to politicians. Seven months later, U.S. Senator Gaylord Nelson visits, returns to Washington DC, and spearheads a movement to establish the first Earth Day. Backmatter includes an Earth Day timeline, facts about Earth Day, and a list of kid-friendly ways to be an environmental activist.

 Little Land (Sudyka, 2023)

About the Book: The book opens with a little girl watering a lush "little bit of land." Then, Diana Sudyka's perfectly paced narration embedded among her striking illustrations traces the changes to the land through periods of geologic time until people literally upend the balance. The hopeful conclusion shows children leading the way to care for the little land so it can begin anew. Backmatter extends the narrative with an author's note, definitions of environmental words and concepts, along with some of the creatures and epochs (periods of geologic time) represented in the book.

Key Vocabulary and Kid-Friendly Definitions:

- **dependable:** something or someone you can trust or count on

- **fragile:** something that is easy to break or hurt

- **insignificant:** very small or not important

Upper Elementary Extension:

Make five copies of the backmatter and divide students into five small groups. Assign each group one section of the backmatter. In a "jigsaw" fashion, each group reads, summarizes, and shares what they learned from their section.

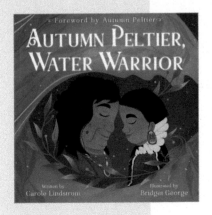

Be Persuasive

Book Title: *Autumn Peltier, Water Warrior* (Lindstrom, 2023)

About the Book: The story of Indigenous water activist Autumn Peltier who, following in the footsteps of her late Aunt Josephine, has been advocating for water rights since she was eight years old. Her respect for and relationship with the water is told from the water's point of view. A call to action at the end of the book invites readers to join the fight to protect this precious resource.

To find a book like this one, look for the following:

- Biographies about activists
- Texts that prompt reflection and action

Learning Targets:

- I notice techniques people use to persuade.
- I ponder the point of view and author's purpose.
- I use what I've learned to persuade people to act.

Comprehension Conversation

Before Reading

Notice the Cover Illustration

What do you think it means to be a water warrior? Have you heard of Autumn Peltier? If not, which person pictured on the cover do you think she might be? At the top of the cover it reads, "Foreword by Autumn Peltier." A foreword is a book introduction written by someone other than the author. Let's read the foreword to *Autumn Peltier, Water Warrior.*

Set a Purpose: This biography is told from a unique point of view. As we learn about Autumn Peltier, listen to determine if you can figure out who is telling her story. We'll also talk about how you, as a writer, can choose who will tell your stories.

During Reading

- *I am nibi* page: According to the glossary in the back of the book, *nibi* means water in Anishinaabe (*ah-nish-in-ah-bay*), an Indigenous language. Turn and tell a friend who you think is narrating this biography. [the water]

- *For a very long time* page: In the glossary, it explains that "looking seven generations into the future" means making decisions based on how they will affect the next seven generations or how our actions today impact those who will come after us. *Generations* are groups of people born around the same time. You and your grownups are from different generations.

- *Over time, more people came* page: Can you infer what is happening to the water on this page?

- *When Grandma Josephine journeyed on to the spirit world* page: "Journeyed on to the spirit world" is another way of saying she passed away. What has Autumn decided to do?

- *Speak for the water* page: Have you heard these lines before? Why do you think Carole Lindstrom is repeating them?

After Reading

- What do you suppose Carole Lindstrom wants us to know and do after reading this book? What was her purpose for writing it?

- How does the author's choice to tell the story from the water's point of view impact your experience as a reader?

Extend the Experience

- Autumn Peltier is speaking for the water because it can't speak for itself. Think of something in our natural world that can't speak for itself. Draw a picture of it. Add a speech bubble. What would it say?

- In the book it says, "Be like Autumn and Grandma Josephine, *leave good footprints,* for me. Draw and/or write how you can leave good footprints to protect the water on the *Leave Good Footprints* printable. (Located on the companion website, http://www.resources.corwin.com/more-rampedup-readalouds.)

Similar Titles

 ***Rose Spoke Out: The Story of Rose Schneiderman* (Berne, 2023)**

About the Book: At age 13, Young Rose, who was known for speaking her mind, started sewing in a factory. After her father passed away, her family needed the money so, for a while, Rose kept her mouth shut about the deplorable working conditions and unfair pay. She began speaking up by organizing the women in her factory, and they were given a fairer wage, but the factory remained dirty, cold, and unsafe. Soon Rose began to organize more of the women factory workers and they staged a protest. After a tragic factory fire claimed 146 workers, Rose spoke up for workers' rights at the Metropolitan Opera House and continued to do so throughout her life. Biographical information and an author's note expand the narrative.

 Spring After Spring: How Rachel Carson Inspired the Environmental Movement (Sisson, 2018)

About the Book: Introduce young readers to the remarkable life of Rachel Carson. Through vivid illustrations and accessible language, the book tells the story of Carson's journey from aspiring writer to pioneering biologist. As Carson delves into the mysteries of the natural world, she uncovers the devastating impact of pesticides on wildlife, ultimately leading to the formation of the Environmental Protection Agency. With its engaging narrative and inspiring message, *Spring After Spring* not only celebrates Carson's achievements but also encourages readers to explore and protect the environment around them.

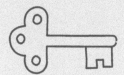

Key Vocabulary and Kid-Friendly Definitions:

- confronting: to face or stand up to someone, something, or your own feelings

- ripple: to make or move in small waves

- summoned: to call to or gather

Upper Elementary Extension:

Students can learn a bit more about Grandma Josephine or Autumn by reading the backmatter and/or accessing online information. Then, reread the book and discuss if the text is more meaningful because they've expanded their content knowledge.

Speak Out Demonstration Text

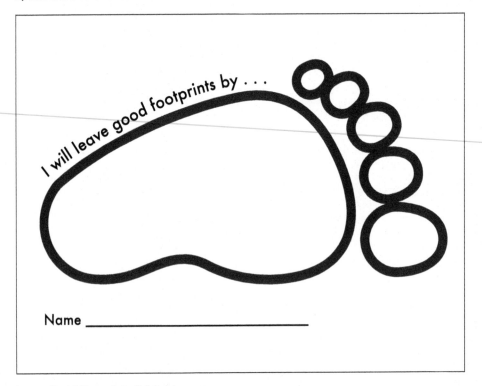

Leave Good Footprints Printable

My Favorite Read Alouds for Teaching Persuasive Writing

Notice, Wonder, and Write

Book Title: *Welcome to the Wonder House*
(Dotlich & Heard, 2023)

About the Book: Acclaimed poets Rebecca Kai Dotlich and Georgia Heard team up and invite readers into their Wonder House. Inside, there are 12 rooms, each containing a few poems for a total of 29. The poems are accompanied by Deborah Freedman's dreamy mixed-media spreads that highlight details found in the poems. A Note About Wonder invites readers to look for, find, and share their wonder. The endpapers feature additional intriguing questions.

To find a book like this one, look for the following:

- Poetry anthologies organized in a unique way
- Poems that include various poetic forms

Comprehension Conversation

Before Reading

Notice the Cover Illustration

- This poetry anthology or collection is called *Welcome to the Wonder House*. What kinds of poems would you expect to find in a Wonder House?
- Is there anything in Deborah Freedman's front cover illustration that makes you wonder?

Set a Purpose: Did you know one of the best ways to learn how to be a poet is to read and study other people's poems? That's exactly what we're going to do today as we explore the poems found inside the Wonder House.

During Reading

[During this read-aloud experience, I will only highlight a few of the poems in the book. Feel free to continue the conversation on another day as you enjoy the remaining poems.]

- Table of Contents: Notice this unique table of contents. It looks like a blueprint that an architect would draw when they are designing a house. Zoom-in on the illustration inside each window as I read aloud the matching names of the rooms. Which room sounds the most interesting to you?
- *Room of Curiosity* page: Let's begin by reading the poems in the Room of Curiosity. Listen to determine if you notice any similarities or differences between these two poems. Tell your friend something you notice about the poem that begins with the line, "Why do diamonds wink and shine?" [Every line except the last one is a question.] That's an interesting way to write a poem! Let's reread Georgia Heard's poem together. Are there any words that rhyme? How is Georgia Heard's poem different from Rebecca Kai Dotlich's poem in this room? [It only has 10 words!]

Learning Targets:

- I notice different kinds of poems.
- I think about how poems are organized.
- I use what I learn about poetry to write my own poems.

- *Room of Ordinary Things* page: Next, I'll share poems found in the Room of Ordinary Things. What are the poems in this room about? [a stone and a stick] How is the poem that begins with "This stone . . ." similar to the first poem we read? [They both have a lot of questions.] Visualize the different items as I reread Georgia Heard's poem. Have you ever used a stick in one of these ways? This is a list poem because it lists all the things a stick could be.

- *Room of Science* page: Georgia Heard's poem describes six different kinds of scientists. If you had to choose, which kind of scientist would you be? Why?

- *Room of Time* page: What do you notice about the poems in this room? [The first poem is a shape poem. The second one begins and ends in a similar way.]

After Reading

- Did the poems we read have anything in common? Can you make any connections among them?

- How did the authors organize the poems in this book? Why do you suppose they chose to do it that way?

Extend the Experience

- Let's make a list of the techniques we noticed while reading the poems.

- Pick something that makes you wonder and write your own poem.

Similar Titles

No World Too Big: Young People Fighting Global Climate Change (Metcalf et al., 2023)

About the Book: Featuring poems by 15 different poets about young environmental activists from across the world, this anthology includes a variety of poetic forms that are explained in the backmatter. Each poem is paired with a prose paragraph about the activist. In the right-hand corner of each two-page spread you'll find a prompt to readers like, "Start a climate club" encouraging them to take individual or collective action.

Poetry Comics (Snider, 2024)

About the Book: A unique anthology that seamlessly blends poetry and graphic-format illustrations. The poems take readers on a journey through the seasons, capturing both the ordinary and extraordinary moments. For poetry writing advice, share the "How to Write a Poem" series of four poems that appear across the seasons. A few other mentor poems to inspire writers include: "Autumn ABCs," "Opposites," and "I Can Be . . .".

Key Vocabulary and Kid-Friendly Definitions:

Will vary based on which poems you read aloud.

Upper Elementary Extension:

Display the questions found on the back endpapers as a jumping-off point for students to write their own questions. Collect their queries on a digital Wonder Wall or on a bulletin board in your room. Use the questions as inspiration for poems.

Poetry Writers Notice

Poems can...

~ be long or short

~ have questions

~ be a list

~ rhyme or not rhyme

~ be shaped like the topic

~ begin and end the same way

Poetry Writers Notice Chart

My Favorite Read Alouds for Teaching Poetry Writing

Ponder Your Purpose

Book Title: *Champion Chompers, Super Stinkers and Other Poems by Extraordinary Animals* (Ashman, 2023)

About the Book: Nineteen animal contestants strut their poetic prowess to convince readers that they are the fastest, biggest, longest, and strongest. Each set of pages begins with an animal's mask poem (learn more about mask poems in the backmatter) along with an illustrated clue of part of that animal. The page turn reveals the animal's distinguishing "award" and a paragraph of key details about that particular creature.

To find a book like this one, look for the following:

- Kid-friendly poems about interesting topics
- Poetry anthologies with unique organizational structures

Comprehension Conversation

Before Reading

Notice the Cover Illustration

- The title of this book is *Champion Chompers, Super Stinkers and Other Poems by Extraordinary Animals*. Can you spot the chomper and the stinker in Aparna Varma's digital illustration?
- Listen to the title carefully: It reads *Poems **by** Extraordinary Animals*. Do you think that means the animals wrote the poems?

Set a Purpose: The word *extraordinary* in the title means something that is not ordinary or usual; instead, it's awesome and unique. Let's read these poems to learn what makes each animal extraordinary and think about Linda Ashman's purpose for writing this poetry collection.

During Reading

[The poems are written as riddles and the illustration that accompanies the poem typically shows a bit of the animal, but some include enough detail to give away the answer. I would suggest reading the poem without displaying the illustration and letting children use the text evidence to guess the animal. Then, reveal the picture to see if they want to stick with or revise their answer. You might also consider splitting this book into thirds and reading about six to seven animals in each read-aloud experience.]

- *Page 5:* I'm going to reread this poem so that you can listen for words or phrases (text evidence) to decide which animal is sharing their skills. [Discuss words and phrases like *lightning speed, limber spine, impressive stride, strong, sleek.* Provide kid-friendly definitions for words as needed.]
- *Page 6:* The cheetah is the best short-distance runner. Do you remember that in the poem it said, "Make sure it's a marathon—You'll never win a sprint"? Did you learn anything new about a cheetah from the paragraph on this page?

Learning Targets:

- I ponder purposes for writing poetry.
- I think about how poems are organized.
- I use what I learn about poetry to write my own poems.

- *Page 7:* If the cheetah was the best short-distance runner, can you guess from the clues in the poem what type of runner this animal is? [long distance] Whisper your animal guess to your neighbor before we turn the page.

[Continue in the same fashion as you enjoy the rest of the book.]

After Reading

- Linda Ashman used a question-answer or riddle-like structure to organize this book of poems. Why do you suppose she structured it this way? What was her purpose for writing this book?

- Share your opinion of the riddle-like structure. Could you try something like this when you are writing about a topic?

Extend the Experience

- As Linda Ashman tells us on page 46, the poems in this book are called *mask poems.* That means she imagined she was the animal and wrote the poem from its point of view. You can write a mask poem about an animal, an object, a place, or even a person. Write a mask poem and we'll see if we can guess who or what it's about.

- Let's perform some of these poems for students in a different class, grade level, or on the morning announcements. If you want to participate, pick a poem you enjoyed and then rehearse it either on your own or with a friend. Once you've polished your performance, we'll share the poems and see if the kids can guess the animal.

Similar Titles

 The Last Straw: Kids vs. Plastics (Hood, 2021) [kid-friendly poems about interesting topics]

About the Book: Poets pen verses for a variety of reasons. In this case, Susan Hood aims to share the truth about plastic. She begins with the poem "Fantastic Plastic" detailing the many uses of plastic and then moves on to poems about the consequences of our overreliance on plastic products. To provide hope and inspiration, she writes about young activists working to find solutions. This multigenre, multilevel text offers poems, tidbits of information, and robust backmatter. In addition, Susan Hood includes "Poetry Notes" explaining the techniques and formats she's used for each poem. [Find book experiences for this book in *Shake Up Shared Reading.*]

 Your One and Only Heart (LaRocca, 2023)

About the Book: Medical doctor and author Rajani LaRocca's clear and concise poems detail the heart's parts and function. Each poem title begins with, "Your heart is . . ." and ends with a different adjective. The poems are paired to highlight the contradictory characteristics of the heart: singular-cooperative, simple-complex, energetic-relaxed, and so on. The vibrant collage illustrations on each set of paired poems feature the same color palette and child.

Key Vocabulary and Kid-Friendly Definitions:

Will vary based on which poems you read aloud.

Upper Elementary Extension:

If you have readers who are connecting with and enjoying poetry, introduce them to verse novels (if you haven't already!). A few to check out include *And Then, Boom!* (Fipps, 2024), *Otter* (Applegate, 2022), and *Something Like Home* (Arango, 2023).

Appendix A: TEXT SETS

TEXT SET: Spread Kindness

Featured Title: *All Kinds of Special* (Sauer, 2023) [Chapter 1]

- *KINDergarten: Where Kindness Matters Every Day* (Ahiyya, 2022)
- *The Power of One: Every Act of Kindness Counts* (Ludwig, 2020)
- *When We Are Kind* (M. G. Smith, 2020)
- *Zero Local Next Stop: Kindness* (Murrow & Murrow, 2020) [Wordless]

TEXT SET: Trees

Featured Title: *The Together Tree* (Saeed, 2023) [Chapter 1]

- *Some Questions About Trees* (Yuly, 2022)
- *Tree Hole Homes* (Stewart, 2022)
- *The Tree* (Layton, 2016)
- *The Tree and the River* (Becker, 2023) [Wordless]

TEXT SET: Rainy Weather

Featured Title: *ZAP! CLAP! ZOOM! The Story of a Thunderstorm* (Salas, 2023b) [Chapter 2]

- *Hello, Rain!* (Maclear, 2021)
- *Mouse Calls* (Pace, 2022)
- *Soaked* (Cushman, 2020)
- *The Umbrella* (Ferry, 2023)

TEXT SET: Community Gardening

Featured Title: *Something, Someday* (Gorman, 2023) [Chapter 3]

- *Harlem Grown: How One Big Idea Transformed a Neighborhood* (Hillery, 2020)
- *In a Garden* (McCanna, 2020)
- *Mary Had a Little Plan* (Sauer, 2022)
- *Thank You, Garden* (Scanlon, 2020)

TEXT SET: My Friend Is Moving Away!

Featured Title: *Friends Beyond Measure* (L. Fisher, 2023) [Chapter 4]

- *Evelyn Del Rey Is Moving Away* (Medina, 2020)
- *Friends Are Friends Forever* (D. Liu, 2021)
- *Goodbye, Friend! Hello, Friend!* (Doerrfeld, 2019)
- *In a Jar* (Marcero, 2020)

TEXT SET: Sloths

Featured Title: *Destiny Finds Her Way* (Engle, 2023a) [Chapter 4]

- *Happy Sloth Day* (Sayre, 2022)
- *Peter & Ernesto: A Tale of Two Sloths* (Annable, 2018) [Graphic Format Text]
- *The Sloth Who Slowed Us Down* (Wild, 2018)
- *The Upside-Down Book of Sloths* (Shreeve, 2023)

TEXT SET: Earth Day/Environmental Action

Featured Title: *To Change a Planet* (Soontornvat, 2022) [Chapter 5]

- *The Day the River Caught Fire: How the Cuyahoga River Exploded and Ignited the Earth Day Movement* (Wittenstein, 2023)
- *Little Land* (Sudyka, 2023)
- *One Little Bag: An Amazing Journey* (Cole, 2020) [Wordless]
- *This Is the Planet Where I Live* (Going, 2023)

TEXT SET: Question-Answer Structure

Featured Title: *Butt or Face?* (Lavelle, 2023) [Chapter 5]

- *Creature Features: 25 Animals Explain Why They Look the Way They Do* (S. Jenkins & Page, 2014)
- *Steve the Dung Beetle: On a Roll* (Stoltz, 2022)
- *Who Am I? An Animal Guessing Game* (S. Jenkins & Page, 2017)
- *Why Do Elephants Have Big Ears?* (S. Jenkins & Page, 2023)

Bibliography

Professional References

Afflerbach, P., Pearson, P. D., & Paris, S. G. (2008). Clarifying differences between reading skills and strategies. *The Reading Teacher, 61*(5), 364–373.

Ahiyya, V. (2022). *Rebellious read alouds: Inviting conversations about diversity with children's books.* Corwin.

ASCD. (2023a, March 7). *The language basis of knowledge.* Scientific Advisory Committee, Knowledge Matters Campaign. https://www.ascd.org/blogs/the-language-basis-of-knowledge

ASCD. (2023b, February 28). *Looking to research for literacy success.* Scientific Advisory Committee, Knowledge Matters Campaign. https://www.ascd.org/blogs/looking-to-research-for-literacy-success

Baker, D. L., & Santoro, L. (2023). Quality read alouds matter: *How* you teach is just as important as *what* you teach. *The Reading Teacher, 77*(3), 310–320.

Beck, I. L., McKeown, M. G., & Kucan, L. (2002). *Bringing words to life: Robust vocabulary instruction.* Guilford Press.

Beck, I. L., McKeown, M. G., & Kucan, L. (2013). *Bringing words to life: Robust vocabulary instruction* (2nd ed.). Guilford Press.

Bishop, R. S. (1990). Mirrors, windows, and sliding glass doors. *Perspectives: Choosing and Using Books for the Classroom, 1*(3), ix–xi.

Burkins, J., & Yates, K. (2021). *Shifting the balance: 6 ways to bring the science of reading into the balanced literacy classroom.* Stenhouse.

Cabell, S. Q., & Hwang, H. (2020). Building content knowledge to boost comprehension in the primary grades. *Reading Research Quarterly, 55*(S1), S99–S107.

Castles, A., Rastle, K., & Nation, K. (2018). Ending the reading wars: Reading acquisition from novice to expert. *Psychological Science in the Public Interest, 19*(1), 5–51. https://doi.org/10.1177/1529100618772271

Cervetti, G. N., & Hiebert, E. H. (2018). Knowledge at the center of English language arts instruction. *The Reading Teacher, 72*(4), 499–507.

Cherry-Paul, S. (2023, February 9). *Cultivating liberatory practices in book clubs* [Conference session]. A workshop at the Colorado Council International Reading Association (CCIRA) conference, Denver.

Cherry-Paul, S. (2024). *Antiracist reading revolution: A framework for teaching beyond representation to liberation.* Corwin.

Cobb, C., & Blachowicz, C. (2014). *No more "look up the list" vocabulary instruction.* Heinemann.

Compton-Lilly, C., Spence, L. K., Thomas, P. L., & Decker, S. L. (2023). Stories grounded in decades of research: What we truly know about the teaching of reading. *The Reading Teacher, 77*(3) 392–400.

Conradi Smith, K., Young, C. A., & Yatzeck, J. C. (2022). What are teachers reading and why?: An analysis of elementary read aloud titles and the rationales underlying teachers' selections. *Literacy Research and Instruction, 61*(4), 383–401.

Cunningham, P. M. (2017). *Phonics they use: Words for reading and writing* (7th ed.). Pearson.

DeBruin-Parecki, A., & Cartwright, K. B. (2023). Supporting inferential comprehension in the preschool classroom: The roles of theory of mind and executive skills. *The Reading Teacher, 77*(2), 146–155.

Duke, N. K., & Cartwright, K. B. (2021). The science of reading progresses: Communicating advances beyond the simple view of reading. *The Reading Teacher, 56*(S1), S25–S44.

Duke, N. K., Ward, A. E., & Pearson, P. D. (2021). The science of reading comprehension instruction. *The Reading Teacher, 74*, 663–672.

Ehri, L. C. (2020). The science of learning to read words: A case for systematic phonics instruction. *Reading Research Quarterly, 55*(S1), S45–S60.

Fisher, D., Frey, N., & Lapp, D. (2023). *Teaching reading: A playbook for developing skilled readers through word recognition and language comprehension.* Corwin.

Gough, P. B., & Tunmer, W. E. (1986). Decoding, reading, and reading disability. *Remedial and Special Education, 7*(1), 6–10.

Hammond, Z. (2015). *Culturally responsive teaching and the brain: Promoting authentic engagement and rigor among culturally and linguistically diverse students.* Corwin.

Hwang, H., Orcutt, E., Reno, E. A., Kim, J., Harsch, R. M., McMaster, K. L., Kendeou, P., & Slater, S. (2023). Making the most of read-alouds to support primary-grade students' inference making. *The Reading Teacher, 77*(2), 167–177.

International Literacy Association. (2018). *The power and promise of read-alouds and independent reading* [Literacy leadership brief]. Author.

International Literacy Association. (2020). *Phonological awareness in early childhood literacy development* [Position statement and research brief]. Author.

Kelly, L. B., & Moses, L. (2018). Children's literature that sparks inferential discussions. *The Reading Teacher (72)*1, 21–29.

Koutrakos, P. (2022). *Mentor texts that multitask: A less-is-more approach to integrated literacy instruction.* Corwin.

Laminack, L. L. (2016). *The ultimate read-aloud resource: Making every moment intentional and instructional with best friend books.* Scholastic.

Lindsey, J. (2022). *Reading above the fray: Reliable, research-based routines for developing decoding skills.* Scholastic.

McClure, E. L., & Fullerton, S. K. (2017). Instructional interactions: Supporting students' reading development through interactive read-alouds of informational text. *The Reading Teacher, 71*(1), 51–59.

Moll, L. C., & Gonzalez, N. (1994). Lessons from research with language-minority children. *JRB: A Journal of Literacy, 26*, 439–456.

Muhammad, G. (2020). *Cultivating genius: An equity framework for culturally and historically responsive literacy.* Scholastic.

Rasinski, T. (2017). Readers who struggle: Why many struggle and a modest proposal for improving their reading. *The Reading Teacher, 70*(5), 519–524.

Rasinski, T., Nichols, W., Paige, D., Rupley, W., Young, C., & Valerio, M. (2020). Teaching reading: A blend of art and science. *Literacy Today, 38*(2), 46–47.

Silverman, R. D., Johnson, E., Keane, K., & Khanna, S. (2020). Beyond decoding: A meta-analysis of the effects of language comprehension interventions on K–5 students' language and literacy outcomes. *Reading Research Quarterly, 55*(S1), S207–S233.

Silverman, R. D., & Keane, K. (2022). Supporting language comprehension: Recommendations for instruction in K–5 based on recent research. *Literacy Today, 40*(2), 24–25.

Varelas, M., & Pappas, C. C. (2006). Intertextuality in read-alouds of integrated science-literacy units in urban primary classrooms: Opportunities for the development of thought and language. *Cognition and Instruction, 24*(2), 211–259.

Venegas, E. M., & Guanzon, A. (2023). A planning tool for improving interactive read-alouds: Why and how. *The Reading Teacher, 77*(2), 207–216.

Walther, M. P. (2019). *The ramped-up read aloud: What to notice as you turn the page.* Corwin.

Walther, M. P. (2022). *Shake up shared reading: Expanding on read alouds to encourage student independence.* Corwin.

Walther, M. P., & Biggs-Tucker, K. (2020). *The literacy workshop: Where reading and writing converge.* Stenhouse.

Walther, M. P., & Phillips, K. A. (2012). *Month-by-month reading instruction for the differentiated classroom.* Scholastic.

Wright, T. S. (2019). The power of interactive read alouds. *American Educator, 42*(4), 4–8.

Young, T. A., Ricks, P. H., & MacKay, K. L. (2023). Engaging students with expository books through interactive read alouds. *The Reading Teacher, 77*(1), 6–15.

Zygouris-Coe, V., Wiggins, M. B., & Smith, L. H. (2004/2005). Engaging students with text: The 3-2-1 strategy. *The Reading Teacher, 58*(4), 381–384.

Children's Literature References

Ackerman, S. H. (2024). *Not just the driver!* (R. Neubecker, Illus.). Beach Lane/Simon & Schuster.

Aguilera, C. (2020). *9 kilometers.* (L. Schimel, Trans., G. Lyon, Illus.). Eerdmans.

Ahiyya, V. (2022). *KINDergarten: Where kindness matters every day.* (J. Chou, Illus.). Random House Studio.

Anganuzzi, C. (2023). *The ocean gardener.* Tiger Tales.

Annable, G. (2018). *Peter & Ernesto: A tale of two sloths.* First Second.

Applegate, K. (2022). *Otter.* (C. Santoso, Illus.). Feiwel & Friends.

Arango, A. B. (2023). *Something like home.* Random House.

Ashman, L. (2023). *Champion chompers, super stinkers and other poems by extraordinary animals.* (A. Varma, Illus.). Kids Can.

Avant-Garde, Z. (2023). *Words of wonder from Z to A.* (K. Morris, Illus.). Doubleday.

Baillie, K. (2022). *Railroad engineer Olive Dennis.* (T. Stephani, Illus.). Innovation.

Baker, J. (2023). *Desert jungle.* Candlewick.

Banyai, I. (1995). *Zoom.* Puffin/Penguin.

Barnett, M. (2023). *Twenty questions.* (C. Robinson, Illus.). Candlewick.

Bates, A. J. (2023). *The welcome home.* Paula Wiseman/Simon & Schuster.

Becker, A. (2023). *The tree and the river.* Candlewick.

Beckmeyer, D. (2023). *I am a tornado.* Atheneum.

Benediktsson, Æ. P. (2023). *Stranded! A mostly true story from Iceland.* Barefoot.

Bentley, T. (2023). *One chicken nugget.* Baltzer & Bray/HarperCollins.

Bergstrom, A. H. (2023). *Tumble.* Orchard.

Berne, E. C. (2023). *Rose spoke out: The story of Rose Schneiderman.* (G. Abeille, Illus.). Apples & Honey/Behrman.

Bernstrom, D. (2020). *Big papa and the time machine.* (S. W. Evans, Illus.). HarperCollins.

Bernstrom, D. (2022). *Song in the city.* (J. Mohammed, Illus.). HarperCollins.

Bingham, W. (2023). *The walk.* (E. B. Lewis, Illus.). Abrams.

Black, M. I. (2009). *Chicken cheeks.* (K. Hawkes, Illus.). Simon & Schuster.

Bluemle, E. (2017). *Tap tap boom boom.* (G. B. Karas, Illus.). Candlewick.

Boxer, E. (2022). *One turtle's last straw: The real-life rescue that sparked a sea change.* (M. Á. Migués, Illus.). Crown.

Brown, M. (2022). *El cuarto turquesa/The turquoise room.* (A. M. Garcia, Illus.). Children's Book Press/Lee & Low.

Bryon, N. (2019). *Rocket says look up!* (D. Adeola, Illus.). Random House.

Bryon, N. (2020). *Rocket says clean up!* (D. Adeola, Illus.). Random House.

Bryon, N. (2023). *Rocket says speak up!* (D. Adeola, Illus.). Random House.

Byrne, R. (2014). *This book just ate my dog.* Henry Holt.

Casal, L. (2023). *Baller Ina.* Knopf/Random House.

Charles, T. (2023). *Ketanji Brown Jackson: A justice for all.* (J. Skidmore, Illus.). Simon & Schuster.

Cho, L. (2023). *Oh, Olive!* Katherine Tegen/HarperCollins.

Cohen, T. (2023). *City beet.* (U. Lugo, Illus.). Sleeping Bear.

Cole, H. (2020). *One little bag: An amazing journey.* Scholastic.

Cornall, G. (2017). *Jabari jumps.* Candlewick.

Cornwall, G. (2020). *Jabari tries.* Candlewick.

Cox, L. (2023). *Yoshi, sea turtle genius: A true story about an amazing swimmer.* (R. Jones, Illus.). Anne Schwartz/Random House.

Crews, N. (2024). *Extraordinary magic: The storytelling life of Virginia Hamilton.* Christy Ottoviano/Little, Brown.

Cronin, D. (2023). *Lawrence & Sophia.* (B. Cronin, Illus.). Rocky Pond/Random House.

Cushman, A. (2020). *Soaked!* Viking.

David-Sax, P. (2022). *Everything in its place: A story of books and belonging.* (C. Pinkney Barlow, Illus.). Doubleday.

de la Peña, M. (2015). *Last stop on market street.* (C. Robinson, Illus.). Putnam.

de la Peña, M. (2021). *Milo imagines the world.* (C. Robinson, Illus.). Putnam.

de Sève, R. (2022). *This story is not about a kitten.* (C. Ellis, Illus.). Random House Studio.

Debbink, A. (2023). *If the rivers run free.* (N. Wong, Illus.). Sleeping Bear.

Deedy, C. A. (2022). *Wombat said come in.* (B. Lies, Illus.). Margaret Quinlin/Peachtree.

Deedy, C. A. (2023). *Carina Felina.* (H. Cole, Illus.). Scholastic.

Denise, A. A. (2019). *Planting stories: The life of librarian and storyteller Pura Belpré.* HarperCollins.

Doerrfeld, C. (2019). *Goodbye, friend! Hello, friend!* Dial.

Doerrfeld, C. (2023). *Beneath.* Little, Brown.

Dotlich, R. K., & Heard, G. (2023). *Welcome to the wonder house.* (D. Freedman, Illus.). Wordsong.

Eady, A. (2024). *The last stand.* (Jerome & J. Pumphrey, Illus.). Knopf.

Engle, M. (2023a). *Destiny finds her way: How a rescued baby sloth learned to be wild.* (S. Trull, Photographer). National Geographic.

Engle, M. (2023b). *Water day.* (O. Sua, Illus.). Atheneum/Simon & Schuster.

Faber, P. (2022). *Special delivery: A book's journey around the world.* (K. Fahlén, Illus.). Candlewick.

Fenske, J. (2020). *The bug in the bog.* Simon & Schuster.

Ferry, B. (2015). *Stick and stone.* (T. Lichtenheld, Illus.). Houghton Mifflin Harcourt.

Ferry, B. (2023). *The umbrella.* (T. Lichtenheld, Illus.). Clarion/HarperCollins.

Finison, C. (2022). *Hurry, little tortoise, time for school!* (E. Kraan, Illus.). Random House Studio.

Fipps, L. (2024). *And then, boom!* Penguin/Paulsen.

Fisher, L. (2023). *Friends beyond measure: A story told with infographics.* HarperCollins.

Fleming, C. (2012). *Oh, no!* (E. Rohmann, Illus.). Schwartz & Wade.

Fleming, C. (2023). *MINE!* (E. Rohmann, Illus.). Anne Schwartz/Random House.

Fong, P. (2023). *When the fog rolls in.* Greenwillow/HarperCollins.

Gardner, K. (2021). *How to find a fox.* (O. Saarinen, Photographer). Running Press/Hachette.

Gardner, M., & Gardner, A. (2023). *Daddy dressed me.* (N. Fisher, Illus.). Aladdin/Simon & Schuster.

Genhart, M. (2023). *Spanish is the language of my family.* (J. Parra, Illus.). Neal Porter/Holiday House.

Gianferrari, M. (2023). *Thank a farmer.* (M. Mikai, Illus.). Norton.

Gilbert, L. (2021). *The perfect plan.* Bloomsbury.

Going, K. L. (2023). *This is the planet where I live.* (D. Frasier, Illus.). Beach Lane/Simon & Schuster.

Gopal, J. R. (2024). *One sweet song.* (S. Sánchez, Illus.). Candlewick.

Gorman, A. (2023). *Something, someday.* (C. Robinson, Illus.). Viking.

Graham, B. (2023). *The concrete garden.* Candlewick.

Gray, G. R., Jr. (2023). *I'm from.* (O. Mora, Illus.). Balzer & Bray/HarperCollins.

Greanias, M. C. (2023). *How this book got red.* (M. Iwai, Illus.). Sourcebooks/Jabberwocky.

Ha, A. K. (2023). *Walter finds his voice: The story of a shy crocodile.* Red Comet.

Hale, S., & Hale, D. (2014). *The princess in black.* (L. Pham, Illus.). Candlewick.

Hammond, T. (2023). *A day with no words.* (K. Cosgrove, Illus.). Wheat Penny.

Harrison, V. (2023). *BIG.* Little, Brown.

Hatke, B. (2010). *Zita the spacegirl.* First Second/Roaring Brook.

Heder, T. (2022). *Sal boat: A boat by Sal.* Abrams.

Heavenrich, S. (2021). *13 ways to eat a fly.* (D. Clark, Illus.). Charlesbridge.

Hillery, T. (2020). *Harlem grown: How one big idea transformed a neighborhood.* (J. Hartland, Illus.). Simon & Schuster.

Hocker, K. (2024). *I was: The stories of animal skulls.* (N. Donovan, Illus.). Candlewick.

Hodgkinson, L. (2023). *The princess and the (greedy) pea.* Candlewick.

Hoefler, K. (2023). *In the dark.* (C. Luyken, Illus.). Knopf.

Holt, B. (2023). *The red jacket.* HarperCollins.

Holub, J. (2023). *Bears are best!* (L. Keller, Illus.). Crown/Random House.

Hood, S. (2021). *The last straw: Kids vs. plastics.* (C. Engel, Illus.). HarperCollins.

Howley, J. (2023). *The animal song.* Random House.

Hrachovec, A. (2023). *Catside up, catside down: A book of prepositions.* Feiwel & Friends/Macmillan.

Jain, M. (2023). *The only astronaut.* (A. Stegmaier, Illus.). Kids Can.

Jenkins, M. (2022). *Puffin.* (J. Desmond, Illus.). Candlewick.

Jenkins, S. (2021). *Disasters by the numbers: A book of infographics.* Houghton Mifflin Harcourt.

Jenkins, S. (2022). *One day by the numbers.* Clarion/HarperCollins.

Jenkins, S., & Page, R. (2014). *Creature features: 25 animals explain why they look the way they do.* Houghton Mifflin.

Jenkins, S., & Page, R. (2017). *Who am I? An animal guessing game.* Houghton Mifflin Harcourt.

Jenkins, S., & Page, R. (2023). *Why do elephants have big ears?* Little, Brown.

Joy, M. (2023). *Wallflowers.* Clarion/HarperCollins.

Kalb, B. (2024). *Buffalo Fluffalo.* (E. Kraan, Illus.). Random House Studio.

Kasza, K. (2003). *My lucky day.* Putnam.

Katstaller, R. (2022). *Skater Cielo.* Orchard/Scholastic.

Krans, A. P. (2023). *Finding Papa.* (T. Bui, Illus.). HarperCollins.

Keating, J. (2022). *The girl who built an ocean: An artist, an Argonaut, and the true story of the world's first aquarium.* (M. M. Nutter, Illus.). Knopf/Random House.

Keely, C. (2017). *A book of bridges: Here to there and me to you.* (C. Krampien, Illus.). Sleeping Bear.

Knowles, J. (2022). *Ear worm.* (G. Berstein, Illus.). Candlewick.

Kulekjian, J. (2023). *KABOOM! A volcano erupts.* (Z. Si, Illus.). Kids Can.

Lanan, J. (2023). *Jumper: A day in the life of a backyard jumping spider.* Roaring Brook.

Langley, K. (2021). *When Langston dances.* (K. Mallett, Illus.). Simon & Schuster.

LaRocca, R. (2023). *Your one and only heart.* (L. P. Conrad, Illus.). Dial.

Lavelle, K. (2023). *Butt or face? Can you tell which end you're looking at?* Sourcebooks.

Layton, N. (2016). *The tree.* Candlewick.

Lee, S. N. (2023). *Lolo's sari-sari store.* (C. Almeda, Illus.). Atheneum/Simon & Schuster.

Li, X. (2024). *I lived inside a whale.* Little, Brown.

Lindstrom, C. (2023). *Autumn Peltier, water warrior.* (B. George, Illus.). Roaring Brook.

Liu, D. (2021). *Friends are friends forever.* (L. Scurfield, Illus.). Henry Holt.

Liu, L. (2023). *Hidden gem.* Henry Holt.

Lodding, L. R., & Pabari, E. (2023). *Flipflopi: How a boat made from flip-flops is helping to save the ocean.* (M. M. Mwangi, Illus.). Beaming Books.

Lower, J. (2023). *The brilliant calculator: How mathematician Edith Clark helped electrify America.* (S. Reagan, Illus.). Calkins Creek/Astra.

Ludwig, T. (2020). *The power of one: Every act of kindness counts.* (M. Curato, Illus.). Borzoi/Knopf.

Mack, J. (2017). *Mine!* Chronicle.

Mack, J. (2024). *Time to make art.* Henry Holt.

MacLean, R. (2023). *More than words: So many ways to say what we mean.* Henry Holt.

Maclear, K. (2021). *Hello, rain!* (C. Turnham, Illus.). Chronicle.

Magruder, N. (2016). *How to find a fox.* Feiwel and Friends/MacMillan.

Majewski, M. (2023). *Bridges.* Abrams.

Marcero, D. (2020). *In a jar.* Putnam.

Markel, M. (2017). *Balderdash! John Newbery and the boisterous birth of children's books.* (N. Carpenter, Illus.). Chronicle.

Markel, M. (2023). *Tomfoolery! Randolph Caldecott and the rambunctious coming-of-age of children's books.* (B. McClintock, Illus.). Chronicle.

Martínez, C. G. (2023). *Not a monster.* (L. González, Illus.). Charlesbridge.

McCanna, T. (2020). *In a garden.* (A. Sicuro, Illus.). Paula Wiseman/Simon & Schuster.

McCarthy, S. (2023). *The wilderness.* Candlewick.

Medina, M. (2020). *Evelyn Del Rey is moving away.* (S. Sánchez, Illus.). Candlewick.

Metcalf, L. H., Dawson, K. V., & Bradley, J. (2023). *No world too big: Young people fighting global climate change.* (J. Bradley, Illus.). Charlesbridge.

Monsen, A. (2022). *Chester van Chime who forgot how to rhyme.* (A. Hanlon, Illus.). Little, Brown.

Mora, O. (2019). *Saturday.* Little, Brown.

Morrison, F. (2022). *Kick push: Be your epic self.* Bloomsbury.

Muhammad, I., & Ali, S. K. (2019). *The proudest blue: A story of hijab and family.* (H. Aly, Illus.). Little, Brown.

Murrow, E., & Murrow, V. (2020). *Zero local next stop: Kindness.* Candlewick.

Newsome, M. (2024). *Sydney's big speech.* (J. Orlando, Illus.). HarperCollins.

Offsay, C. (2024). *The quiet forest.* (A. Cushman, Illus.). Paula Wiseman/Simon & Schuster.

Otis, C. (2023). *The bright side.* Rocky Pond/Penguin Random House.

Pace, A. M. (2022). *Mouse calls.* (E. Kraan, Illus.). Beach Lane/Simon & Schuster.

Parra, J. (2022). *Growing an artist: The story of a landscaper and his son.* Simon & Schuster.

Paschkis, J. (2021). *The wordy book.* Enchanted Lion.

Paul, M. (2023). *365: How to count a year.* (J. Chung, Illus.). Beach Lane/Simon & Schuster.

Penfold, A. (2018). *All are welcome.* (S. Kaufman, Illus.). Knopf/Random House.

Penfold, A. (2021). *Big feelings.* (S. Kaufman, Illus.). Knopf/Random House.

Penfold, A. (2022). *All are neighbors.* (S. Kaufman, Illus.). Knopf/Random House.

Piedra, T., & Joy, M. (2023). *One tiny treefrog: A countdown to survival.* Candlewick.

Pizzoli, G. (2024). *Lucky duck.* Knopf.

Pumphrey, J. (2022a). *It's a sign!* (J. Pumphrey, Illus.). Disney/Hyperion.

Pumphrey, J. (2022b). *Somewhere in the Bayou.* (J. Pumphrey, Illus.). Norton.

Raczka, B. (2023). *You are a story.* (Kristen & K. Howdeshell, Illus.). Neal Porter/Holiday House.

Raúl the Third. (2023). *¡Vamos! Let's go read.* (E. Bay, Illus.). Versify/HarperCollins.

Reynolds, J. (2021). *Stuntboy, in the meantime.* (R. the Third, Illus.). Atheneum/Simon & Schuster.

Richmond, S. E. (2023). *Night owl night.* (M. Lechuga, Illus.). Charlesbridge.

Rocco, H. (2022). *How to send a hug.* (J. Rocco, Illus.). Little, Brown.

Rogers, K. (2023). *A letter for Bob.* (J. Nelson, Illus.). Heartdrum/HarperCollins.

Ruzzier, S. (2023). *The real story.* Abrams Appleseed.

Saeed, A. (2023). *The together tree.* (L. Pham, Illus.). Salaam Reads/Simon & Schuster.

Salas, L. P. (2023a). *Finding family: The duckling raised by loons.* (A. Neonakis, Illus.). Millbrook/Lerner.

Salas, L. P. (2023b). *ZAP! CLAP! BOOM! The story of a thunderstorm.* (E. Mackay, Illus.). Bloomsbury.

Salati, D. (2022). *Hot dog.* Knopf/Random House.

Santamaria, S. (2023). *Yenebi's drive to school.* Chronicle.

Santat, D. (2022). *The aquanaut: A graphic novel.* Graphix/Scholastic.

Sauer, T. (2022). *Mary had a little plan.* (V. Brantley-Newton, Illus.). Union Square Kids.

Sauer, T. (2023). *All kinds of special.* (F. Martin, Illus.). Paula Wiseman/Simon & Schuster.

Sayre, A. P. (2022). *Happy sloth day!* Beach Lane/Simon & Schuster.

Scanlon, L. G. (2020). *Thank you, garden.* (S. Shin, Illus.). Beach Lane/Simon & Schuster.

Schmitt, K. R. (2023). *I ship: A container ship's colossal journey.* (J. Dong, Illus.). Millbrook/Lerner.

Schu, J. (2023). *This is a story.* (L. Castillo, Illus.). Candlewick.

Scott, J. (2023). *My baba's garden.* (S. Smith, Illus.). Neal Porter/Holiday House.

Shaffer, J. J. (2023). *Creep, leap, crunch! A food chain story.* Knopf/Random House.

Shreeve, E. (2023). *The upside-down book of sloths.* (I. Grott, Illus.). W. W. Norton.

Sidman, J. (2023). *We are branches.* (B. Krommes, Illus.). Clarion/HarperCollins.

Siqueira, A. (2023). *Abuela's super capa.* (E. Chavarri, Illus.). HarperCollins.

Sisson, S. R. (2018). *Spring after spring: How Rachel Carson inspired the environmental movement.* Roaring Brook.

Slade, S. (2023). *Behold the octopus!* (T. Gonzalez, Illus.). Peachtree.

Slade, S. (2024). *Behold the hummingbird!* (T. Gonzalez, Illus.). Peachtree.

Slater, S. (2023). *Down the hole.* (A. Ming, Illus.). Clarion/HarperCollins.

Smith, L. (2022). *A gift for Nana.* Random House Studio.

Smith, L. (2023). *Stickler loves the world.* Random House Studio.

Smith, M. G. (2020). *When we are kind.* (N. Heidhardt, Illus.). Orca.

Smith, N. (2023). *The artivist.* Kokila/Penguin Random House.

Smith, S. (2023). *Do you remember?* Neal Porter/Penguin Random House.

Snider, G. (2022). *One boy watching.* Chronicle.

Snider, G. (2024). *Poetry comics.* Chronicle.

Soontornvat, C. (2022). *To change a planet.* (R. J. Bell, Illus.). Scholastic.

Stead, P. C. (2022). *Every dog in the neighborhood.* (M. Cordell, Illus.). Neal Porter/Holiday House.

Stelson, C. (2023). *Stars of the night: The courageous children of the Czech kindertransport.* (S. Alko, Illus.). Carolrhoda.

Stewart, M. (2022). *Tree hole homes: Daytime dens and nighttime nooks.* (A. Hevron, Illus.). Random House Studio.

Stewart, M. (2023a). *Thank you, moon: Celebrating nature's nightlight.* (J. Lanan, Illus.). Knopf.

Stewart, M. (2023b). *Whale fall: Exploring an ocean-floor ecosystem.* (R. Dunlavey, Illus.). Random House Studio.

Stith, S., & Stith, J. (2023). *Black beach: A community, an oil spill, and the origin of Earth Day.* Little Bee.

Stoltz, S. R. (2022). *Steve the dung beetle on a roll.* (M. Bailey, Illus.). Pygmy Giraffe/Lyric and Stone.

Stremer, J. (2023). *Great carrier reef.* (G. Wright, Illus.). Holiday House.

Sudyka, D. (2023). *Little land.* Little, Brown.

Tang, M. (2022). *Yuna's cardboard castles.* (J. Chen, Illus.). Beaming.

Tate, D. (2023). *Jerry changed the game: How engineer Jerry Lawson revolutionized video games forever.* (C. Harris, Illus.). Paula Wiseman/Simon & Schuster.

Tatsukawa, M. (2023). *Mole is not alone.* Henry Holt.

Tekiela, S. (2012). *Whose butt?* Adventure.

Thompkins-Bigelow, J. (2022). *Abdul's story.* (T. Rose, Illus.). Salaam Reads/Simon & Schuster.

Towler, P. (2024). *Mysterious, marvelous octopus.* National Geographic.

Tripplett, N. (2024). *The blue pickup.* (M. Mikai, Illus.). HarperCollins.

Vere, E. (2023). *The artist.* Doubleday.

Vickers, E. (2023). *How to make a memory.* (A. Aranda, Illus.). Simon & Schuster.

Vo, Y. (2022). *Gibberish.* Levine Querido/Chronicle.

Wallace, S. N. (2023). *Love is loud: How Diane Nash led the civil rights movement.* (B. Collier, Illus.). Paula Wiseman/Simon & Schuster.

Wallmark, L. (2023). *The queen of chess: How Judit Polgár changed the game.* (S. Lewis, Illus.). Little Bee/Simon & Schuster.

Wang, A. (2021). *Watercress.* (J. Chin, Illus.). Neal Porter/Holiday House.

Weatherford, C. B. (2023). *All rise: The story of Ketanji Brown Jackson.* (A. Evans, Illus.). Crown/Random House.

Weatherford, C. B. (2024). *Bros.* (R. Brown, Illus.). Candlewick.

Weber, F. (2024). *More dung! A beetle tale.* Disney/Hyperion.

Wenzel, B. (2023). *Every dreaming creature.* Little, Brown.

White, D. (2014). *Blue on blue.* (B. Krommes, Illus.). Beach Lane/Simon & Schuster.

White, E. B. (1952/1980). *Charlotte's web.* HarperCollins.

Wild, M. (2018). *The sloth who slowed us down.* (V. To, Illus.). Abrams.

Wilder, D. (2023). *I made these ants some underpants.* (K.-F. Steele, Illus.). Chronicle.

Wilkins, E. J. (2023). *Zora, the story keeper.* (D. Coulter, Illus.). Kokila/Penguin Random House.

Windness, K. (2023). *Bitsy bat, school star.* Paula Wiseman/Simon & Schuster.

Wittenstein, B. (2023). *The day the river caught fire: How the Cuyahoga River exploded and ignited the Earth Day movement.* (J. Hartland, Illus.). Paula Wiseman/Simon & Schuster.

Wong, J. (2023). *When you can swim.* Orchard/Scholastic.

Wood, A. (1984). *The napping house.* (D. Wood, Illus.). Harcourt.

Woodson, J. (2018). *The day you begin.* (R. López, Illus.). Penguin.

Wynter, A. (2021). *Everybody in the red brick building.* (O. Mora, Illus.). Balzer & Bray/HarperCollins.

Yolen, J. (2016). *What to do with a box.* (C. Sheban, Illus.). Creative Editions.

Yolen, J., & Stemple, H. E. Y. (2020). *I am a storm.* (Kevin & K. Howdeshell, Illus.). Rise x Penguin Workshop.

Yuly, T. (2022). *Some questions about trees.* Atheneum.

Index

Because...
ALL TEACHERS ARE LEADERS

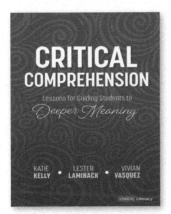

KATIE KELLY, LESTER LAMINACK, VIVIAN VASQUEZ

Expand students' understanding of a text with an accessible, three-step lesson process that gives them the life skills to discuss just about anything with critical curiosity.

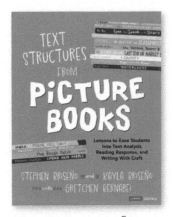

STEPHEN BRISEÑO, KAYLA BRISEÑO, WITH GRETCHEN BERNABEI

Boost students' reading comprehension and writing skills with 50 low-prep, quick-access lessons within the context of beautifully illustrated, engaging picture books.

NANCY AKHAVAN

Support students at all levels of English language proficiency as they learn and grow more confident.

WILEY BLEVINS

Implement effective phonics instruction with these powerful routines that help teachers differentiate whole-class lessons, so students at every skill level can engage.

DOUGLAS FISHER, NANCY FREY

Put away the word-list mindset, and embrace active modeling, peer work, and independent practice to build vocabulary success.

SONJA CHERRY-PAUL

Foster identity-inspiring learning experiences where students can show up completely as themselves and recognize the full humanity of all people.

To order your copies, visit corwin.com/literacy

At Corwin Literacy we have put together a collection of just-in-time, classroom-tested, practical resources from trusted experts that allow you to quickly find the information you need when you need it.

BRETT VOGELSINGER

Spark classroom creativity and transform students' writing skills with a genre we too often ignore—poetry!

JARRED AMATO

Create a classroom environment where independent reading thrives to help students achieve huge gains in all areas of literacy, learning, and civic engagement.

TRICIA EBARVIA

Make important intentional anti-bias shifts in pedagogy to help students become more critical readers, writers, and thinkers.

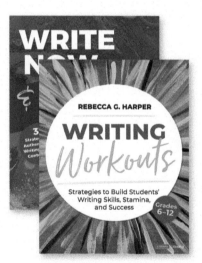

REBECCA HARPER

Give students the fun they want and the targeted practice they need to hone skills in persuasive writing, argument, fiction, poetry, memoir, and more.

JEFFREY D. WILHELM, MICHAEL W. SMITH, HUGH KESSON, DEBORAH APPLEMAN

Help students become more critical consumers of digital media through lessons designed to provide engaging collaborative reading and discussion experiences, no matter what content you teach.

CHRISTINA NOSEK, MELANIE MEEHAN, MATTHEW JOHNSON, MATTHEW R. KAY, DAVE STUART JR.

This series offers actionable answers to your most pressing questions about teaching reading, writing, and ELA.

A Sage Company

CORWIN HAS ONE MISSION: to enhance education through intentional professional learning.

We build long-term relationships with our authors, educators, clients, and associations who partner with us to develop and continuously improve the best evidence-based practices that establish and support lifelong learning.